5TH E

MW00514104

THE

LONG PATH

GUIDE

NEW YORK-NEW JERSEY TRAIL CONFERENCE

Published by
New York-New Jersey Trail Conference
156 Ramapo Valley Road
Mahwah, New Jersey 07430
www.nynjtc.org

Library of Congress Cataloging-in-Publication Data

New York - New Jersey Trail Conference.
The Long Path guide -- 5th ed.
    p. cm.
  Rev. ed. of: Guide to the Long Path. 4th ed. 1996.
  Includes index.
  ISBN 1-880775-31-X (pbk.)
    1. Hiking -- Long Path (N.J. and N.Y.) -- Guidebooks. 2. Long Path Region
(N.J. and N.Y.) -- Guidebooks. I. New York-New Jersey Trail Conference Guide
to the Long Path. II. Title.

GV199.42.N52 L666 2002
917.47'38--dc21

                                                                2002069249

Contents

President's Foreword

Welcome to the newest edition of the Long Path Guide. The Trail Conference's mission is to protect the outdoors and educate people in its wise use. This book plays a role in fulfilling that mission as it describes one of the two long distance hiking trails entirely in New York State.

There are three main reasons why this trail is important to us. First, it offers opportunities for hikers to experience different types of terrain and passes through urban, suburban, rural, and wild areas. The road walks show how vulnerable our landscape is. Second, the trail shows how public and private interests can work together to preserve our open spaces. The trail passes through more private land than any other trail maintained by the Trail Conference. This would not have been possible without us learning how to interact with private landowners and other environmental groups to obtain rights-of-way for the trail. Third, by forming the Long Path North Hiking Club to construct the northern parts of the trail, it showed how we could create more trails to be maintained by the Trail Conference and create public support through trail construction.

Thank you and enjoy the Long Path and this guide. Your purchase provides support for Trail Conference activities such as its conservation and advocacy efforts.

— Jane Daniels
President, Board of Directors

Preface

It is now six years since the last edition of the Long Path Guide. In that time much has happened, both to the trail and to technology that keeps track of it. Work on the Shawangunk Ridge Trail was completed so that it now forms a continuous path from High Point State Park in New Jersey to the traditional Long Path route near Sam's Point Preserve. Two major relocations in the Catskills completed in 2001 have removed many miles of road walking.

Technology has made easily possible for the first time an accurate trace of the entire route of the Long Path. The maps in this book are produced from a complete GPS trace of the entire Long Path, both on the traditional route and along the Shawangunk Ridge Trail route. The thickness of the line representing the Long Path route on the maps greatly exceeds the error of the GPS units in marking its actual trace.

There are many changes in the presentation in this edition of the Long Path Guide. First of all, it's larger in overall dimensions, reducing the amount of page turning and making room for larger photographs and more readable maps. This edition features all new maps designed specifically for it. The section maps now all overlap each other so that there is no ambiguity in how to go between sections. Also new are the section profiles showing how the elevation changes with distance traveled. The Guide includes GPS co-ordinates for the official parking areas for those that are inclined to using the latest technology. Ed Walsh has allowed me to add his "Backpacking the Long Path" booklet as a new part of this book so that more people can take their wandering spirit a little farther afield. Finally, all of the photographs are new.

— Herb Chong
Cartographer and Editor

The route of the Long Path is in a constant state of flux. As this book goes to press, there are two major relocations planned for the Long Path, one at the northern end of Minnewaska State Park in Sections 12 and 13, and the other near Woodland Valley State Campground in Sections 16 and 17. Each of the relocations will eliminate most of the road walking in these sections. Many more changes may take place between the publication of this book and the next edition. The latest information on the Long Path is always available from the Trail Conference at http://www.nynjtc.org/trails/longpath/index.html.

Acknowledgments

One person, no matter how large their pretensions may be, simply can't do a project of the size of producing this book. Listed below are the different specialized tasks that go into the making of this book and the people who worked on each task. Everyone here pulled hard and made this book into a reality. However, the technical aspects of the book are only one part of producing a hiking trail guidebook. There are also the many people who provided moral support and companionship as I walked many sections of the Long Path myself to see how things really were on the trail. Of these dozens of people, I'd like to single out a few for special thanks: Ed Walsh, who seemed to walk everywhere with his GPS to check out just where things really went now that they had finished moving the trail again; Mike Warren for setting the standard by which all of the other photographers, including myself, had to meet; John Jurasek for putting up with my demands for "more GPS data, more GPS data;" and finally Jane Daniels for letting me convince myself that I could do this book, for letting me do the book with so many new things in it, and then helping me see the project through to the end.

—HC, *January 9, 2002*

Cartography and Overall Editing: Herb Chong.

GPS Data: Elie Bijou, Herb Chong, Kay Cynamon, Jakob Franke, Ed Goldstein, John Jurasek (coordinator), Eric Meyer, Terry Murphy, and Ed Walsh.

Trail Checking: Herb Chong, Kay Cynamon, Jakob Franke, John Jurasek, Pete Senterman, and Ed Walsh.

Photography: Herb Chong, Loren Dobert, Jakob Franke, Todd Schreibman, Ed Walsh, and Michael Warren.

Text Proofing: Kay Cynamon, Walt Daniels, Jakob Franke, and Pete Senterman.

Indexing: Jakob Franke

Book Design: Nora Porter

THE LONG PATH

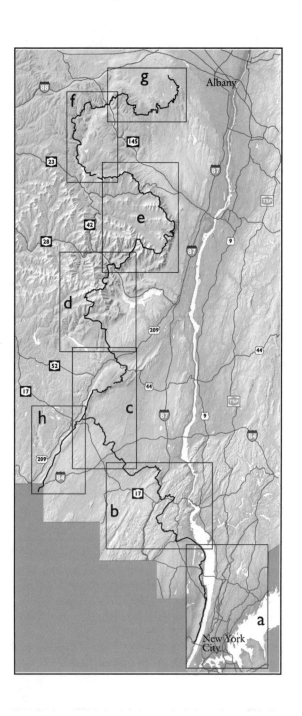

Overview

The Long Path begins in Fort Lee, New Jersey, on the west side of the George Washington Bridge. For the first 12 miles of trail north to the New York State line, it follows the Palisades Escarpment through the lands of Palisades Interstate Park. There are many spectacular views of the Hudson River, New York City and Yonkers.

After crossing into New York, the Long Path turns away from the Hudson River to follow the ridge of the Palisades Escarpment to its end in Mt. Ivy. Much of this route passes through units of the Palisades Interstate Park system in addition to county and town parks. However, some of the vital links take the trail through private property, and there is some road walking through the towns of Piermont and Nyack. The route has extensive views of the lower Hudson River valley with the most dramatic views from Hook Mountain and High Tor.

Leaving the Palisades, the Long Path enters Harriman State Park, traversing nearly the entire length of the park in a northwesterly direction. Since Harriman is only 30 miles from New York City, many hikers from the city frequent it. An abundance of trails and old woods roads crisscross the park, giving many opportunities for circular hikes where the Long Path forms part of the route.

The Harriman part of the trail has intersections with several other important hiking trails passing through the same area. One meets through-hikers on the Appalachian Trail near Island Pond Mountain as they traverse the park from its western edge to the northeastern corner, making their way from Georgia to Maine. More information on the Appalachian Trail can be obtained from the Appalachian Trail Conference at 799 Washington Street, Harpers Ferry, WV 25425, or http://www.appalachiantrail.org. Those who want to treat themselves to some Trail Conference history can trace parts of the Ramapo-Dunderberg Trail[1], the first hiking trail constructed by the Trail Conference (between 1920 and 1921), from the junction at Times Square.

At the northern end of the park, the Long Path goes over Long Mountain, the site of the Raymond H. Torrey Memorial, commemorating one of the founders of the Trail Conference and an early supporter of the Long Path. Torrey served as President of the New York-New Jersey Trail Conference from 1931 to until his unexpected death in 1938. When Vincent Schaefer of the Mohawk Valley Hiking Club originated the Long Path idea in the 1930's as New York's version of Vermont's Long Trail, Torrey's weekly column in the New York Post, "The Long Brown Path," helped popularize the idea and spotlighted the hiking community.

North of Harriman, the trail descends to the Wallkill Valley in Orange County,

---

[1] The original name of this trail was the Tuxedo-Jones Point Trail.

NY. For the next 50 miles, the Long Path largely follows roads. Once consisting primarily of farms, this area rapidly developed into a bedroom community for New York City. The trail follows less busy rural roads where possible. Only in two sections of Orange County, Schunemunk Mountain State Park, and Highland Lakes State Park, does the Long Path travel off-road.

Schunemunk Mountain, the core of the State Park named after it, is the dramatic long ridge of the westernmost mountain in this vicinity. A distinct conglomerate rock forms the upper parts of the mountain. Its flattened top has many spectacular views both east to the Hudson River and north to the Shawangunks and the Catskills.

Beyond Schunemunk Mountain State Park, the Long Path follows rural roads until it reaches Highland Lakes State Park. It passes through the latter park on footpaths and woods roads before returning to rural roads. Not until it intersects the Shawangunk Ridge Trail (SRT) along the Wurtsboro Ridge does the Long Path resume its course on footpaths. The Trail Conference is in continuous negotiation with landowners to move the trail in Orange County off roads but no major changes are expected for the foreseeable future.

From the Wallkill River valley, the Long Path climbs the southern part of the Shawangunk Mountains escarpment. Characterized by beautiful white cliffs and spectacular waterfalls, the Shawangunks, with five mountaintop lakes distributed on its flattened tops, are among the gems of the eastern United States. The Long Path passes near two of the Shawangunks' lakes, Mud Pond and Lake Awosting. The trail climbs up and over many of the cliffs and passes Verkeerder Kill Falls. It affords many spectacular views of the Hudson Valley and the Catskills, sometimes with Lake Awosting in the foreground. Unfortunately, a critical section of the Long Path near Mud Pond crosses private property that has been closed by the owner, forcing either an uncrossable gap or a long detour on an already long section of the trail.

Beyond the Shawangunks, the Long Path crosses the Rondout Valley entirely on roads. To date, this rural area has avoided the development pressures that have hit the Wallkill Valley.

North of the Rondout Valley, the Long Path enters Catskill Park. The Catskills were once thought to be the highest mountains in New York as they rise abruptly from the Hudson River valley. The Long Path continues through the Catskill Forest Preserve for more than ninety miles, going over eleven of the thirty-five peaks whose summits are higher than 3,500 feet. There are many views along the way, and one gets a true sense of wilderness here. The Catskill Forest Preserve permits camping throughout the park while on state land except within 150 feet of a trail or stream and in areas above 3,500 feet. The Long Path passes near several lean-tos for those who intend to backpack portions of the trail. There are road-walking sections, but these generally go through undeveloped areas. Just south of Slide Mountain, near Denning, the Long Path meets the eastern end of the Finger Lakes Trail, another long distance hiking trail that heads west, connecting with other trails that lead all the way to North Dakota. There is also a connector to head north into Canada to join the Bruce Trail. For more information on the Finger Lakes Trail, contact the Finger

Lakes Trail Conference at 6111 Visitor Center Road, Mount Morris, NY 14510 or http://www.fingerlakes.net/trailsystem.

North of Catskill Park, the trail follows a series of mountains that form the northernmost edge of the Catskill Mountains. While noticeably lower than the main peaks, these mountains and ridges still offer a beautiful hiking experience. About eight miles north of the Catskill Forest Preserve, the Long Path enters several State Reforestation areas, working forests where logging is permitted (as opposed to the Catskill Park, which must be kept "forever wild"). At the western edge of Huntersfield Ridge, the last mountain encountered traveling northwards whose summit is over 3,000 feet, the trail makes a gradual descent to the Schoharie Reservoir.

Once reaching the Schoharie Reservoir, the northern-most outpost of the New York City water system, the Long Path heads north for 30 miles through the beautiful Schoharie Valley. This area was once a major Native American travel route and became home to many early European settlements. As the trail passes through the valley and the highlands to the west, it encounters many remnants of that early period. At the northern end of the valley, the trail goes over the sentinel of Vroman's Nose, a rocky crag with magnificent views, before descending to Middleburgh.

In Middleburgh the Long Path turns east and traverses a region known as the "Endless Mountains," largely through State Reforestation areas. Farming is still viable in this region and the trail passes along the edge of many open fields. In the east, the Endless Mountains end abruptly at the Helderberg Escarpment. After the trail meets the upper edge of the escarpment, it turns north to follow the escarpment into John Boyd Thacher State Park. From there, it continues on to near Altamont, and further on rural roads to reach Adirondack State Park. Once in Adirondack Park, it is possible to reach Whiteface Mountain via existing trails.

History

Vincent J. Schaefer of the Mohawk Valley Hiking Club originally conceived the Long Path. He proposed that New York establish its own "Long Path" similar to the Long Trail in Vermont. The Long Trail was America's first long distance hiking trail and was often described as a footpath in the wilderness. The Long Path was intended to be an alternative route from Bear Mountain for the Appalachian Trail hiker. Unlike other trails, Schaefer wanted the Long Path to be an unmarked route connecting scenic or historic points of interest. These points of interest themselves would be described in a guidebook describing these points of interest. He wanted hikers to "enjoy the sense of uncertainty, exploration, and achievement that reaches its highest level when the individual is dependent on the use of compass, marked map, and wood knowledge to reach an objective". The challenge for the hiker was to use topographic maps and compass to connect these points in any way they could, using whatever they found along the way.

The Long Path started receiving much public support from Raymond Torrey in 1933. W. W. Cady[2] took on the assignment of scouting the route from the George Washington Bridge through the Catskills. From Gilboa north, Vincent Schaefer and his brother Paul worked out a route through the Adirondacks to Whiteface Mountain. Every week, Torrey would write a description of the newly scouted section of the route in his column "The Long Brown Path" in the NY Post. However Schaefer's concept of an unmarked route being called a path proved to be difficult for the general hiking public to grasp.

In 1935, the Palisades Park Commission began to acquire property for the construction of the Palisades Interstate Parkway, greatly increasing access to the cliffs of the Palisades Escarpment. This renewed interest in the Long Path project. By 1943, Alexander Jessup had marked the trail as far as Peekamoose Mountain in the Catskills, but World War II distracted people's minds. The project languished for nearly twenty years after that.

In 1960 Robert Jessen of the Ramapo Ramblers and Michael Warren of New York City urged revival of the project. By now the post-war boom and the growth of suburbia had changed the original concept of the Long Path from an unmarked path in the wilderness into a blazed and cleared trail. There was now too much civilization to pass through. Many of the back roads and woodlands that Schaefer had planned to use for the trail corridor were now in private hands, subdivided into homes, or otherwise unusable for use as backcountry hiking.

During the 1960's and 1970's construction of the trail proceeded as far

---

[2] Cady was born in Kansas, lived in Colorado, and moved to the NYC area in the 1920s. Currently, nothing more is known about him.

north as the Catskills. In the Catskill Forest Preserve the Long Path followed existing trails as much as possible. However, new trail construction was needed over Peekamoose and Table Mountains. The last part of new trail construction in the Catskills of this era completed when the "missing link" section around Kaaterskill High Peak opened in 1987. It became possible to continuously hike the then-225 miles of the Long Path from the George Washington Bridge to East Windham at the northern end of the Catskill Park, although there were still road walking sections even in the Park.

The 1990's have become another great period of trail building. With assistance from the National Park Service's River and Trail Conservation Assistance Program the Long Path North Hiking Club was formed. Members of this organization have built and maintained over 75 miles of the Long Path through Schoharie and Albany Counties. Additionally the Shawangunk Ridge Trail (SRT) was built connecting High Point, New Jersey with Minnewaska State Park in New York. The SRT provides an alternative route for the Long Path from Harriman State Park northwards. One can hike the Appalachian Trail from Harriman west to High Point State Park in New Jersey before heading north on the SRT to rejoin the main Long Path near Bear Hill Nature Preserve.

As of January, 2002, the main section of the Long Path is a near-continuous 349-mile hiking trail that extends from the George Washington Bridge to the village of Altamont, about 15 miles west of Albany. While plans go ahead to extend the trail to the Mohawk River and the Adirondacks, the existing trail route constantly changes to adapt to private land changes. The alternate section of the Shawangunk Ridge Trail adds another 28 miles to the total.

In the late 1970s and in the 1980s, the northward movement of suburbia began to have a major impact on the Long Path's trail system. Where it was once possible to get permission to build a trail with just a knock on a door and a handshake, formal agreements were now required. The ridge tops where the trail passed were no longer immune to development. In some areas, the trail had to be moved from the woods to public roadways. In other places, bucolic country roads followed by the trail became suburban thoroughfares.

About 90 miles of the Long Path currently follow public roadways. The Trail Conference is working on several plans to reduce the amount of road walking. Particularly difficult is the Orange County section between Schunemunk Mountain State Park and the Shawangunks. Because of the lack of public lands and much suburban development, finding a suitable trail route is a challenge. Two strategies have developed to address the Orange County "problem."

In 1989, the New York-New Jersey Trail Conference, in cooperation with the National Park Service, initiated a study to determine the feasibility of relocating the Long Path from the roads of Orange County to the Shawangunk Ridge. The proposed route would follow the Appalachian Trail from Harriman

State Park to High Point State Park in the northwest corner of New Jersey and then continue along the Kittatinny-Shawangunk Ridge to Minnewaska State Park. After two years of study, a report was issued that demonstrated the feasibility of this route. The Trail Conference quickly negotiated agreements with landowners, and 30 of the 36 miles of the trail were constructed during 1992 and 1993[3]. Today, there are two Long Path routes from Harriman State Park to Minnewaska State Park: the traditional Orange County lowland route and the Shawangunk Ridge Trail with its breathtaking views.

At the same time another study began to look for an alternative lowland route. With the creation of Highland Lakes State Park, the Long Path in Orange County rerouted through the park and a series of less busy roadways. However, with the large number of private landowners needing to be convinced to allow a hiking trail to pass along or through their properties, the dream of a completely off-road footpath is unlikely for now.

In Rockland County, the Long Path passes through a series of state, county, and town parks before entering Harriman State Park. While most of the trail in Rockland County is on public land, there are vital links across private property. Only 30 miles from New York City, this section is the most threatened. Together with the Rockland County Planning Board, the Trail Conference prepared in 1989 a report entitled The Long Path in Rockland County. This report, which views the Long Path as "the spine of a Rockland County Greenway," provides guidelines to local planning boards for long-term protection strategies for the trail. The Long Path has received greater protection as it was put on the official county map.[4]

In Catskill Park, the Long Path follows some public roadways in the central Catskills area, primarily near Phoenicia. This road walking exists because there are no pre-existing trails for the Long Path to follow, not due to the absence of public land. Because Article 14 of the New York State Constitution protects the Catskill Forest Preserve, mandating that it be kept "forever wild," the New York State Department of Environmental Conservation (DEC) strictly regulates new trail construction in the park.

In the summer of 2000, a major relocation was completed eliminating 3 miles of road walking and the use of the Mink Hollow Trail. Plateau Mountain was added. In the summer of 2001, the Long Path was rerouted over Indian Head Mountain and north through the Catskill Center's Platte Clove Preserve, eliminating another mile of road walking and the Jimmy Dolan Notch Trail. Camping is not permitted in the Platte Clove Preserve.

Relocation has been approved which will move the Long Path from Woodland Valley Road to the ridgeline from Terrace Mountain over Mt. Pleasant and Romer Mountain to Lane Street in Phoenicia. Another relocation will happen in the area near Vernooy Falls as the trail is moved to recently acquired land.

---

[3] The remaining 6 miles were finished in 1997.
[4] Interested people can obtain a copy of the report by pointing their web browser to http://www.co.rockland.ny.us/bull/osmap.htm.

The Trail Conference has also begun a concerted effort to extend the Long Path to the Mohawk River and the Adirondack Park, thus enabling the Long Path to achieve its original goal of a long-distance trail from New York City to the northern Adirondacks. After a two-year study conducted by the Trail Conference and the National Park Service, the trail is being built along the original route as envisioned by Vincent Schaefer in the 1930s.

Navigation

The Long Path is marked with a 2" x 4" paint blaze for most of the route. The blaze color is Long Path Aqua, a trade name of the New York-New Jersey Trail Conference. It is a light blue-green that many people term turquoise. Turns are marked with two blazes, one over the other, with the top blaze offset in the direction of the turn. For important locations, the Long Path uses plastic marker disks (often abbreviated to "markers") that approximate the paint blaze color.

The only major exceptions to the blazing described above are in Catskill Park and on the Wurtsboro Ridge DEC parcels near Wurtsboro on the Shawangunk Ridge. These are areas where the Trail Conference maintains the trails on behalf of the DEC. In the both areas, the Long Path follows existing Forest Preserve trails marked in red, blue or yellow plastic disks, depending upon the trail. In certain sections of private land inside the park, the Long Path blazes revert to Aqua paint blazes. In the oldest parts of the park, some of these markers are made of painted metal. Be sure to read the descriptions carefully, as the disk colors often change in the middle of a section.

Three main sources of maps cover the areas traversed by the Long Path: ones produced by the New York-New Jersey Trail Conference, ones produced by the United States Geological Survey (USGS), and Jimapco, a commercial map vendor. The Trail Conference's maps are specialized for hiking. They contain all of the officially maintained trails in their areas of coverage with markings for features of special interest to hikers. The maps are printed on Tyvek, a waterproof and tear resistant material, to enable their use in all weather conditions. However, only about half of the Long Path crosses areas covered by these maps. The USGS 7.5' 1:24,000 series of topographic map quads cover all areas crossed by the Long Path but are printed on paper and thus need protection from wet and windy weather. Also, the vast majority of these maps were produced in the 1950's or 60's and are sometimes well out of date, even when taking into account special "photo-revised" updates produced in the early 1980's. The third source is Jimapco. They are a company specialized in making road maps of the northern part of the Hudson Valley and surrounding areas. They produce the best road maps available for navigating to and from the trailheads for each of the sections of the Long Path. Jimapco maps are available at many small stores from Orange County northwards or on the web at http://www.jimapco.com.

The maps in this book are a combination of USGS data with some corrections to areas important for navigating the Long Path. They are designed to be a supplement to the Trail Conference's hiking maps and the USGS topographic maps. As such, they are neither as detailed nor as complete in coverage. However, they contain enough detail that a hiker should not need continual reference to other maps to navigate the trail if they are following the trail descriptions in this guidebook.

Modern technology has become a useful accessory to hikers with small, handheld Global Positioning System (GPS) units now being quite inexpensive and reliable. The trail section descriptions contain GPS coordinates to aid in navigating the Long Path and allow the hiker to reliably place themselves relative to the important points on the trail. This includes all of the major named features and all of the official parking areas.

Each GPS coordinate in this book is given in Universal Transverse Mercator (UTM), a worldwide standard for specifying a location on the Earth. UTM has become popular among GPS users because the coordinates are north and east specifications in meters. Knowing the UTM coordinates for two positions allows one to easily estimate the distance between the positions.

One caveat of using a GPS for navigation is that there are many different references for specifying a position. Nearly all United States Geological Survey (USGS) topographic maps are referenced to NAD27 while all GPS units in this country come from the factory set to NAD83/WGS84 (the later two standards are identical for practical use in North America). All of the coordinates in this book are given using the NAD83/WGS84 standards. In the area covered by the Long Path, the difference in position using a given coordinate amounts to several hundred feet when switching between NAD27 and NAD83/WGS84.

The second caveat for using a GPS for navigation is that there is an inherent error in GPS positions that depend on the satellite configuration and signal reception conditions at the time of measurement. Although under ideal conditions, a consumer GPS unit can be as accurate as ten feet, twenty to fifty feet is more typical. The GPS positions in the descriptions in this book specify location information to more precision than the accuracy allows. This means that using a GPS unit to move to the position exactly as stated in the trail descriptions in this book will place one very close to the intended point, but not necessarily closer than one hundred feet, depending on conditions.

A third caveat for GPS users is that USGS topographic maps can contain systematic positional errors. Some of the older maps completed from aerial photographs taken during World War II, which includes many of the quads required to obtain coverage of the Long Path, can have average horizontal errors of as much as 200 feet compared to a GPS or recent aerial photographs of the same area.

Thus, although a GPS unit can be very precise for navigation, it may not correspond to topographic or any other map sources based only on USGS data.

End-to-End

The New York-New Jersey Trail Conference offers a certificate and an End-to-End "rocker" to anyone who hikes the entire length of the Long Path. Hikers have the option of using the traditional Orange County route or the more scenic Shawangunk Ridge route. The trip can be completed in one continuous trip or in a number of hikes over many years. As of November 2001, there are 69 Long Path End-  to-Enders. The certificate is free to members of the Trail Conference, but there is a $5.00 handling charge for nonmembers.

Since the Long Path is continually expanding, the requirements for completing the trail are constantly changing. For information on current requirements, a tally sheet, or more information, contact The Long Path End-to-End Committee, c/o Ed Walsh, 11 Kwiecinski Street, West Haverstraw, NY 10993.

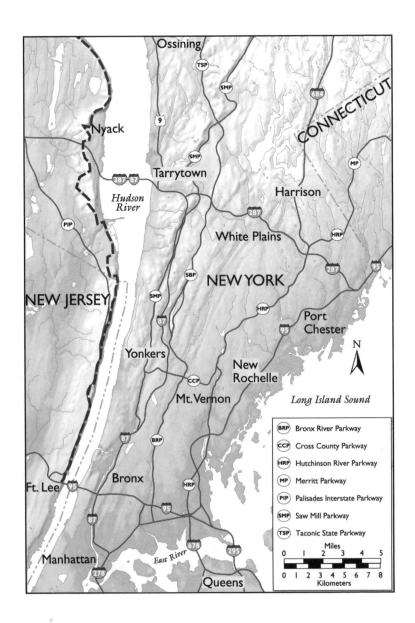

Hudson Palisades

The southernmost sections of the Long Path follow the Hudson River and the Hudson Palisades north, staying close to the river and to civilization. Although the trail does have some quiet forests and lakes, the majority of its scenic vistas look out over the Hudson River and the works of civilization. Its most impressive views encompass towns and villages along the way, but the most conspicuous ones are of the cities and villages on the east side of the Hudson River, not the least of which include the Borough of Manhattan and the City of Yonkers. On most days, it is possible to see barges and tugboats plying the river, and occasionally a small freighter passing as it connects points along the navigable portions of the Hudson River from Albany on south to the great port of New York City. These southernmost sections of the Long Path are the main ones easily accessible by public transportation, making them attractive and easily reachable weekend jaunts into nature for those who live in New York City.

Forest view, New Jersey Palisades

MICHAEL WARREN

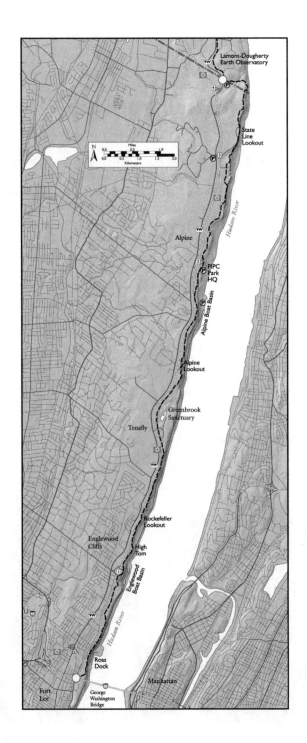

1. George Washington Bridge to NY-NJ State Line

Feature: New Jersey Palisades
Distance: 12.70 miles
USGS Map Quads: Central Park, Yonkers, and Nyack
Trail Conference Map: Map 4A, Hudson Palisades Trails, New Jersey Section

General Description

The Long Path follows the crest of the spectacular Palisades Escarpment on the western bank of the Hudson River near New York City, wandering between the cliff edge and the Palisades Interstate Parkway. The route affords stunning views of the basaltic face of the Palisades, the Hudson River and the City of New York and its suburbs. The trail passes through rich forests, with occasional streams and swamps. Old roads, rock walls and foundations along the route are remnants of past settlement along the Palisades. Several side trails lead down to the Shore Trail along the Hudson River. These allow the hiker to make a number of interesting circuits; the *New York Walk Book* and the *New Jersey Walk Book*, both published by the New York-New Jersey Trail Conference, can be consulted for additional information. The trail is generally wide and nearly level (except for some steep sections near the New York-New Jersey border). Unfortunately, the trail is almost always within sound of the Palisades Interstate Parkway. In 1971 this section of the Long Path was designated a National Recreational Trail by Secretary of the Interior, Roger C. B. Morton.

Access

From New York: Take the George Washington Bridge to the first exit after the Palisades Interstate Parkway.
From New Jersey: Take any road, including the Palisades Interstate Parkway, I-95, NJ 4 and US 1-9, that leads to the George Washington Bridge. The trail begins on Hudson Terrace, the easternmost north-south road in the vicinity of the Bridge, just north of the overpass that carries the approach to the Bridge over Hudson Terrace.
By public transportation: Take any bus or subway to the George Washington Bridge Bus Terminal and walk over the bridge or take a bus to Bridge Plaza in Fort Lee, NJ. From Bridge Plaza North, walk south to the first cross

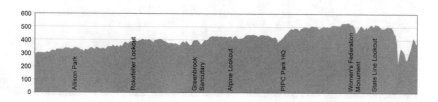

street, turn left towards the river, and turn left on Hudson Terrace to reach a stairway and the start of the trail. The Red and Tan Lines buses 9W and 9A give access to many points along the trail from US Route 9W.

Parking

0.00 Fort Lee Historic Park, about two blocks south of the trailhead on Hudson Terrace (fee charged April-November); street parking along and near Hudson Terrace (free on Sundays and holidays; meters with one-hour limit on other days). (18T 587325E 4522705N).
1.40 Allison Park (when open). (18T 588250E 4524884N).
3.30 Rockefeller Lookout (20-minute limit). (18T 589185E 4527341N)
6.50 Alpine Lookout (20-minute limit). (18T 590350E 4531621N)
10.40 Parking along Route 9W in Alpine near overpass leading to Women's Federation Monument. (18T 591394E 4537120N)
11.25 State Line Lookout. (18T 591990E 4538017N)
12.70 Parking along Route 9W at NY-NJ state line, just south of the access road to Lamont-Doherty Earth Observatory. (18T 591566E 4539432N)
Parking is also available at Ross Dock and the Englewood and Alpine Boat Basins on the Hudson River (fee charged in season); side trails lead up to the Long Path.

Manhattan and the George Washington Bridge

Trail Description

0.00 The Long Path begins on Hudson Terrace at the steps leading to the northern pedestrian walkway of the George Washington Bridge. Three Aqua blazes at the foot of the steps mark the start of the trail. The trail climbs two sets of steps, turns left to cross a bridge roadway, and enters the woods on a broad gravel track to the right of a chain-link fence. The Long Path follows the "Trail to River" signs while several side paths lead left and right. There are a few views of the Hudson River.

0.50 At the last of several signs for "Trail to River," the Carpenters Trail (blue on top and white on the bottom) heads right, leading to the Shore Trail (white). The Long Path continues to the left on a narrower track near the cliff edge. In 300 feet, a side trail (white on top and blue on the bottom) leads left to a footbridge over the Palisades Interstate Parkway. The Long Path continues on past the former site of an old mounted cannon from the Spanish-American War. The trail then goes by several old stone walls and crosses a stream.

1.15 The trail passes a gas station (water, vending machines, food, phone) on the left and then crosses a stream after a short while.

1.40 The trail passes to the left of the iron fence surrounding Allison Park to reach the entrance to Allison Park. This park was developed by the trustees of the Estate of William O. Allison (1849-1924), who was born and spent his life

nearby.[5] When open, the park offers water, restrooms, phone, and overlooks. The Long Path continues along the paved access road to the park, enters a narrow strip of woods near the Parkway, and passes the entrance road to St. Peters College. It briefly follows the Parkway's shoulder before heading back toward the edge of the Palisade's cliffs on what becomes an abandoned asphalt drive.

2.10 The trail descends steps to Palisade Avenue, turns right, turns left at the corner and goes up another set of steps to the right. It then turns left to follow the cliff edge. Views across the river include the Henry Hudson Bridge over the Harlem River and Manhattan's Inwood Hill Park. The medieval-looking monastery is the Metropolitan Museum of Art's Cloisters.

2.75 As the Long Path turns left, an unmarked trail straight ahead leads to the High Tom promontory with its magnificent views up the river.

3.25 The Long Path reaches Rockefeller Lookout and its tremendous views. Not long after, it crosses a small stream and briefly follows an old gravel road. There are many fine river views. Clinton Point, reached by a short walk toward the right away from the Long Path immediately after it passes an open

---

[5] William O. Allison was a native of the small group of small fishing villages that developed at the base of the Palisades during the 19th century. He was born in Undercliff Village in 1849 and became a successful journalist in his early twenties. He started a trade journal (the *Oil, Paint, and Drug Reporter*) and became very successful at acquiring more trade journals, making him a wealthy man. In his later years, he interviewed old-timers from the Undercliffs, but a large part of his historical collection burned along with his mansion in 1903. The trustees of his estate established Allison Park, and some of the land he owned is now a part of the Flatbrook Sanctuary in Englewood.

Blackledge-Kearny House, Alpine Boat Basin

MICHAEL WARREN

Women's Federation Monument

area, is one of the best viewpoints. Just after the trail crosses another stream, reach the fence for the Greenbrook Sanctuary on the right of the trail.

5.10 The trail crosses the entrance road to the Greenbrook Sanctuary. The Sanctuary, open to interested parties by membership, preserves a splendid example of the forests and other habitats that once ranged along the top of the Palisades. The Long Path continues along the Sanctuary's fence, twice plunging below the grade of the Parkway to cross over streams that run through woodland swamps.

5.95 The Huylers Landing Trail (red), which connects to the Shore Trail (white) at the Hudson's edge, leads right at a very sharp angle shortly after leaving the Sanctuary fence. The Long Path then returns to the edge of the Palisades.

6.45 Reach Alpine Lookout, with many fine views. The trail runs past the lookout point and enters the woods at the end of the cliff-edge railing. It then passes a series of old stone walls and foundations and travels briefly on an old road as it meanders between the Parkway and the cliff edge. It is never far from either, but there are plenty of river views.

7.85 A tunnel leaves to the left under Palisades Interstate Parkway to US Route 9W.

8.05 The trail uses a tunnel to pass below Alpine Approach Road. Immediately after the tunnel, the Alpine Approach Trail (orange blazes) leads right and down the hill to the Alpine Boat Basin. The Long Path shifts left at this point and exits the woods. (For reverse direction, a sign reading "Path to River" shows where the Long Path leaves the paved road and enters the woods.)

8.25 The trail passes the headquarters of the New Jersey section of Palisades Interstate Park. There are water, telephone, bathroom facilities, and information about the Park and Greenbrook Sanctuary in the Park Commission headquarters building. The Long Path enters the woods on a wide path at the north end of the headquarters parking lot, past the building. Once in the woods, it goes through a variety of hardwood and hemlock forests that afford river views, some quite fine.

10.00 The trail reaches the end of Ruckman Road. To the right is an overlook above the Hudson (with a concrete block wall). The Long Path turns left on Ruckman Road and, in another 50 feet, turns right on a gravel road into well-developed forest. Meet a second gravel road leading right to run along the cliff edge. This road, not part of the Long Path, ends in about 900 feet at the terminus of a great split off the main face of the Palisades. With its many splendid views, it makes a worthwhile excursion.

10.40 The trail turns right on a narrow gravel road. In another 500 feet, the Long Path reaches a second gravel road. The left branch, marked with blue-and-white rectangles, leads to a footbridge over the Parkway to parking on 9W and to the Bergen Boy Scouts Council's Camp Alpine. To the right, these markers run concurrently with the Long Path.

10.55 Reach a clearing with stone monument shaped like a castle, a reminder of the preservation works of the New Jersey State Federation of Women's Clubs. They played an instrumental part in creating Palisades Interstate Park at the beginning of the 20th century. Beyond the clearing, the trail descends on rock steps. A few hundred yards farther, the blue-and-white trail, now called the Forest View Trail, leaves to the right and descends to the river to connect with the Shore Trail (white). The Long Path continues ahead to cross a stream and begin an ascent on steps to reach the concrete access road to State Line Lookout. (This road was originally part of US Route 9W). The trail bears right past large stones that block vehicle access and follows the concrete road.

11.25 The State Line Lookout's snack bar, with restrooms, food, water, and phone, is on the left. The concession remains open all year. The trail continues along the edge of the concrete road and passes Point Lookout on top of Indian Head, the highest point in the New Jersey section of Palisades Interstate Park. In another 225 yards, the Long Path bears right into the woods, just past the end of the rock wall along the roadside.

11.90 Continue straight ahead as a cross-country ski trail comes in from the left. In another 300 feet, the Long Path turns right, up four steps, and continues on a narrower path. It turns right at a chain-link fence marking the New Jersey-New York state boundary (to the left, there is a stone boundary monument placed in 1882). The trail descends along the fence on stone steps, turns left, and passes through a gate in the fence to enter NY. It continues to descend on steps, often quite steeply, close to the edge of the cliffs.

12.20 The steps end and the Long Path turns left to descend more gradually to a stream crossing.

12.35 The Shore Trail (white) goes right and follows the stream for 0.75 miles to a beautiful cascade and remnants of Lawrence Garden (or Italian Garden, designed after a garden in Amalfi). The Long Path turns left to follow the stream uphill, ascending gently but steadily. Another unmarked trail leaves to the left 0.2 miles farther along the Long Path as the ascent ends.

12.70 The Long Path reaches US Route 9W at the entrance road to Lamont-Doherty Earth Observatory, just north of the New Jersey-New York state line. To continue, cross the entrance road.

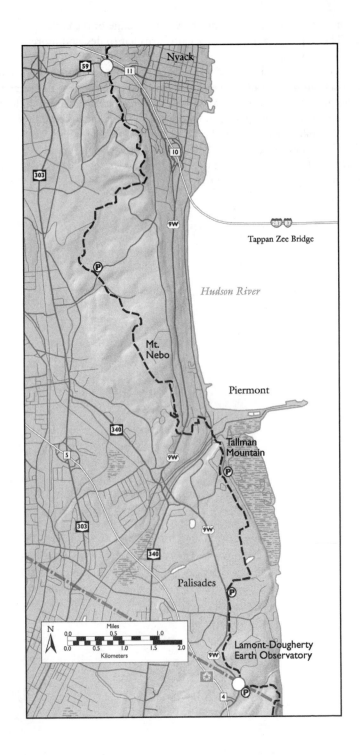

2. NY–NJ State Line to Nyack

Features: Tallman Mountain State Park, Clausland Mountain County Park, Tackamack Town Park, and Blauvelt State Park
Distance: 10.30 miles
USGS Map Quads: Nyack
Trail Conference Maps: Map 4B, Hudson Palisades Trails, New York Section

General Description

After following the Palisades through New Jersey, the Long Path continues into New York along the Palisades Escarpment. This section is a mix of state, county and town parks and some suburban road walking. The trail begins along US Route 9W in the hamlet of Palisades, continues to Tallman Mountain State Park, descends to the Village of Piermont, ascends to Mt. Nebo, Clausland Mountain County Park, Tackamack Town Park, and Blauvelt State Park, and finally descends into Nyack. This section is rich in history with the trail passing close to historic places such as Sneden's Landing, the Revolutionary War hamlet of Palisades, Rockland Cemetery (General Frémont's Grave) and the abandoned rifle ranges in Blauvelt State Park.

Access

Take the Palisades Interstate Parkway to Exit 4, just south of the New York–New Jersey state line. Turn north onto Route 9W and continue to the entrance of Lamont-Doherty Earth Observatory.
By public transportation: The Red and Tan Lines buses 9W and 9A give access to many points along the trail from Route 9W.

Parking

0.00 Parking along Route 9W at the NY–NJ state line, just south of access road of Lamont-Doherty Earth Observatory. (18T 591566E 4539432N)
1.00 Route 9W at Rockland County bike trail near the south entrance to Tallman Mountain State Park. (18T 591378E 4540991N)
2.60 Tallman Mountain State Park picnic area. (Unlocated)
3.45 Street parking in Piermont. (18T 591117E 4543586N)
6.70 Tackamack Park on Clausland Mountain Road. (18T 589147E 4546229N)
10.30 Street parking in Nyack. (Unlocated)

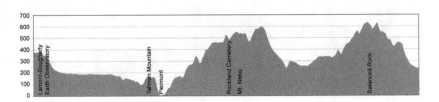

Trail Description

0.00 The Long Path crosses the entrance to Columbia University's Lamont-Doherty Earth Observatory near the gatehouse. The observatory has departments for research into climatology, geochemistry, oceans, and climate, and seismology. The trail veers right, then left, and stays close to Route 9W. Pass a swamp to the right. The trail then crosses a stone wall and ascends over a small knoll.

0.25 Turn right onto a woods road and continue downhill, roughly paralleling Route 9W.

0.45 The Long Path turns left into the woods and reaches the parking lot of a building, the former Tree Ring Lab of the Lamont-Doherty Earth Observatory, but now a daycare facility. Turn left toward Route 9W and then right onto the highway. Hikers should exercise extreme caution along this road. It has frequent high-speed traffic. Keep to the left of the road, well within the white line.

0.55 Reach intersection with Washington Spring Road and Oak Tree Road in the Hamlet of Palisades, New York. This is an area rich with history. To the right is Sneden's Landing. Today, it is a well-known enclave for artists and actors escaping from New York City. Historically, Sneden's Landing was the site of ferry service to Dobbs Ferry. Exactly 2 miles west on Oak Tree Road are historic sites such as the De Wint house in the Hamlet of Tappan, Washington's headquarters in the Revolutionary War, and the 1776 House where the British spy Major André was kept prisoner prior to his execution. The Long Path continues north along Route 9W.

1.00 The Long Path turns right, leaving Route 9W, and enters Tallman State Park, passing a parking area to the left. It heads towards the river on a gravel road, part of the Tallman Bike Path.

1.30 With ruins of a brick-and-concrete building visible to the right, the Long

Winter view of the Sparkill Marsh

JAKOB FRANKE

Bridge on the footpath, Tallman Mountain State Park

Path turns left and continues along a raised berm. These elevated mounds of dirt were built in the early 20th century to retain seepage from a never-constructed oil storage facility that was to be established in the area. The Long Path crosses a marshy section on plank bridging and passes a pond on the right.

1.95 The Long Path curves to the right and crosses the Tallman Bike Path. After crossing it, the trail turns left and follows the Palisades Escarpment parallel to the river. There are views through the trees of Sparkill Marsh, filled with *Phragmites communis* (common name "giant reed") extending out into the river.

2.45 The Long Path skirts the South Picnic Area of the Park, passing a stone comfort station to the left. It descends stone steps and a paved path to cross a wooden bridge over a stream. With the park swimming pool visible below to the right, the Long Path turns sharply left and goes up a paved path with a wooden railing.

2.70 At a traffic circle, the Long Path crosses the park road leading down to the river. On the other side of the road, it ascends railroad-tie steps and continues to climb, steeply at times, to the North Picnic Area. At the top, it turns right and follows the park road that runs close to the edge of the escarpment.

3.00 The Long Path reaches an outstanding viewpoint on the trail's right over the Hudson River. The Tappan Zee Bridge and Hook Mountain are visible to the north. Directly below are the mile-long Piermont Pier (the original terminus of the Erie Railroad) and the extensive Sparkill Marsh. The villages of

Irvington and Dobbs Ferry may be seen across the river, with the gothic tower of the Lyndhurst mansion on the skyline to the northeast. Turn right, leaving the road, and begin a steep, rocky descent towards Piermont. Interesting restaurants and shops are found in the village.

3.15 At the bottom of the descent, the Long Path turns left on a gravel road, the route of the Tallman Bike Path. In 200 feet, the bike path ends, and the Long Path turns right on Ferdon Avenue. It immediately crosses Sparkill Creek and enters the Village of Piermont. At a traffic light, the trail crosses South Piermont Avenue (left) and Paradise Avenue (right) to continue straight ahead on Piermont Avenue.

3.45 At the old railroad crossing in the center of Piermont, the trail turns left onto Tate Avenue and climbs uphill, then right and parallels the river. The trail veers left and climbs up an old concrete staircase, emerging onto Ash Street adjacent to the former railroad station. (The station building, which is over 100 years old, is now unused.) The abandoned Erie Railroad right-of-way that crosses the Long Path here is a rail trail and an official side-trail to the Long Path. It provides an interesting alternative path, with Hudson River views, north to Nyack. The Long Path turns left and continues west along Ash Street to Piermont Place. Turn left on Piermont Place and then right on Crescent Road. At the end of Crescent Road turn left, and follow the path past several houses on the right. Turn right on an old fire road and, in 75 yards, reach US Route 9W. Turn right on Route 9W and follow it for a few yards to Castle Road, a rural road.

3.90 Turn left on Castle Road, which then bends north. This part of the road is private. Before reaching the last house, the trail heads to the right into the woods and rejoins the old fire-road. Turn right and follow this road into Rockland Cemetery. It has fine views west toward the Ramapos in the distance. About 500 feet after passing the last house, the path meets a paved cemetery road. The trail makes a 180-degree turn and continues uphill on the cemetery road to reach the top of the Palisades and a seasonal view of the Hudson. At the top, the trail passes the obelisk memorializing Henry Honeychurch Gorringe, who transported Cleopatra's Needle from Egypt, as well as the monument to General John Charles Frémont, better known as the "Pathfinder." Also buried at the cemetery, almost within touching distance of the Long Path is George Zoebelein, a long-time trail supervisor of the Long Path in Rockland County, and a former president of the Trail Conference. George's gravesite is approximately 30 feet from where the trail makes the 180-degree turn.

4.80 The Long Path leaves the cemetery and gradually regains the Palisades ridge where heads northwest along the ridge. It continues on a level path through the woods, crossing several stone walls and intermittent streams.

5.50 The Long Path arrives at a three-way trail intersection. An orange-marked trail, built and maintained by Rockland County, goes to the right to Mt. Nebo, once an Air Force Nike missile site and now a recreation area for the Town of Orangetown. The same trail will rejoin the Long Path in 0.40 miles. The Long Path continues straight ahead and heads downhill, crosses a streambed, makes a left jog, and then goes right. An old woods road goes left and leads to NY Route 303, near the Kings Highway intersection. The trail ascends gradually and then undulates through the woods of Clausland Mountain County Park.

5.90 The orange-marked trail comes in from the right. The Long Path continues, crossing a couple of streams along the way, the last one on a wooden bridge.

6.70 The trail crosses Clausland Mountain Road and enters Tackamack Town Park in the Town of Orangetown. Tackamack was the Indian name of Jan Claus, a trader who lived in the area.[1] The trail passes through a metal gate and descends, first on a gravel road and then on a woods road, until it reaches a small water impoundment. Here the Long Path goes right into the woods, following the water impoundment. The trail follows the stream for a while and finally crosses it on a wooden bridge. Not long afterwards, the Long Path crosses Marsico Court.

7.20 The trail enters Blauvelt State Park, passes through a stand of evergreens, and veers right, after which it joins a woods road. A nearby embankment was the site of the firing line for the pre-World War I National Guard Camp Bluefield's rifle range. They were forced to close the camp because the lead from the bullets kept landing in Grand View, to the east along the river. All the trees in this section were planted after the National Guard abandoned it. The Long Path turns right, following the stone wall, and then follows a series of woods roads around the rifle range. The trail parallels a target wall of the rifle range.

7.75 The Long Path climbs over a small embankment and descends a set of wooden steps to a woods road. This embankment is actually the earth-covered concrete tunnel that provided safe passage from the firing line to the target wall. The trail continues to the right along the woods road, passing the entrance to the tunnel off to the right. It continues straight ahead, turns right at a split in the road, and turns sharply left on another woods road, then, at a stream crossing, turns right uphill into the woods before finally emerging onto Tweed Boulevard (Rockland County Route 5). The Long Path crosses the boulevard and climbs a staircase onto the crest of the Palisades ridge.

8.70 There is a 180-degree view here, with the Tappan Zee, Piermont Pier, New York City and the Hackensack River valley visible. This was the site of the famous "Balanced Rock." Because vandals managed to unbalance it, park officials were forced to remove it in 1966. From here, the trail continues along the ridge before finally descending to a gravel road. The road leads left to Tweed Boulevard and right to a water tank.

9.10 The Long Path continues by crossing the gravel road and making a sharp ascent to gain the ridge. The trail starts descending, crosses an open woods road, and continues north. It passes a grove of evergreens just before reaching

---

[1] Although a Native American of the Wicqaskeek tribe on the east side of the Hudson, Tackamack adopted the Dutch name of Jan Claus (or Jan Klase). He was a very active signer of Native American deeds and his name can be found on the deeds establishing the Tappan patent, the Demarest patent, and the Wawayanda patent. One wonders how he had established the right to sign these patents on behalf of Native Americans.

Bradley Hill Road (Rockland County Route 38).

9.60 The trail turns right on Bradley Hill Road and, after a few paces, turns left into the woods just past a driveway and regains the Palisades ridge crest. If heading for historic Nyack instead of staying on the Long Path, continue on Bradley Hill Road and turn right onto South Highland Avenue, at the entrance to Nyack College. Turn right onto Upland Drive; turn right onto South Boulevard, and then left onto Central Avenue. Left onto Prospect Avenue, right onto Terrace Drive, and left onto Lowland Drive. Following a switchback, US Route 9W is reached. Turn left to a bridge across the New York State Thruway and cross the bridge. At a blinking red light (corner of Franklin Street and Clinton Avenue) the rail-trail from Piermont to Nyack is reached. Follow the rail-trail to the left to reach the center of Nyack. Broadway, where buses, shops, and restaurants are available, is one block to the right.

9.85 The Long Path passes an opening in an old stone wall. It has good views into the Village of Nyack. The trail descends west off the ridge and turns right to pass a residential area.

10.05 The trail emerges onto the end of paved Towt Road. It follows Towt Road and then continues onto Waldron Avenue.

10.30 The trail reaches the intersection of Waldron Avenue and NY Route 59. Here there are a number of motels, stores and fast food restaurants. To continue, proceed straight ahead (the road beyond this point is known as Mountainview Avenue).

3. Nyack to Long Clove

Features: Hook Mountain
Distance: 8.90 miles
USGS Map Quads: Nyack and Haverstraw
Trail Conference Maps: Map 4B, Hudson Palisades Trails, New York Section

General Description

The first two miles of this section are suburban and the trail frequently runs along roads or near houses. After leaving US Route 9W, the Long Path ascends Hook Mountain. Its bare summit affords splendid views up and down the Hudson River. The trail then continues through gentle woodlands and along ridges, passing an old cemetery and some old quarries.

Access

Take the New York State Thruway to Exit 11, Mountainview Avenue.
By public transportation: The Red and Tan Lines buses US 9W and 9A give access to many points along the trail from US Route 9W.

Parking

0.00 Strip shopping centers near Mountainview Avenue may provide parking. (Unlocated)
2.00 Christian Herald Road at Route US 9W. (18T 590067E 4551298N)
5.60 Landing Hill Road (limited, tends to fill up on weekends). (18T 591294E 4555293N)
6.25 Golf course parking lot. (Unlocated)
8.90 Long Clove Road and US Route 9W (limited parking). (18T 588510E 4558666N)

Trail Description

0.00 The section begins where Waldron Avenue/Mountainview Avenue crosses NY Route 59. There is a traffic light at the intersection. The Long Path continues north on Mountainview Avenue and heads uphill to the bridge over the New York State Thruway. This is a busy commercial area with food and phones widely available. Once crossing the Thruway, Mountainview Avenue becomes a quiet street and passes a driveway on the right.

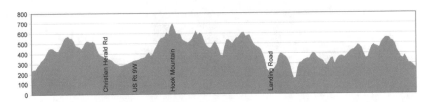

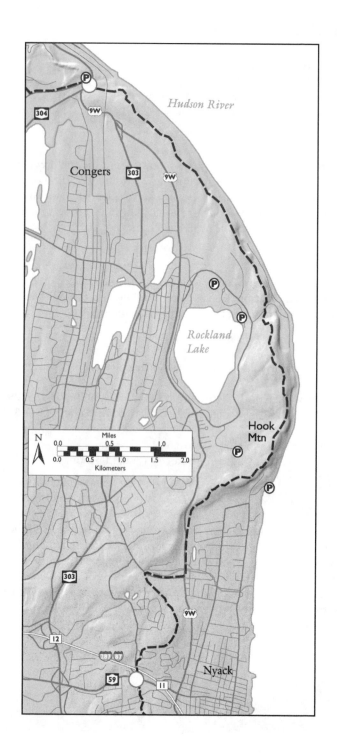

0.25 The trail turns right into woodland after passing the driveway. Next, the trail crosses a road from an apartment complex and ascends the steep pitch on the other side. It quickly bears right and passes through a narrow strip of woods with housing complexes on both sides. At the next junction, continuing eastward on a woods road leads to a corner of Oak Hill Cemetery where there are spectacular views of the Tappan Zee, one of the widest parts of the Hudson. The trail turns left instead and climbs the woods road on a series of switchbacks to a water tank.

0.70 Now on the level, the trail continues northward along a stone wall. It skirts another garden apartment complex on the left through adjoining woodland. An unmarked trail drops down on the right to the Nyack High School, but continue on the level. Finally, the trail makes a dramatic turn downhill on a pathway created through the fallen talus and reaches Christian Herald Road.

1.60 Turn right onto Christian Herald Road.

2.00 The Long Path turns left onto Route US 9W at a traffic light.

2.40 Leave US Route 9W through a gap in the guardrail. After about 20 feet, the trail turns right into the woods, and moves diagonally away from the road. Pass an intersection on the right where the Upper Nyack Trail (white) descends downhill through the woods. It ends after 0.75 miles at the entrance to Nyack Beach State Park. This permits a circular hike using the Long Path and the Shore Path at the base of Hook Mountain. Views of the Hudson River and the Tappan Zee Bridge appear, and the trail begins the often steep and rocky climb up Hook Mountain.

3.15 The open, rocky summit of Hook Mountain affords a tremendous view up and down the Hudson River with the Palisades visible to the south on the right bank of the river. The trail now descends through dry woods. Many fine

Chicken mushroom (Laetiporus sulphureus)

JAKOB FRANKE

View from Hook Mountain

views occur as the trail trends downward along a broad woods road on the west side of Hook Mountain's ridge. As the trail approaches the recreation areas of Rockland Lake State Park, it passes an old stone wall and several unmarked side trails leaving to either side. After a final steep descent, reach Landing Hill Road.

5.65 Turning right downhill, Landing Hill Road will meet the Shore Trail (white). It can be used for a circular hike over and around Hook Mountain. Turning left leads to Rockland Lake State Park and US Route 9W. The Long Path crosses the Landing Hill Road and begins to climb. It quickly passes a tiny, old cemetery, the Wells Family Cemetary, with faded headstones from the 19th century. After passing the cemetary, the trail begins to go up and down, following the crest of the ridge. There are several beautiful views, some from precipices, of Croton Point Park and Croton Dam on the other side of the Hudson River. The trail passes tennis courts and a stone wall to the left.

6.25 An unmarked trail leads left to the parking lot of the State Park golf course. When open, the concession provides water, phone and food. The Long Path continues along the ridge, often changing from upward to downward, with views through the trees both to the left and to the right.

8.50 The Long Path makes a sharp left, up a slight grade, as an unnamed trail (white) continues straight ahead. This trail leads down to the Shore Path. The Long Path crosses under a power line, beneath which there is a railroad tunnel, and descends to US Route 9W.

8.90 The trail reaches US Route 9W just east of its intersection with NY Route 304. To continue, cross US Route 9W and follow Long Clove Road.

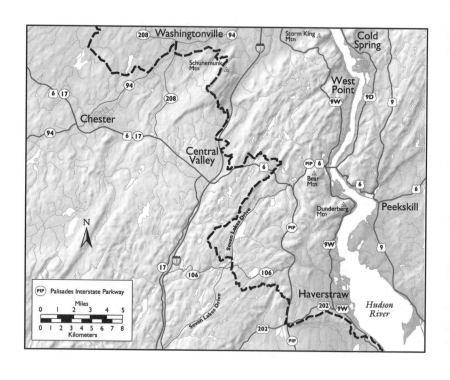

The Hudson Highlands

The Long Path makes its first foray into genuine mountains as it passes through the Hudson Highlands. It is the first time that the trail passes above 1000 feet elevation above sea level. As part of its journey north through this region, it traverses the length of two major New York State Parks, Harriman, one of the oldest, and Schunemunk Mountain, one of the newest. It also enters a part of New York State that is steeped in Trail Conference history. Many of the trails created by the Trail Conference in its infancy are contained in Harriman and Bear Mountain State Parks. The very first section of the Appalachian Trail lies in Harriman and that first section crosses the Long Path near Island Pond Mountain in Section 6. There are many, many trails throughout the Harriman and Bear Mountain State Parks, making endless loop possibilities incorporating portions of the Long Path.

Lake Kanawauke from Pine Swamp Mountain

HERB CHONG

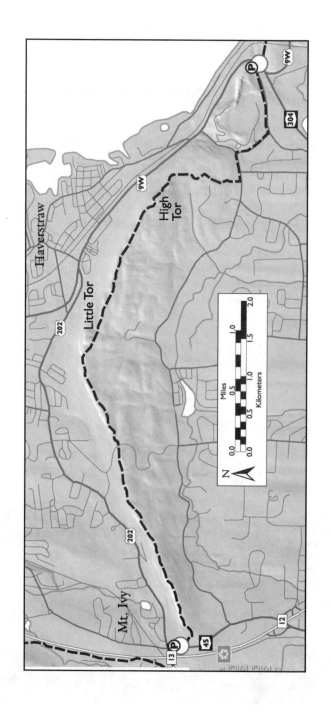

4. Long Clove to Mt. Ivy

Features: High Tor
Distance: 7.00 miles
USGS Map Quads: Thiells
Trail Conference Maps: Map 4B, Hudson Palisades Trails, New York Section

General Description

In this section, the Long Path travels along little used roads for a mile, passing dramatic quarried cliffs of the Palisades, and then enters the woods and ascends High Tor. The ascent is often steep, with several good viewpoints. The open summit affords a 360-degree view up and down the Hudson Valley. The trail then descends from High Tor, ultimately passing Little Tor while following the ridge. After crossing Central Highway, the trail enters Rockland County's South Mountain Park. The section ends by descending off the western curving edge of the Palisades just before that feature plunges below the ground.

Access

This section begins on US Route 9W about 100 yards east of its junction with NY Route 304. The trail crosses Route 9W in the center of an "S" curve on the highway.
By public transportation: The Red and Tan Lines 11A bus stops at the intersection of Ridge Road and South Mountain Road, which the trail crosses.

Parking

0.00 Long Clove Road and Route 9W (limited parking). (18T 588510E 4558666N)
1.10 Along South Mountain Road west of Scratchup Road (limited to 4-5 cars). (18T 587000E 4558935N)
4.75 Central Highway (limited parking). (18T 583470E 4560575N)
7.00 Mt. Ivy commuter parking lot, open to those with Trail Conference or member club affiliation on non-business days; phone Haverstraw Police at 845-354-1500 on morning of hike. (18T 580796E 4559834N)

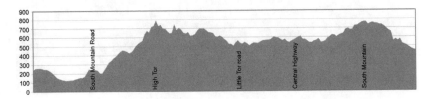

Trail Description

0.00 The section begins at the intersection of Long Clove Road and US Route 9W. The trail proceeds northward on Long Clove Road and follows the road uphill around a sharp left hook. The name of the street changes to Scratchup Road after a short while.

0.60 Follow the road along a sharp right turn. The trail passes the gates for the Tilcon New York quarry.

1.00 The trail swings left and uphill to reach South Mountain Road. Turn left here onto the road. This is a twisting road with narrow shoulders. Remember to walk single file facing traffic.

1.10 Reach a small parking area (4-5 cars) on the right. Then pass Ridge Road on the left.

1.20 After an open area, the trail turns right into the woods. It continues uphill, sometimes climbing steeply, meandering beside and sometimes over stone walls.

1.70 The trail levels off and passes through a stand of mountain laurel. After a brief descent, the trail resumes uphill climbing to reach the ridge top near another stone wall.

1.95 Turn left at the top of the ridge and follow a well-trodden route near the cliff edge. The trail turns away from the cliff face to begin the first of four short, extremely steep climbs that often require hand pulls.

2.30 After the fourth steep rise, reach the summit of High Tor. High Tor is the highest peak on the Palisades and its open, rocky summit affords spectacular views in all directions. The Hudson River vanishes to the north behind Dunderberg Mountain. Directly below, along the Hudson, is the Town of

Haverstraw

MICHAEL WARREN

Deer by the trailside

Haverstraw. Entergy's Indian Point nuclear plant is visible across from Tomkins Cove. To the west, the rolling hills of the Ramapos and Harriman State Park may be seen. The polygonal pattern visible on the summit's rocks is a natural result of the cooling of the diabase that forms the Palisades. Colonists used the summit as a signal point during the Revolution, and it later was the site of an airplane beacon; the remains of the tower are still visible. The peak was subject of Maxwell Anderson's play *High Tor*. The Long Path leaves High Tor and drops steeply into the woods.

2.45 The trail reaches the end of a fire road that it will follow gently downhill all the way to Central Highway. On the way, it runs through deciduous woods on or near the top of the ridge of the Palisades. The slope is steep to the right of the trail and gentle to the left.

3.05 The Long Path meets an unmarked trail to the right. This trail leads to a summit over the cliff edge.

3.70 The trail crosses a dirt road. To the right, the road heads briefly uphill and swings to the front of the open summit of Little Tor. To the left is a small artificial pond. It was the water source for the Kaatz mansion, a building demolished in the early 1970's during the construction of High Tor State Park. There is a fine view to the north, with Haverstraw directly below. As the Long Path continues gradually descending along the ridge, it is crossed by many unmarked side trails and dirt roads.

4.45 Cross beneath a power line.

4.75 Cross Central Highway and enter Rockland County's South Mountain Park. The trail enters the woods on a gravel road, but just after passing the car barrier, it leaves the road and turns right onto a steep path. The trail is gener-

Tilcon quarry

ally close to and parallel with the gravel road and crosses it once.

5.20 Join the gravel road briefly as it curves left. Follow the road for about 50 feet and than leave it to descend gently to the right. The Long Path is now a wide, well-cleared path through the woods following the cliff edge of the Palisades. There are extensive views to the south.

6.55 A precipice affords a view of Cheesecote Mountain and Limekiln, Catamount and Horse Stable Mountains. An old quarry and the edge of the Palisades can be seen looking down along the direction of the trail.

6.65 A view over an old quarry shows the end of the Palisades. Beyond, the Palisades ridge dips into the ground. The trail follows this last curving ridge downhill.

6.85 Reach NY Route 45, cross it and turn right. (For reverse direction, the trail enters the woods just south of a dirt road and a county park sign). The trail passes the entrance to the Mt. Ivy commuter parking lot.

7.00 Reach the intersection of NY Route 45 and US Route 202. To continue, turn left onto Route 202.

5. Mt. Ivy to Lake Skannatati

Features: Harriman State Park
Distance: 9.30 miles
USGS Map Quads: Thiells
Trail Conference Maps: Map 3, Southern Harriman-Bear Mountain Trails

General Description

The Long Path heads north along the Palisades Interstate Parkway for about a mile, crosses the South Branch of Minisceongo Creek, turns west, and climbs up the side of Cheesecote Mountain before descending past Cheesecote Pond and Letchworth Village Cemetery. The trail briefly follows Calls Hollow Road before turning west into Harriman State Park. Harriman State Park is a stunningly beautiful preserve of lakes, hemlock and hardwood forest, historical trails and sites, wetlands, mountains and ridges. With its proximity to the New York metropolitan area, many parts of Harriman become crowded on weekends and holidays. On the portion of its route through the Park covered in this section, the Long Path keeps largely to gentle grades until it reaches Lake Skannatati.

Access

This section begins at the intersection of NY Route 45 and US Route 202, just east of Exit 13 of the Palisades Interstate Parkway. The trail turns west off Calls Hollow Road, about 2.6 miles north of Old Route 202 in Ladentown. The section ends at a fisherman's access parking area beside Lake Skannatati on Seven Lakes Drive, about 0.75 miles north of Kanawauke Circle.

Parking

0.00 Mt. Ivy commuter parking lot, open to those with Trail Conference or member club affiliation on non-business days; phone Haverstraw Police at 845-354-1500 on morning of hike. (18T 580796E 4559834N)
3.50 Calls Hollow Road (room for 1-2 cars). Not recommended because of possible vandalism. (18T 579587E 4563388N)
9.30 Lake Skannatati parking area. (18T 575219E 4566012N)

Camping

5.60 Big Hill Shelter

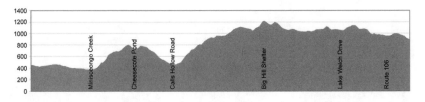

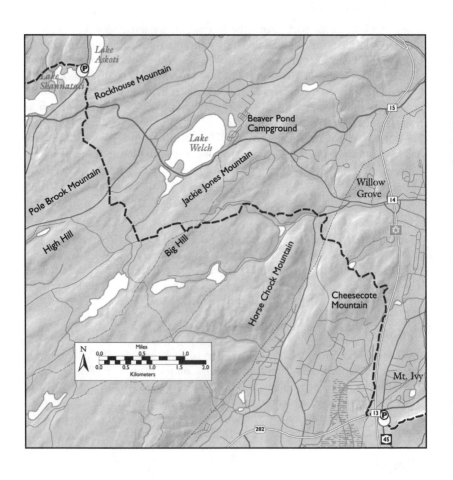

Trail Description

0.00 At the intersection of NY Route 45 and US Route 202, turn west on Route 202 to go under Palisades Interstate Parkway.

0.20 The trail turns right and follows the entrance ramp to the Parkway. After passing Quaker Road to the left, cross the entrance ramp and enter the woods at a small pine grove. The turn is indistinctly marked. The trail follows a narrow, forested strip of land between the Palisades Interstate Parkway on the right and a chain-link fence on the left that separates the trail from a housing development.

0.55 The trail passes under a power line and continues north along the narrow strip.

1.15 The route becomes very swampy as you reach a corner in the chain-link fence. It veers to the left away from the trail.

1.30 The trail turns right onto a grassy woods road, and begins to parallel the South Branch of Minisceongo Creek.

1.45 Walk along the top of a stone arch over the South Branch of the Minisceongo Creek that carries the creek under the Parkway. Continue along a small tributary stream for approximately 75 yards. Cross the stream, turning away from the Parkway, to intersect a woods road. Turn right onto the road and ascend gently through a hardwood forest along a hill slope.

1.60 The trail turns left and heads up the hill. The grade moderates and the trail continues uphill, with many turns along the way.

1.90 Turn left on a grassy woods road and continue uphill. The road changes from grass to cinders. For the next 1.6 miles until Calls Hollow Road, many dirt roads diverge from the road that the Long Path follows. However, the trail stays with the largest and most developed road as it twists and turns.

2.35 Reach the crest of a knob on the shoulder of Cheesecote Mountain and begin to descend, still on the woods road.

2.45 Reach Cheesecote Pond and turn left. The trail goes along the eastern and southern sides of the pond, keeping the pond on the right.

2.60 Reach a large turnaround at the southwest corner of the pond.[7] The trail bears left and uphill for a short distance, away from the pond. It then begins a steady descent and changes to a rough cobble base.

2.90 Bear left at a Y-intersection and follow the steeper road downhill.

3.30 Shortly after crossing a power line right-of-way, the trail reaches Letchworth Village Cemetery. Only numbers mark most of its graves. The Long Path turns left and skirts the cemetery, then turns left again at an intersection of gravel roads. The grade levels off.

3.50 Reach Calls Hollow Road and turn left along the pavement.

3.60 Turn right, leaving the road, and re-enter woods. The trail crosses Horse Chock Brook. After crossing the brook, make a short ascent straight up the slope to meet a woods road. The trail turns left to follow the road.

4.15 After a brief drop into the valley of an intermittent stream, the Long

---

[7] Parking at the pond is restricted to Haverstraw residents.

St. Johns-in-the-Wilderness Church

Path veers right on a narrow track to ascend the valley while the woods road continues left across the valley. The trail crosses the stream and a rock wall as it continues to climb. The forest becomes much more open, with a low understory.

4.40 Reach a crest, with the hiker's reward for a climb of 500 feet, a large patch of lowbush blueberry. From here it is a short drop and rise to the crest of another small knoll.

4.55 The Long Path reaches the dirt road of an AT&T buried telephone cable right-of-way. Cross the road and enter the woods on the other side. After 250 feet, turn right onto an old woods road headed toward a stream. Cross the stream (last sure water before Big Hill Shelter) and turn left as the trail begins a gradual climb.

4.90 Continue climbing over open rock with a seasonal view of the Hudson behind you.

5.00 Pass a small swamp on the left. It may be dry in summer.

5.15 After passing some small glacial erratics, the Long Path enters mountain laurel, turns left and begins a gradual downhill.

5.30 Turn left as the trail drops downhill.

5.35 Reach an intersection with the Suffern-Bear Mountain Trail (SBM) (yellow). The Long Path and SBM continue jointly over ledges to climb up to Big Hill Shelter. The woods road leading left from this junction leads to Second Reservoir.

5.60 Arrive at Big Hill Shelter. Built in 1927, this stone shelter has three fireplaces. The Long Path veers right at the shelter as the SBM continues straight ahead. The Long Path follows a fire road back to the AT&T right-of-way.

5.75 Cross AT&T right-of-way and continue through laurel.

5.85 Begin a short climb up a grassy slope.

6.00 Turn right onto a woods road.

6.25 Cross an intermittent stream on the rocks and contour around a small hill. The trail then passes through a clearing that was the site of a jet plane crash in 1974. The plane had been en-route to Buffalo to pick up the Baltimore Colts football team.

6.50 After passing through a boulder field, turn right on an old woods road. The trail passes under a telephone line and then through a red pine grove before descending through a swamp, crossing its outlet on a wooden bridge. The trail goes up and down through a hardwood forest rich in oak. Open forest alternates with patches of dense mountain laurel and occasional boulder fields.

Note: The USGS Thiells topographic map of the area from mile 6.95 to mile 7.80 is well out-of-date and shows incorrect road locations.

6.95 The Long Path makes a left turn uphill. Straight ahead, an unmarked trail leads in 0.15 miles to St. John's-in-the-Wilderness Church, the site of the hiking community's annual Palm Sunday pilgrimage.

7.45 Turn right and, in 250 feet, cross a grassy road. (In the opposite direction, one must bear right a bit when crossing the road.) The trail becomes wide and grassy as it approaches Lake Welch Drive.

7.60 Cross Lake Welch Drive near its intersection with Johnsontown Road. The Long Path ascends on an old woods road, at first steeply and with several turns, through open, glade-like forest.

7.80 Bear right, still heading uphill, as another woods road goes left. In 200 feet, the trail turns left on a narrow path as the woods road continues straight ahead. After crossing a rock wall, the trail reaches an open knoll with an old stone foundation on the left. This was the farm of Charles Conklin. Once past the foundation, the trail enters brushier woods and begins to descend.

8.15 The Beech Trail (blue) starts to the right. A few hundred feet farther on, an unmarked trail goes off to the right as the Long Path bears left and begins to descend to an intermittent stream.

8.70 Cross the rocky outlet stream of a large marsh that is all but hidden to the right. The trail continues on a grassy woods road.

8.80 Reach Rockland County Route 106 (also known as Gate Hill Road or Old Route 210), turn right and follow the road for 250 feet. The trail then crosses the road and heads diagonally uphill into the woods. Not long after, it makes a left turn onto a woods road. Cross under a telephone line. Two additional left turns bring the trail past the south end of Lake Askoti.

9.25 Reach Seven Lakes Drive. Turn right, go over the bridge over the outlet of Lake Askoti and enter the woods on the opposite side of the road. The trail descends and swings to the right, passing Lake Skannatati on the left.

9.30 The trail reaches a paved parking lot beside the lake. To continue, follow the shore of Lake Skannatati north through the parking lot.

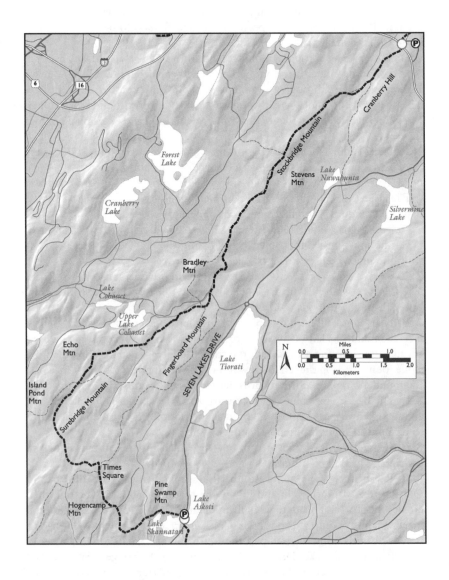

6. Lake Skannatati to US Route 6

Features: Harriman State Park, Surebridge Swamp, Appalachian Trail Crossing, and Stockbridge Mountain
Distance: 10.15 miles
USGS Map Quads: Thiells and Popolopen Lake
Trail Conference Maps: Map 4, Northern Harriman-Bear Mountain Trails

General Description

This section of the trail continues through Harriman State Park. The Long Path crosses many woods roads and other trails within the park, making possible various loop hikes. The trail traverses hemlock forests and rhododendron groves, and passes by large swamps. After these, the trail climbs and follows along the long, linear ridge of Stockbridge Mountain. Upon descending from the mountain, the trail passes another swamp before reaching US Route 6.

Access

To reach the beginning of the section from the New York State Thruway, take Exit 15, Suffern. Continue north on NY Route 17 to Sloatsburg. Just north of the village, turn right onto Seven Lakes Drive. This section starts at the fishing access parking lot off of Seven Lakes Drive at Lake Skannatati, about 0.75 miles north of Kanawauke Circle. From the Palisades Interstate Parkway, take Exit 15, go west on Gate Hill Road and Rockland County Route 106 to Kanawauke Circle, and then go north for 0.75 miles on Seven Lakes Drive.

Parking

0.00 Lake Skannatati parking area. (18T 575219E 4566012N)
5.75 Tiorati Circle picnic area, about 0.5 miles east of the Long Path crossing of Arden Valley Road (fee charged seasonally). (18T 576301E 4569666N)
10.15 Parking area off Route 6. (18T 579286E 4574266N)

Camping

8.00 Stockbridge Shelter.

Trail Description

0.00 The section begins at the Lake Skannatati parking area off of the Seven Lakes Drive. Follow the shore of Lake Skannatati north through the parking area. At the northeast end of the lake, where the Arden-Surebridge Trail (A-SB) (red triangle on white) starts to the right, turn left into the woods and follow its north shore. About halfway along the north shore, the Long Path veers away from the lake, crests over a small ridge and drops back to the west arm of the lake. After undulating up and down along the lake's western shore, the trail crosses the lake's swampy inlet stream and begins a series of longer ups and downs.

1.25 The Long Path turns left and joins a woods road, the route of the Dunning Trail (yellow). After 250 feet, the Long Path turns right on a footpath, as the Dunning Trail continues along the woods road. The Long Path goes over a grassy ledge perched on a hill slope and passes a shaft of the abandoned Hogencamp Mine, one of the largest iron mines inside the Park boundary. Stone foundations on the side of the trail are remnants of this mining community.

1.40 The trail turns right near an overhanging rock, known as Cape Horn, to continue up an old stone-lined road. After passing through a saddle, the trail begins to descend through forest rich in hemlock and mountain laurel. It joins an old woods road, the continuation of the Surebridge Mine Road.

2.00 Reach Times Square, the junction of the Long Path, the A-SB Trail (red triangle on white) and the Ramapo-Dunderberg Trail (red dot on white). The Long Path continues west jointly with the A-SB Trail on the Surebridge Mine Road through fairly level terrain.

Lake Skannatati

2.10 The Long Path and the A-SB Trail turn left, leaving Surebridge Mine Road, and rises gently through a forest of hemlock and white pine. Surebridge Swamp becomes visible below to the right. The trail now alternates through laurel, hardwoods, hemlocks and large rhododendrons.

2.60 The Lichen Trail (blue L on a white square) starts to the left as the Long Path and A-SB continue on a downgrade to pass a swampy area on the right. The trails approach and veer away from a hemlock swamp and then run along the swamp's intermittent outlet stream before crossing the stream. The descent ends as the combined trails begin to pass a marsh on the right.

2.90 The White Bar Trail (horizontal white rectangle) starts to the left. In another 30 feet, the

ED WALSH

Appalachian Trail Junction

Long Path turns right as the A-SB continues straight ahead along the side of a marsh. The Long Path crosses an outlet stream and runs between the marsh and a steep, hemlock-covered slope. Upon reaching the head of the marsh, which becomes a wooded swamp, the trail follows an inlet stream. The trail then turns left and uphill, away from the stream.

3.60 Cross the Appalachian Trail (vertical white 2x6 rectangle) in a slight dip at a prominent signpost. The Long Path now rises to a broad knob, dips to a marsh, and climbs a knoll. The sign has distances to various landmarks on each of the Long Path and Appalachian Trail routes.

4.30 The trail reaches the top of the knoll and begins to descend, passing a partial view of Upper Lake Cohasset on the way down.

4.45 Pass shelter, with no water, on the left as the descent continues. This shelter was built in 1937 for the girls' camps on Upper Lake Cohasset. The trail crosses Surebridge Mine Road and, in another 0.25 miles, crosses a stream leading from a marsh on the right to Upper Lake Cohasset. The trail now crosses a series of intermittent streams and boulder fields as it approaches the road.

5.75 Cross Arden Valley Road at a horseshoe bend. The Long Path jogs left to cross the pavement opposite a wide woods road. Follow this woods road as it passes to the left of a beautiful hardwood swamp.

6.15 After the swamp ends, the Long Path climbs to the left as the woods road continues straight ahead. The trail now ascends, sometimes steeply, to the long ridge of Stockbridge Mountain. Once on the bedrock outcrop of the ridge, the trail follows the gentle ups and downs of the crest northeast.

7.80 The trail passes under a large cantilevered rock, known as Hippo Rock, which juts toward the trail from the west

8.00 The trail reaches the Stockbridge Shelter after crossing the Menomine Trail (yellow) in a valley. Stockbridge Shelter is a handsome rock-and-mortar structure with a plank floor. It sits on a rock outcrop with a fine view to the south. No water is available.

8.30 The Long Path drops steeply over a boulder slope. The Cave Shelter is set into an overhang near the base of its rock face. It is damp and hardly an inviting place to spend the night. Again, no water is available. From here, the trend is downhill to US Route 6. As the descent progresses, trees get larger and form a closed canopy; blueberry becomes more dominant in the under-story.

9.10 The trail turns left and passes to the left of a small knob that is the point of a large saddle. After crossing from the right to the left side of a valley and back again, the trail climbs out of the valley. It reaches and turns left on a woods road. Upon reaching an embankment above Route 6, the trail turns left and follows it above the highway.

10.00 At the base of the slope, turn right to drop to the highway. The trail crosses the road and continues up the exit road from the parking area on the north side of US Route 6. (This road is the old Route 6, used until 1967, when the present road was opened to traffic).

10.15 The section ends shortly after the pavement widens to allow parking. To continue, turn left and enter the woods.

7. US Route 6 to Woodbury

Features: Harriman State Park, Howell, Brooks and Blackcap Mountains, and the Torrey Memorial on Long Mountain
Distance: 11.10 miles
USGS Map Quads: Popolopen Lake
Trail Conference Maps: Map 4, Northern Harriman-Bear Mountain Trails, and Map 8, West Hudson Trails

General Description

This section is the last of the three within Harriman State Park, and is by far the most rugged. The Long Path climbs four peaks, often on steep grades both up and down. The exertion is worth the effort because views of dramatic geology, especially in the U-shaped valley between Howell and Brooks mountains. The trail frequently borders West Point Military Reservation. The last part of this section is outside of Harriman State Park and generally follows suburban and rural roads.

Access

Take the New York State Thruway to Exit 16, Harriman. Continue east on US Route 6. Or take the Palisades Interstate Parkway to Exit 18, and continue west on Route 6. The section starts at a parking area in a narrow, unmarked loop on the north side of Route 6. Entry by car is one way from the east side of the loop, about 1.2 miles west of the Long Mountain Circle.

Parking

0.00 Parking area off Route 6. (18T 579286E 4574266N)
11.10 Intersection of Quaker Road and NY Route 32, about 0.2 miles south of the Long Path's crossing of Route 32 at a railroad trestle. (18T 574643E 4579193N)

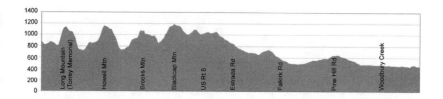

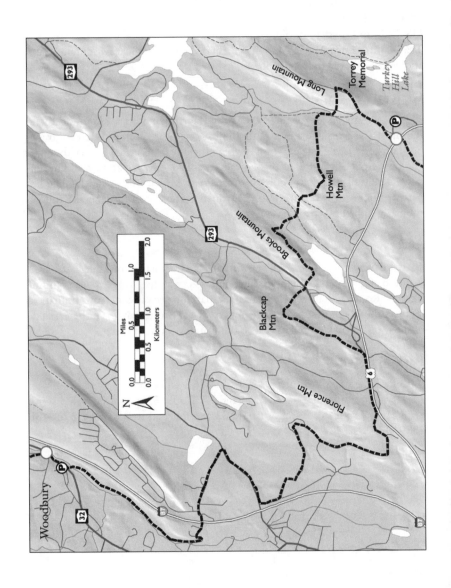

Trail Description

0.00 The Long Path leaves the pavement of the parking area loop road at the interpretive kiosk honoring Raymond H. Torrey and the Long Path. It heads north into the woods on a wide gravel road. The road becomes grassy as it passes through oak forest with open, short and shrubby understory. The descent into a hollow steepens as traffic noises fade.

0.30 Pass an old woods road going down to the left. Immediately thereafter, the Popolopen Gorge Trail (red square on white) leaves to the right. The Long Path turns left after this and begins to climb toward the summit of Long Mountain, steepening rapidly.

0.50 The grade levels off as the trail approaches the summit and the vegetation becomes sparse.

0.60 The Long Path reaches the summit of Long Mountain, the site of the Torrey Memorial. There is a spectacular 360-degree view from the summit with Bear Mountain visible to the east and Turkey Hill Lake directly below.

0.65 The Long Path continues past the Torrey Memorial and starts a gradual descent from Long Mountain. In another 500 feet, the trail turns left and descends through a series of long switchbacks.

1.10 The trail intersects an old woods road to the left and crosses Deep Hollow Brook (the crossing can be difficult after a heavy rain). It then turns right and continues on a path alongside the stream. Meet a second stream paralleling the trail on the left. Shortly thereafter, the trail turns left at an opening in the woods and crosses the stream on rocks. It then ascends and approaches a cleared swath along the West Point boundary. The trail follows the boundary

Final ascent of Long Mountain

TODD SCHREIBMAN

Torrey Memorial

line, with some detours to the left and back again, for about half a mile. The trail eventually leaves the boundary permanently and heads left to top out at a knoll with lots of blueberries.

2.15 Reach a viewpoint on Howell Mountain with Brooks Mountain visible to the west and Blackcap Mountain beyond. Route 6 is visible straight ahead. The trail briefly continues its gentle descent on a curve, slabbing a rise to the right. Then, it abruptly turns left and begins a steep plunge into Brooks Hollow. The Long Path traverses a flat terrace before another left turn over the edge completes the descent, this time with switchbacks.

2.55 Cross the outlet stream from Lake Massawippa in the middle of Brooks Hollow, a classic U-shaped post-glacial valley. Its broad, flat floor with several intermittent streambeds curves upward on both sides at a rapidly increasing pitch. Once over the log bridge, the trail turns left and goes upstream for a short distance before continuing across the valley floor. It reaches the valley wall and the trail begins a steep ascent of Brooks Mountain, principally by two long switchbacks. The second switchback becomes gentler in grade as it merges with the southwest trending crest of Brooks Mountain. Once on the crest, the grade is gently uphill with views of the steeply plunging valley to the left.

3.20 The ridge ends suddenly at a rocky knob. The Long Path turns to descend steeply to the left at first and then curves to the right around the end of the ridge. It reaches and climbs out of the small valley to views of Lake Massawippa a few hundred feet downhill to the left. The trail next undulates up and down through laurel and then blueberry as the dominant understory plants.

3.70 Reach NY Route 293 near a stream. Cross the road at the end of the guardrail and re-enter the woods. The trail now ascends, often steeply, up the shoulder of Blackcap Mountain. Once attained, it follows the ridge crest southwest, closely paralleling the West Point boundary, until the trail descends toward Route 6.

5.05 The trail approaches US Route 6 and turns west along the highway. The next blazes are about 30 feet inside the woods bordering the road, next to a chain-link fence bordering the highway. (In the reverse direction, the trail enters the woods about 30 feet west of the "Yield" sign for Route 293 traffic entering US Route 6.)

5.60 Just before a large grassy clearing with a power line on the north side of the highway, the trail passes through a gap in the chain-link fence. It veers to the right and crosses the clearing on a diagonal to the northwest. At the opposite side of the clearing, there is a telephone pole at the end of an abandoned paved road (the old Route 6). Turn right and follow this road.

6.20 Reach a barricade across the road with a small vehicle turnaround on the opposite side. There is currently no parking allowed here. The trail continues straight ahead on what is now known as Estrada Road, a quiet residential street, past several houses. Thomas Estrada-Palma, the first president of Cuba (1902–06), lived here from 1879 to 1902 while he headed a junta that financed the Cuban Revolution.

6.65 The trail continues straight ahead as the road becomes paved where several driveways join it.

7.15 Continue straight, staying on Estrada Road. In 200 feet, in sight of the New York State Thruway, turn right onto Falkirk Road. The trail now follows quiet rural roads.

7.95 At a T-intersection, go right on Smith Clove Road (Orange County Route 9) and head away from the Thruway.

8.45 Pass a golf course entrance on right.

8.55 Go left on Pine Hill Road.

8.80 Pass Pearce Road on the right.

8.95 Pass Pine Hill Court on the right.

9.05 Pass De Santis Drive on the left.

9.15 Pass Skyline Drive on the right. Cross the Thruway and follow Pine Hill Road downhill as it curves.

9.35 Pass Pine Place on the right.

9.45 Follow Pine Hill Road under the railroad.

9.55 Just before Pine Hill Road crosses Woodbury Creek, the Long Path turns right on a gravel road which runs between the railroad tracks and Woodbury Creek.

10.45 Cross a seasonal stream

11.05 Cross Woodbury Creek. This stream crossing may be difficult during periods of high water. If it can't be crossed at the pipeline, follow the shore downstream under the trestle to the road. Do not cross the trestle! (Metro-North now uses this railroad trestle, part of what was formerly known as the Graham Line of the Erie Railroad, for passenger service). The trail is heavily overgrown in this section.

11.10 Reach NY Route 32. Turn right and go under the trestle. The section ends about 50 feet north of the trestle, where the Long Path turns left and climbs an embankment.

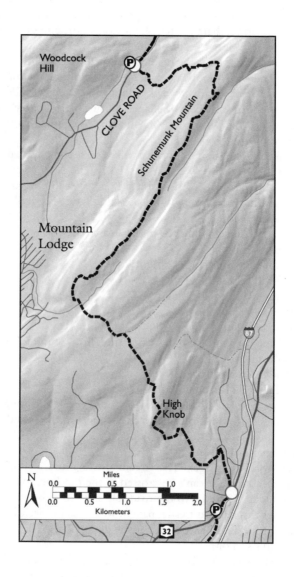

8. Woodbury to Salisbury Mills

Feature: Schunemunk Mountain State Park and the Highlands Trail
Distance: 7.00 miles
USGS Map Quads: Popolopen Lake, Cornwall, and Maybrook
Trail Conference Maps: Map 8, West Hudson Trails

General Description

The trail continues for a short distance along a Metro-North railroad right-of-way before turning into the woods to go up the often-steep ascent of Schunemunk Mountain. Schunemunk (pronounced "skun-uh-munk") is a northeast-southwest trending ridge, with sharp sides and a nearly level top. The mountaintop, formerly owned by Open Space Institute, became New York's 163rd State Park in 2001, securing its lasting protection and ensuring public access for future generations of New Yorkers The north half of the mountain is divided by a cleft into two ridges. The Long Path follows much of the length of the western ridge, often with splendid scenery, before it descends to the valley to the west, emerging onto Clove Road at the Hil-Mar Lodge.

While most of Schunemunk Mountain is closed to hunters, the western areas of the mountain are open for hunting. Hikers should be aware of the dates of the various hunting seasons and plan accordingly. Deer and turkey are often seen on Schunemunk.

Access

Take the New York State Thruway north to Exit 16, Harriman. Continue north on NY Route 32. Approximately 1.8 miles north of the Woodbury Police sign in the town of Highland Mills, you will pass under a high railroad trestle painted black. The Long Path leaves the west side of the road about 50 feet north of the trestle.

Parking

0.00 At the intersection of Evans Drive and NY Route 32, about 0.2 miles south of the railroad trestle. (18T 574643E 4579193N)
7.00 At the Hil-Mar Lodge off Clove Road. Hikers should park in a grassy area just south of the main entrance; do not park in the paved parking lot. Camping is available at Hil-Mar Lodge, call first 845-486-4869. (18T 573446E 4585058N)

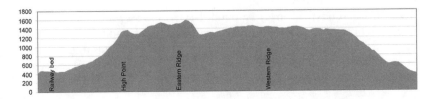

Trail Description

0.00 The Long Path leaves the west side of NY Route 32 at the end of the guardrail about 50 feet north of where the high railroad trestle goes over the road. It almost immediately climbs a wooded embankment, crosses under the trestle on a gravel road, climbs a steep embankment (watch for poison ivy), and turns right to follow the left side of the trestle. After it reaches the grade of the tracks, the trail turns and follows them north. **Stay away from the center of the trackbed.** The Metro-North passenger trains travel very quickly and very quietly. They can easily overtake a hiker without warning, leaving little time to move to safety.

0.30 Pass the access road to sand pits.

0.35 Turn sharply left onto old road. This road ends at a steep gully and the trail continues to the right into the woods from there, meeting up with another woods road. Follow this second road to the right as it begins a meandering ascent of Schunemunk Mountain, crossing several stone walls along the way.

0.85 The trail turns left onto a narrow track and heads uphill. It now ascends steadily, sometimes steeply, up the slope and then more gently across it. Along the way are several good views, including one at Little Knob.

1.40 Reach the crest of High Knob. This open ridgetop has fine views up and down the valley and of the Hudson River to the north. The trail continues on the top of this flat ridge and then goes left on rocks forming the west side of the ridge. It descends to approach the head of the valley between High Knob and the main ridge to the west. As the gap between the ridges closes, the trail drops into the woods to cross two valleys before ascending a boulder-strewn slope to the opposite ridge.

1.80 The trail reaches the top of the ridge and turns north to follow it for about 0.4 miles before dropping into a small valley.

2.40 The trail crosses Dark Hollow Brook, usually dry, and climbs to the main ridge of Schunemunk Mountain.

2.60 The Jessup Trail (yellow) crosses near the top of the ridge. This trail is also the Highlands Trail (teal diamond). It stretches northeast to Storm King Mountain and southwest through Sterling Forest State Park to reach the Delaware River at the Delaware Water Gap. In another 300 yards, the Long Path reaches an open area of exposed rock, turns left and enters the woods. The descent for the next quarter-mile is on a talus slope, often very steep. An opening in the canopy on the way down affords views of the lowlands below Schunemunk. Once reaching the base of the talus slope, the descent moderates. Striped maple, a small tree with beautiful variegated bark, is abundant here and well worth looking for.

2.95 Cross a woods road on level ground. The trail crosses a sometimes-swampy intermittent stream, turns left on the next woods road, and takes a right fork up a small hill. Turning right on the second woods road leads to the Barton Swamp Trail (red dot on white). Less than 50 yards beyond the fork, a narrow track leads diagonally off the woods road to the right (pay careful attention to

The wooded slope of Schunemunk Mountain

blazes here). The trail now goes gently uphill through sparse woods with lots of chestnut oak to gain the westernmost ridge of Schunemunk Mountain. It continues to ascend gently with occasional views both east and west. The many crevices in the rock cause the trail to zigzag quite a bit for the next 3 miles.

4.10 The Barton Swamp Trail (red dot on white), which follows a valley between the eastern and western ridges of Schunemunk Mountain, leaves to the right. The Long Path continues straight ahead.

4.20 The Western Ridge Trail (blue dot on white) leaves to the right. For the next 1.5 miles, the Long Path takes advantage of the many fine viewpoints and interesting rock formations along the way, leading to frequent shifts in direction. Both blazes and cairns mark the trail. Scattered over the windswept top of Schunemunk are pitch pine, birch, oak, elm and many other stunted trees. Blueberry bushes abound, and mountain laurel is found along the lower portions of the trail. The geology of this area is unique since Schunemunk is younger than its neighbors. Also, the pink conglomerate rock forming the top of Schunemunk is very different from the rocks found in the other surrounding mountain ranges.

4.90 Reach an open area on top of the ridge with fine views to the west toward Woodcock Hill and beyond to Washingtonville and, on clear days, all the way to the ridge of the Shawangunks. To the east are the steep cliffs of the eastern ridge of Schunemunk. These cliffs are favorites of hawks who glide in the warm updrafts.

5.10 The Sweet Clover Trail (white) leaves to the right to cross to the eastern ridge and continue down to Mountainville.

5.60 The Long Path turns left as the Barton Swamp Trail (red dot on white) leaves to the right, and the Trestle Trail (white) continues straight ahead along the ridge. Just a short detour along the Trestle Trail brings you to a glorious viewpoint northward to the Catskill Mountains. After traversing some more rock outcroppings, the Long Path begins a gradual descent down the western slope of the mountain.

6.00 The trail widens and becomes an abandoned woods road cut into the slope of the mountain and built up with rocks on the downhill side. The road descends gradually on switchbacks.

6.50 The road curves sharply to the right, just before reaching a stone wall. The Long Path continues straight ahead through a break in the wall and heads into the woods to descend gradually.

6.65 The trail goes through an opening in another stone wall and left onto a broad woods road.

6.70 The trail crosses over a stream and turns to the right, still following the woods road.

6.90 Pass a private dwelling. The trail continues straight, passing the southern edge of the Hil-Mar Lodge property.

7.00 The owner of Hil-Mar Lodge allows hikers to park on a meadow off Clove Road, just south of the main entrance to the Lodge. Look for the parking sign. Do not park in the paved parking lot without speaking to the owner first. To continue on the Long Path, turn right on Clove Road.

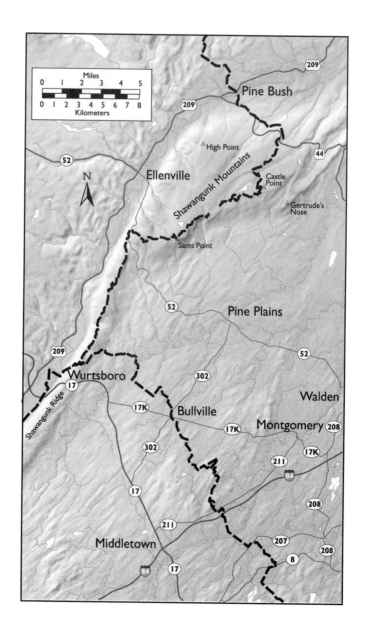

Orange County
and The Shawangunk Ridge

These sections of the Long Path provide the bridge between the low mountains of the Hudson Highlands in the south and the beginnings of the Catskills in the north. In between lie many small village and towns set in the slowly rolling hills of Orange County. Although not as exciting as sections further north or south, walking the backroads of Orange County move one into an older time and a different way of life from the frenetic pace of city living. It is only by walking the roads ordinarily driven that one can appreciate the different pace of rural living and its dependence on the pace of nature and not of people. The northern sections pass along the Shawangunk Ridge into Minnewaska State Park, one of the most beautiful and interesting areas of the Hudson Valley. Though certainly not the tallest or the most exotic park in New York, it is one of the most colorful in character with its rich and varied flora, fauna, and vistas.

Pool on the Sanders Kill, Minnewaska State Park

HERB CHONG

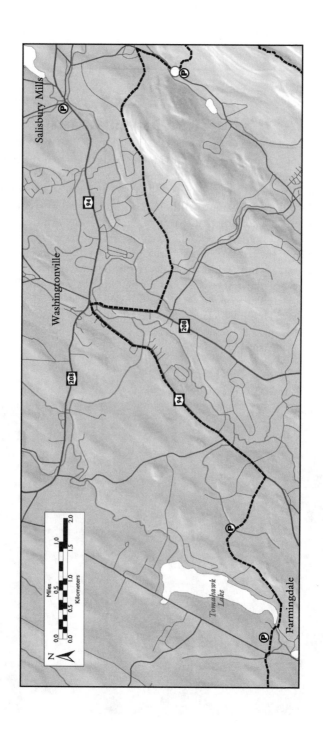

9. Salisbury Mills to NY Route 211

Feature: Road walk through hilly farm country
Distance: 18.30 miles
USGS Map Quads: Cornwall, Maybrook, and Goshen.
Trail Conference Maps: none

General Description

This section follows roads that run parallel to the Moodna Creek and an abandoned railroad. Initially the trail passes north of Woodcock Hill through the town of Washingtonville. Then, as the area becomes open country, the Long Path passes several horse and dairy farms. The trail along NY Route 94 affords wonderful views east to Schunemunk Mountain with expanses of open fields and small woods in the foreground. It passes Tomahawk Lake, a residential community, and several horse and dairy farms, offering frequent views to the higher hills in the distance. It crosses the Wallkill River, the most significant watercourse in the area. This section is suitable for bicycling since it is relatively free of truck traffic. Future plans are to place the footpath off the roads.[8]

Access

Take the New York State Thruway to Exit 16, Harriman. Go west on NY Route 17/future Interstate 86 three miles to Exit 130. Follow NY Route 208 north to Clove Road (Orange County Route 27). Turn right on Clove Road and continue for about 4 miles until reaching Hil-Mar Lodge in Salisbury Mills.

Parking

0.00 Hil-Mar Lodge (18T 573446E 4585058N)
7.30 Farmingdale Road (limited parking). (18T 565849E 4584057N)
8.90 At Hulsetown Road. (18T 563851E 4583476N)
13.90 To right at Metro-North passenger station. (18T 561269E 4589178N)
18.30 On Hidden Drive at NY Route 211. (18T 556904E 4591745N)

---

[8] Side-trips can be made to Thomas Bull County Park and historic sites, as well as to the picturesque county seat of Goshen and the Trotting Horse Museum.

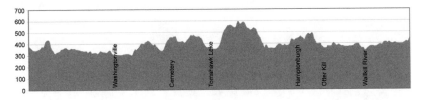

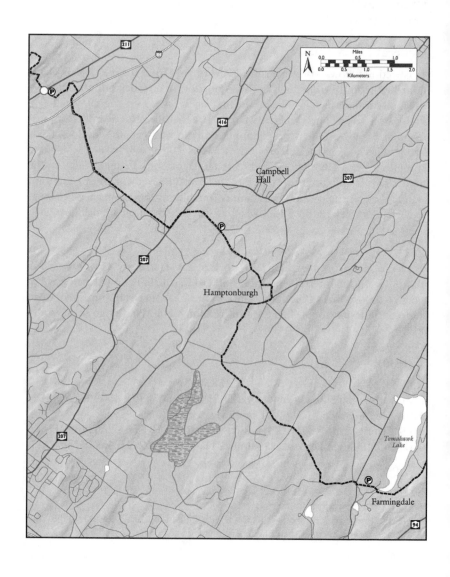

Trail Description

0.00 Turn right onto Clove Road (Orange County 27) and continue north along the road.

0.50 The trail turns left onto an abandoned paved road, a private driveway. The condition of the pavement worsens as the road continues, gradually ascending. The road goes mainly through woods but also passes several fields and a small pond.

0.90 The road begins to descend.

1.10 The trail turns right, leaving the road, and enters an open field. Follow the right side of the field. The trail re-enters the woods at the far end of the field. The trees here are very thin and the blazes may be difficult to see. The trail meanders; crosses stone walls in several places, and follows streambeds that are frequently muddy.

1.40 Cross a rutted woods road.

1.60 Reach paved Woodcock Mountain Road. Turn left onto it.

4.20 Reach Route 208. Turn left and then turn right when Route 208 reaches the light onto Hudson Street.

4.80 Reach NY Route 94. Turn left and follow this busy road north. Be sure to stay to the left and well outside the white line as you walk this road. This is a major artery and there are several blind turns where speeding cars have little warning of people on the side of the road.

6.00 Pass Tuttle Road. The area opens up and a view of the long ridge that characterizes Schunemunk Mountain appears to the east.

6.60 Turn right onto Farmingdale Road. There is a large farm with a County Gift Shop on the corner.

7.30 Reach the abandoned Erie Railroad rail bed as it crosses a wetland. There is limited parking along the road here. The Long Path continues west after passing the rail bed, following Farmingdale Road past wetlands and scattered residences.

7.80 Heard Road goes right. Continue on Farmingdale Road.

8.20 Pass a small old cemetery on the left.

8.60 Reach a bridge crossing the southern end of Tomahawk Lake.

8.90 Cross Hulsetown Road onto Goshen Road. Cross Conrail Maybrook-Warwick Line railroad tracks and head uphill.

9.40 Turn right onto Purgatory Road. Not long after, distant hills and farmlands come into view.

10.20 Cross Ridge Road. After cresting the hill, there are distant views of the Shawangunks. Pass several farms.

11.70 There is a large horse farm on the left. Turn right onto Pische Road.

12.50 Turn right onto Sarah Wells Trail, (Orange County Route 8). Sara Wells and her husband Thomas Bull were the founding settlers of Orange County. (Having had 17 children they did it almost single-handed!) Be sure to stay well on the shoulder.

12.70 Turn left onto Egbertson Road (Orange County Route 77).

13.90 Cross under the Marcy-South Power Lines, then cross Station Road,

Campbell Hall. To the right is the Metro-North passenger station; to the left is an abandoned rail bed heads south to Goshen.

14.50 Turn left onto NY Route 207. This is a major road, so stay on the shoulder.

14.70 Turn right onto Stony Ford Road (Orange County Route 53).

15.80 Reach the bridge across the Wallkill River.

16.00 Stony Ford Road goes off to the left; continue straight on County Route 53.

16.90 Cross under the Metro-North Port Jervis Line railroad bridge.

17.10 Cross under Interstate 84. Continue to the end of a guardrail on the left side.

17.75 Turn sharply left after the guardrail and follow the cut path through the field.

18.10 Turn right onto Hidden Drive.

18.30 Arrive at NY Route 211. To continue on the Long Path, cross Route 211 and stay on Hidden Drive. Parking is possible along one side of Hidden Drive.

10. NY Route 211 to Shawangunk Ridge Trail

Features: Highland Lakes State Park, Town of Wallkill, Orange County, Road walk with views of Shawangunk Ridge in the distance, and the gradual ascent of the Shawangunk Ridge.
Distance: 17.05 miles
USGS Map Quads: Goshen, Pine Bush, and Wurtsboro
Trail Conference Maps: none

General Description

The Long Path passes through Highland Lakes State Park, an undeveloped property acquired by the Palisades Interstate Park Commission in the 1960s. Geologically, the park consists of a series of low parallel ridges with lakes and wetlands in between. In the park, the Long Path follows old woods roads that are unpaved and frequently muddy because they are also used by horses and mountain bikes. A part of the park near the lakes was known as Camp Orange and was a summer recreation area with many homes. The ruins of the old dwellings have long ago been removed but the foundations are still visible. The Long Path follows several roads in western Orange County as it approaches the Shawangunks. This is still a fairly unpopulated area of the county and the trail passes many farms and fields with expansive views. The best views on the road-walking section are eastward across Orange County. Just before reaching the top of the ridge, the Long Path heads south and then enters the woods via an abandoned gravel road and ascends to the ridgetop. It intersects with the Shawangunk Ridge Trail at one of the most expansive, panoramic viewpoints on the Long Path.

Access

Take New York State Thruway to Exit 16, Harriman. Follow NY Route 17/ future Interstate 86 north nineteen miles to NY Route 211 at Exit 120, Middletown. Head north on Route 211 for 3.5 miles to Hidden Drive on the right. Park on the side of the road.

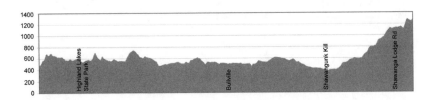

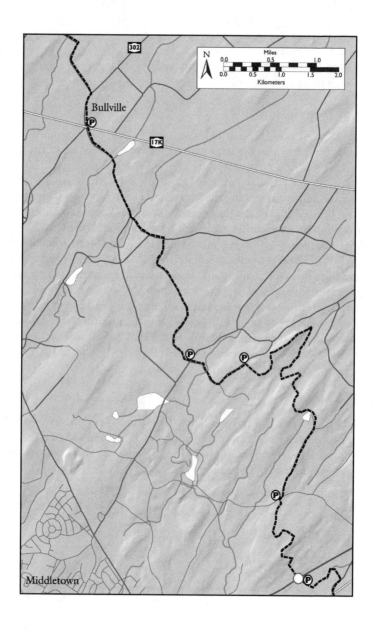

Parking

0.00 At Hidden Drive and NY Route 211. (18T 556904E 4591745N)
1.50 At Camp Orange Road. (18T 556586E 4592967N)
4.10 At Tamms Road. (18T 556006E 4595229N)
4.90 At Scotchtown Road and Tamms Road. (18T 555044E 4595276N)
8.10 NY Route 17K and NY Route 302 in Bullville. (18T 553248E 4599149N)
12.80 Shawangunk Kill along Stone School House Road. (18T 550350E 4603227N)
13.00 At Orange County Route 61. (18T 550198E 4603421N)
16.55 Along Shawanga Lodge Road. (18T 546074E 4603144N)

Camping

Camping on DEC land.

Trail Description

0.00 Cross NY Route 211 onto a driveway for a mobile home community. When the driveway turns to right, the trail continues straight ahead, skirting the edge of a field.

0.20 Turn right just inside the woods at the end of the field and continue uphill near the edge of the woods.

0.30 Turn left onto a well-used woods road to enter Highland Lakes State Park.

0.50 Turn right onto one of the main north-south roads in the park. This road meanders up and down, sometimes steeply, as it traverses the first ridge, and reaches a stone wall.

1.20 The road cuts through a stone wall.

1.50 Turn right onto Camp Orange Road.

1.60 Turn left to head northward once again.

2.25 Arrive at an intersection with large oak tree in center and stone walls along each of the roads. Continue straight ahead.

2.40 Bear to the left as another road comes in from the right. (This road provides another access point to the park.)

2.55 Pass by one of the small lakes that give the park its name. There is a road that circles the lake. The Long Path continues on this road heading uphill to another ridgetop, and then drops down into a small wetland before heading uphill again.

3.10 Turn right onto another road and begin heading down from this ridge.

3.30 Turn left at a road crossing. Going straight leads out of the park.

3.50 Bear to the right at an intersection in a particularly wet low-lying area.

3.70 Reach a clearing where there are many roads crisscrossing along the slopes of another ridge. This is a very popular site for mountain bikes. Continue straight ahead, following the blazes to avoid going in circles.

4.00 Arrive at the west end of the meadow, somewhat higher up. Look for a trail going off to the left through one of the stone walls.

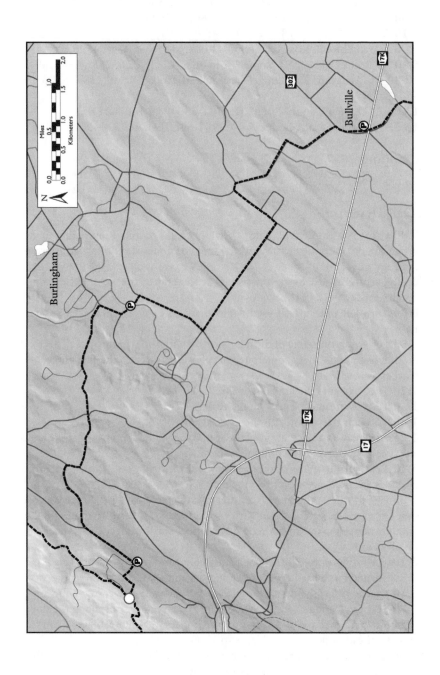

4.10 Exit Highland Lakes State Park and turn left onto Tamms Road. It skirts the western border of the parkland. The Shawangunk Ridge becomes visible in the background and can be seen frequently during the next several miles.
4.90 Reach Scotchtown Road. Cross Scotchtown Road and follow King Road.
6.50 Turn left onto Gordon Road.
7.00 Bear right onto Lybolt Road toward the crossroads of Bullville. The Bull family was one of the most prominent landowners in the county and many historic locations, parks and schools carry the Bull name.
8.10 Cross NY Route 17K at the traffic light and continue north on NY Route 302. Just before this intersection there is a seasonal farm stand where fruits and vegetables and other goodies can be purchased.
8.40 Turn left onto Burlingham Road. Pass more farmland. There are views toward the Shawangunks.
9.80 Crans Mill Road bears to the right. Continue left on Burlingham Road.
9.90 Turn left onto Long Lane.
10.50 Turn right onto Petticoate Lane.
11.90 Turn right onto Stone School House Road. This is known as Miller's Crossing. Sha-Wan-Gun Airport, a small gliderport/airport, is located here.
12.70 Arrive at an intersection with Bible Camp Road. It goes off to the right. Turn left and continue on Stone School House Road.
12.80 Arrive at a bridge crossing the Shawangunk Kill. The Long Path crosses the Shawangunk Kill on Stone School House Road.
13.00 Turn right after crossing the Kill and reach North Street (Orange County Route 61). This short stretch of road changes its name from Stone School House Road to Larson Road and forks as Rouis Road; keep bearing to the right. Follow North Street to Roe Road just before a stream crossing.
13.20 Turn left onto Roe Road, which is a narrow, steep, one-lane road and follow it uphill.
14.50 Cross Nashopa Road and continue steeply uphill, now following Pantelop Road.
15.10 Turn right at Roosa Gap Road. Berentsen's Campground, seasonal, is located 1.4 miles south from here on Roosa Gap Road (phone 845-733-4984).
15.20 Turn left onto Crane Road and continue to the top of the hill.
15.90 Turn left onto Shawanga Lodge Road, heading south.
16.55 Just past Flaherty Drive the trail turns right and goes uphill before entering the woods. The trail is marked with blue DEC disks. It follows old roads to the ridgetop via switchbacks. Layers of the light-colored rock characteristic of the Shawangunks can be seen in the cuts near the top.
16.75 Turn left onto another of the gravel roads, following it around a 90-degree curve to pass a road on the right and then on the left. As the road begins to make another 90-degree turn, the Long Path heads straight through some bushes and continues to join with the Shawangunk Ridge Trail.
17.05 The Long Path intersects the Shawangunk Ridge Trail[9] (SRT) at a mag-

---

[9] The Shawangunk Ridge Trail starts at the Appalachian Trail at High Point, NJ and heads north to Sam's Point Preserve, following the Shawangunk Ridge for 40 miles. The trail is also

nificent panoramic viewpoint. From this viewpoint you can look south to see the Basha Kill Wildlife Management Area. Basha Kill is an excellent area to watch migratory birds. To the west the Village of Wurtsboro is visible below and, in the distance, Route 17 crossing the mountains to the west. Just to the north is Wurtsboro Airport. It is common to see planes from the airport towing gliders aloft to float above the updrafts created by the ridge. To the far north are the Catskill Mountains. Beyond this vantage point, the trail follows the western slopes of the ridge. Unlike the northern Shawangunks, where the most interesting topography is in the east, the southern Shawangunks are much more interesting on the western side. Development reaches high up on the ridge on the east side. The Long Path turns right and follows the Shawangunk Ridge Trail north.

---

blazed with blue disks on DEC land and Aqua rectangles on private land. Use sections G1-G4 in reverse to head south from here 28 miles to High Point where, at the intersection with the Appalachian Trail, you can then proceed to Harriman State Park to rejoin the main Long Path, or continue south along the Kittatinnies.

11. Shawangunk Ridge Trail to Sam's Point Preserve

Features: Wurtsboro Ridge and Bear Hill Nature Preserve
Distance: 11.90 miles
USGS Map Quads: Wurtsboro, Ellenville, and Napanoch
Trail Conference Maps: Map 9, Southern Shawangunk Trails

General Description

The Long Path follows the Shawangunk Ridge Trail north for the next twelve miles. This section is primarily ridgetop with many spectacular views in all directions. These are among the most dramatic in southern New York. The forest is primarily scrub oak, blueberry and occasional pitch pine. The low forest frequently places the hiker above the trees with unlimited visibility. There are also sections of Shawangunk slab, though not as common as found further north. The trail traverses the ridge to NY Route 52. Then it ascends to the Bear Hill Nature Preserve and follows roads through Cragsmoor until it reaches the Sam's Point Preserve entrance gate.

Access

Take the New York State Thruway to Exit 16, Harriman. Take NY Route 17/ future Interstate 86 west 29 miles to Exit 114, Highview. Turn right at the end of the exit ramp onto Old Route 17 (Sullivan County 171) and go uphill for 0.4 miles. Turn left on Shawanga Lodge Road and follow it for 1.1 miles. Walk uphill along the Long Path starting from mile 16.55 in Section 10.

Parking

0.00 Shawanga Lodge Road, 0.5 miles from the intersection of the Long Path and the Shawangunk Ridge Trail. Walk uphill on the trail to meet the Long Path, entering state land. (18T 546074E 4603144N)

3.05 Ferguson Road (still called Roosa Gap Summitville Road on most maps), 0.7 miles west of top of ridge (Shawanga Lodge Road). (18T 547142E 4606751N)

9.05 NY Route 52 at overlook. (18T 549619E 4613761N)

10.15 Bear Hill Nature Preserve at Dellenbaugh Road. (18T 550495E 4613333N)

11.90 Sam's Point Preserve entrance gate (fee charged). (18T 553137E 4613363N)

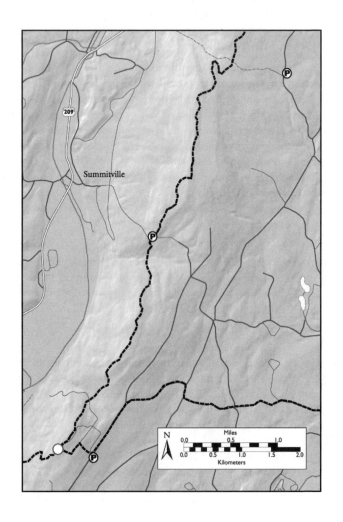

Camping

Camping on DEC land.

Trail Description

0.00 The Long Path turns right and follows the Shawangunk Ridge Trail north just to the left of the slab into and through the scrub oak. For the next quarter-mile or so, the trail alternates between scrub oak forest with views and denser woods. It then begins to descend, gradually at first, followed by a steeper descent to a col.

0.70 The trail reaches a gravel road that leads down to Wurtsboro Airport. After crossing the road, the trail crosses a stream, reaches an abandoned logging road and then begins climbing back to the ridgetop on a series of switchbacks. As the trail reaches the scrub oak, views again open up to Wurtsboro Airport and to the south.

1.35 The trail crosses another gravel road that leads down to an abandoned lead mine. It then reaches a rock outcropping with a spectacular view north and south across the valley to the west. This point is just north of Wurtsboro Airport. Below is the water-filled Summitville section of the old Delaware and Hudson Canal, now a state park. The towpath of the old canal has been restored here.

1.90 The trail reaches another dramatic viewpoint. From here it is possible to see northwest to the Catskills and northeast to Roosa Gap and Sam's Point. Beyond here the trail begins a gradual descent toward Roosa Gap with many views along the way.

2.30 The trail reaches a large overhanging boulder. Again there are views into Roosa Gap and northwest to the Catskills. Beyond the boulder, the trail turns right and descends to a seasonal stream. At the seasonal stream, the trail turns left and descends more steeply along the left bank. At the bottom of the grade, the trail crosses the stream, passes through a wet area and then crosses a larger stream at the bottom of Roosa Gap.

2.90 After the stream crossing the trail begins to ascend and comes to the end of the State-owned Wurtsboro Ridge parcels. As it crosses into private land, the blazes change into the standard Long Path Aqua blaze. Beyond the land boundary the trail climbs to Ferguson Road through a series of switchbacks.

3.05 The trail reaches Ferguson Road. Just to the left of the trail, there is room to park several cars. The trail crosses the road about 0.7 miles west of the height of land. Beyond Ferguson Road, the trail ascends steeply back up to the ridgetop. As you climb, views open up to the south. The ridge north of Ferguson Road is higher and is thus more populated with scrub oak.

3.55 The trail levels out and reaches a spectacular view to the south. This vantage point is higher than any point since the New Jersey border, yielding a view all the way down the ridge to the High Point Monument in New Jersey. There are also views north to the Catskills. From here the trail continues north, remaining about 100 vertical feet below the ridgetop. On the ridgetop is an old fire-lookout tower that has been converted to a State Police radio tower. It

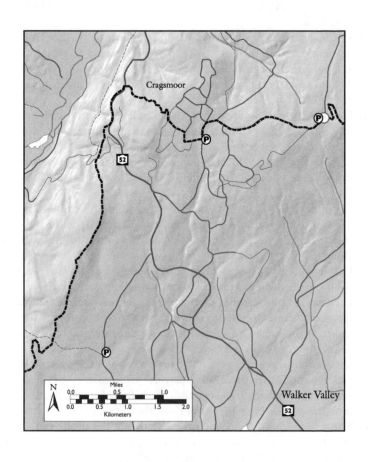

MICHAEL WARREN

Bear Hill Preserve

is off limits. Once the trail is past the former fire tower, it climbs back up to the ridgetop.

4.00 The trail reaches the top of the ridge and continues north. The forest is thicker here so the views are more restricted. At this elevation, mountain laurel mixes in with blueberry and scrub oak.

4.85 The trail climbs over a knoll and reaches a 360-degree view, the best yet on this section. To the south is a view of Roosa Gap, High Point and the Basha Kill. To the northwest, the Catskills are visible, and directly north are Sam's Point and Gertrude's Nose. Northeast are the Taconics, and southeast are Breakneck Ridge and Storm King Mountain, twin sentinels at the entrance to the Hudson Canyon. The trail continues north, comes to a boulder and descends east into a col between two ridges of the mountain.

5.20 After a short climb, the trail reaches the top of the lower eastern ridge and turns back north to descend to another col. There is another view from the eastern ridge northwards. The trail continues to descend from the scrub oak and enters the forest.

5.60 The trail reaches the small DEC Roosa Gap Parcel and the blazes change to blue DEC disks. After entering State land, the trail descends through an interesting rock wall, and then turns right to parallel it uphill to a height of land. At the height of land, the trail turns left and continues to a woods road.

5.95 The trail crosses the woods road and goes through hardwood forest crisscrossed by stone walls, slowly heading uphill in a generally northern direction. During the next 0.3 miles the trail crosses six stone walls, and, after a further third of a mile, leaves State land. The markings change from blue disks to Aqua blazes.

6.55 The trail makes a sharp left turn and climbs up the ridge. Here the trail goes through scrub oak with an occasional pine tree. Some of its markings are painted on the rocks. Once on the ridge, the first good views appear with the Shawangunk Ridge and Basha Kill south and the Catskill Mountains northwest. During the next 1.15 miles the trail winds itself over the ridge, sometimes affording views to the west and northwest, other times northeast to southeast. On the east side of the ridge are steep ledges of 20-40 ft in height and beautiful loose-standing rock formations.

7.25 An old woods road becomes visible on the bottom of the ledges.

7.65 There are some fine last views of the Catskills, Ellenville, and Bear Hill.

7.75 The trail starts heading down through a nice stand of laurel. The trail is quite steep at places.

8.35 Crosse an old road, the former connector between NY Route 52 in Cragsmoor and US Route 209 in Spring Glen. After about 0.1 miles, the trail reaches a stream that cascades very nicely from a steep slope. The trail follows the stream down for about 200 ft, and then crosses the falls. After another 0.1 miles, the trail crosses the old road again and starts heading uphill.

8.75 Reach NY Route 52. Turn left and follow Route 52. What is road marker sign nearest exit point?

9.05 Pass a spectacular overlook high above the valley. The Catskills are visible in all their grandeur in the distance. This is a popular spot to hang glide in the updrafts created by the Shawangunk Ridge. There is a large parking area here. The trail continues past the overlook, reaching a turnoff to the right by a guardrail.

9.15 Turn right off NY Route 52, 0.1 miles past the parking area, at a place where the guardrail ends on the right, and head uphill paralleling Route 52. After a short distance, the trail climbs steeply through a series of switchbacks. The forest understory is primarily mountain laurel and blueberry. As the trail climbs, the forest begins to thin out.

9.70 The trail turns right and emerges on the slab as it continues to climb. From the slab, there are views across the Rondout Valley to the Catskills. After about 0.2 miles, the trail reaches the top of the hill and turns left along the slab. After a short distance, the trail turns right to descend into the woods.

10.05 The trail intersects a wood road. If you were to turn right and follow the woods road for 0.5 miles, you would reach the Bear Hill cliffs. These cliffs are a spectacular example of Shawangunk topography. The area is filled with crevices as you hop from boulder to boulder. From the cliffs, there is a spectacular view to the south. The Bear Hill Nature Preserve was set aside as a park by the community of Cragsmoor. The trail turns left and follows the woods road past boulders that block motor vehicles from accessing the cliffs. Just past the boulders is a parking area where several cars may be left.

10.15 Turn right on Dellenbaugh Road.

10.35 Circle Road goes to the right. Continue to the left on Dellenbaugh Road.

10.45 Meadow Lane is to the left. Continue on Dellenbaugh Road to the right.

10.55 Intersect Cragsmoor Road. To the right is the Cragsmoor Library. Turn left and follow Cragsmoor Road.

10.70 Cragsmoor Road continues ahead as South Gully Road. Bear to the right and follow Sam's Point Road.

11.80 Cross Sam's Point Preserve boundary.

11.90 Reach large parking area for Sam's Point Preserve (owned by the Open Space Institute; managed by The Nature Conservancy). There is a gatehouse here and a parking fee must be paid.

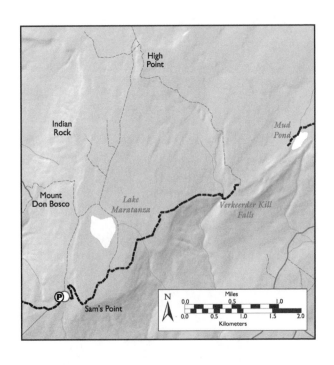

12. Sam's Point Preserve to Jenny Lane

Features: Shawangunk Mountains
Distance: 13.70 miles
USGS Map Quads: Napanoch
Trail Conference Maps: Map 9, Southern Shawangunk Trails

General Description

The Long Path enters the northern Shawangunks by Lake Maratanza on the Nature Conservancy's Sam's Point Preserve. The Shawangunks are one of New York's most popular scenic destinations. Capped by a hard, white conglomerate, the Shawangunks form a long mountain ridge with gently dipping slopes along the surface of the conglomerate that give way suddenly to great white cliffs. A favored spot for rock climbers from all over the northeastern US, the cliffs provide wonderful views of forested and farmed land in the valley below. In addition, the many miles of carriageways provide unparalleled mountain biking and cross-country skiing opportunities. The trail is quite rugged where it traverses cliff sections. It passes by three lakes: Lake Maratanza, Mud Pond and Lake Awosting. Lake Awosting especially is a gem with wooded shores that plunge into clear, deep blue water. In this section, the Long Path also passes two of the Shawangunk's finest waterfalls: Verkeerder Kill Falls and Rainbow Falls.

Access

Take the New York State Thruway to Exit 17, Newburgh. Continue west on Interstate Route 84 to Exit 5. Follow NY Route 208 north to NY Route 52. Turn left onto Route 52 and follow it west to the top of the ridge at Cragsmoor. Turn right on Cragsmoor Road and follow it 1.3 miles to the middle of the Hamlet of Cragsmoor. At a three-way intersection, bear right and again make a right onto Sam's Point Road. Follow Sam's Point Road one mile to parking lot at end.

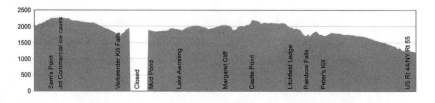

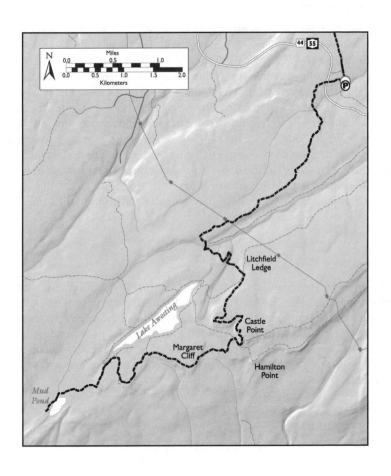

Parking

0.00 Sam's Point Preserve entrance (fee charged). (18T 553137E 4613363N)
13.45 Minnewaska State Park parking area on US Route 44/NY Route 55, about 0.75 miles south of the trail crossing (fee charged). (18T 562860E 4620571N)
13.75 Parking area at Jenny Lane. (18T 562229E 4621346N)

Trail Description

0.00 The Long Path passes through the gate beyond the parking lot at the north end of Sam's Point Road. It then turns right and follows the right fork of the road that loops around Lake Maratanza.
0.10 The trail reaches a hairpin turn in the road and continues along the road as it climbs through the woods towards Sam's Point.
0.50 The Long Path passes under the cliffs of Sam's Point on the left and comes to a spectacular view to the right. From here you can see south along the ridge to High Point, New Jersey. You can also see across the Wallkill Valley to the Hudson Highlands to the south and east. After the view, the trail turns left and ascends along the road to the top of the cliffs.

0.60 To the left is a road that leads a short distance to Sam's Point. It is worth the detour as the view is even better than along the road. Here you are high enough to see above the high point of Cragsmoor and can see west as well as south and east. Just to the west of the ridge and ten miles south is Basha Kill Wildlife Management Area. On a clear day, you can see all the way into New Jersey and Pennsylvania. The Long Path continues straight ahead on the road, passing through a dense pitch pine forest.
1.00 Reach the intersection with the road that led down to the former commercial ice caves. The side trip to explore the ice caves and return to this junction takes less than

Verkeerder Kill Falls

HERB CHONG

Castle Point

an hour and is well worth the time. The Long Path turns right and follows this road a short distance.

1.05 The Long Path turns left and leaves the road. The trail ascends through the blueberry bushes for a short distance and then descends gradually through a mixed blueberry-pitch pine forest.

1.25 The trail gradually turns left and goes through an open area covered with blueberry bushes. There are continuous views north towards Mud Pond and Minnewaska State Park with Gertrude's Nose and Castle Point prominent on the skyline.

1.45 The trail enters a denser forest of pitch pine and blueberry.

1.65 The trail enters a hardwood forest with a stream running through the middle. This stand of birch is highly unusual in the middle of the pitch pine and blueberry woods.

1.75 The trail exits the hardwood forest and reemerges in the pitch pine and blueberry scrub. Again there are views towards Minnewaska State Park.

2.00 The Long Path intersects the old trail that once ran from Lake Maratanza to Verkeerder Kill Falls. The trail left to Lake Maratanza is now closed. The Long Path turns right and follows the other branch of the old trail as it descends towards the falls. The forest gradually changes from one of pitch pine and blueberry to a hardwood forest.

2.60 The trail passes a large glacial erratic on the right. To the right, there are limited views to the valley. The trail enters a hemlock forest.

2.80 The trail crosses Verkeerder Kill. Here there are several channels and the crossing may be difficult in times of high water.

2.85 The trail reaches an intersection. To the right, a path leads in several hundred feet to a spectacular overlook above Verkeerder Kill Falls. Be careful here, as a misstep will send you plunging to the base of the falls 100 feet below. Please do not proceed beyond the falls as the landowner has closed the trail beyond this point. The falls and the overlook are also on private property. The landowner has graciously allowed us access to the falls, so please respect his rights and keep the area as you found it. The Long Path turns left back at the intersection and begins to climb to the top of another ridge. The climb is gradual at first, then steep.

3.10 The climb becomes gentler as it gains the ridge crest. After a viewpoint to the left on a conglomerate shelf, the trail turns away from the edge and passes through an area covered with blueberry bushes and small trees.

3.20 The Long Path reaches open slab. There is an intersection with the High Point Trail (red). The High Point Trail follows the original Long Path route to High Point and the High Point Carriageway 2.65 miles away.

Note: The Long Path is temporarily closed between its intersection with the High Point Trail and Mud Pond ahead. The Trail Conference is investigating

Azaleas growing wild on the trail

alternate routes. Blazes and cairns between this intersection and Mud Pond have been removed and following this route without the permission of the landowner is illegal. Please check on the Trail Conference web page at http://www.nynjtc.org for more information. Those wishing to take the High Point Trail to the other side of Mud Pond, an 8-mile detour, must consult the Southern Shawangunk Trails map to follow the carriage roads around the gap.

4.15 The trail reaches and drops to the level of Mud Pond and begins to run through swampy ground, sometimes on boardwalks.

4.25 Cross the outlet of Mud Pond and continue on a nearly flat table through blueberry, with scattered pine and birch.

5.15 Just as the trail makes the short descent to the western end of Lake Awosting, make a sharp turn to the right. The trail parallels the lake for a short distance to reach a carriage road. Turn right. Farther down the shore is a swimming beach that may be used when a lifeguard is present. Continuing along the shore will cut some distance and time off the hiker's route, but at the expense of wonderful scenery. The Long Path now ascends gently through

Hamilton Point Carriageway

scrubby pine forest, following the route of the former, and exceptionally well named, Scenic Trail. Some faded yellow blazes may still be visible.

5.55 Reach the edge of the ridge, with views to the south and west. The ledges are vertical faces of white, bedded conglomerate. The carriage road twists uphill to reach a higher outlook ledge on Murray Hill with its 270-degree view that includes the Wallkill Valley to the southeast and the great ridge of the Shawangunks to the northeast. The carriage road ends here and the Long Path follows a footpath along the ledge. The route, which is often bare and marked by cairns, is nearly flat, with occasional sharp, short climbs or drops. The vegetation is generally short and scrubby.

5.80 Reach a high point with a 360-degree view that includes Lake Awosting. After a short drop, the trail goes left on the overgrown remnants of a carriage road for about 125 feet, and then turns right onto a footpath.

6.20 The Long Path turns right, onto another carriage road. In 250 feet, it turns left and uphill on a path to reach a decayed carriage road.

6.45 After the carriage road ends, the trail emerges onto Margaret Cliff with its many good views. The trail continues to run along the edge of the cliff.

6.95 The trail drops steeply, at first through a cleft in the rock, until reaching the base of the rock cliff. It moves away from the cliff, crosses a carriage road and then a stream, and ascends through the woods.

7.15 The trail goes through a natural tunnel in the rock. It can be dark, narrow and damp. Hikers with large packs can detour around the tunnel by going about 15 feet to the right. The trail emerges in a cleft between rocks and passes below an overhanging rock to reach a cliff top with several views.

7.60 Turn right onto the Hamilton Point Carriageway. In 20 feet, the Castle Point Carriageway leaves to the left as the Long Path bears right on the Hamilton Point Carriageway. (For reverse direction, continue straight ahead on the Hamilton Point Carriageway, as the Castle Point Carriageway leaves to the right.)

7.70 Turn left off the carriageway onto a footpath and climb. The ascent becomes very steep and requires hand-pulls up ledges. Very good views appear.

7.80 Reach Castle Point and turn left onto the Castle Point Carriageway. The splendid view here includes Lake Awosting. (In the reverse direction, the Long Path drops off the ledge at a sharp left turn in the carriageway.) In 25 yards, take the right fork in the carriageway. The carriageway twists gently downhill with several splendid views. After following the cliff edge toward a narrowing notch, the road turns away from the edge.

8.30 A few hundred feet past a sharp switchback turn in the carriageway, the Long Path turns right, goes up two stone steps and enters the woods on a footpath. It passes a small ledge on the left. After that, a tremendous view to the south and west opens up. The ledge curves gradually clockwise and affords views of Lake Awosting as it begins to run above a small ravine.

8.70 The Long Path turns right and leaves the ledge. A worthwhile detour follows the ledgetop clockwise for a short distance, providing yet more spectacular views of Lake Awosting, the Catskills, and Huntington Ravine below. Until 1994, the Long Path followed this portion of the cliff-top until it was rerouted to remove a long walk along the Upper Awosting Carriageway ahead.

8.80 The trail reaches a rock outcropping on the top of the ridge where there is a view north toward the Catskills and

Wild apple blossoms by the trailside

east toward Castle Point. The trail continues north following the slab and pitch pine for a short distance before descending through the laurel into a hemlock forest. Upon reaching the hemlocks, the trail turns right and follows the top of Litchfield Ledge. The trail is now in deep in a hemlock grove.

9.35 The trail descends and reaches an exposed part of Litchfield Ledge where there is a spectacular view of the Rainbow Falls and the Catskills. The trail continues along the ledge and then descends to the Upper Awosting Carriageway.

9.50 The trail crosses the Upper Awosting Carriageway and descends toward a small stream. The trail crosses the stream as the forest becomes dominated by hemlock.

9.70 Rainbow Falls plunges over the cliff wall just after another stream crossing. After the falls, the trail turns right and continues down the valley of Huntington Ravine.

9.85 The trail turns left and climbs steeply out of the valley. The ascent gradually becomes gentler as several views appear.

10.10 Reach the top of a conglomerate rock plane with a tremendous view to the north. The trail now descends at a moderate pitch down the rock plane with small pines and blueberries growing in patches of soil on the bare rock. On the way down, the trail briefly passes through better-developed woods and crosses a stream. Toward the bottom of the drop, the trail enters scrubby pine woods.

10.40 Turn right onto the Peters Kill Carriageway (it provides the most direct access to Lake Awosting from the Park parking area) and cross the valley of Fly Brook on a causeway. Once over the causeway, the Long Path turns right at the clearing with a large pine tree at its southern edge. In a short distance, it turns left to leave the carriageway and crosses a grassy clearing.

10.55 At the end of the clearing, the trail enters the woods on a slight upgrade and almost immediately turns right onto a wider, rocky trail. The trail follows gentle grades near the top of a gentle slope.

10.95 The trail crosses and briefly follows a power line right-of-way. It then turns left into the woods at a pair of poles just before a sharp drop-off and continues near the top of an asymmetrical ridge that is gentle to the left and sharp to the right. There are occasional views of a parallel ridge across the valley to the right.

11.60 The Blueberry Run Trail (blue) begins to the right, leading down to the Peters Kill Carriageway. The Long Path regains the ridge crest as it passes through short pines.

11.80 Turn left away from the edge of the ridge and into hardwoods. The trail descends gently through forest rich in mountain laurel.

13.40 Cross a stream on rocks.

13.50 Cross US Route 44/55.

13.65 The trail crosses a stone wall and passes through a grassy field.

13.70 Reach Jenny Lane, a gravel road that was the old Wawarsing Turnpike. To continue, turn left and follow the road.

13. Jenny Lane to Riggsville

Features: Road walk
Distance: 12.80 miles
USGS Map Quads: Napanoch, Kerhonkson
Trail Conference Maps: Map 9, Southern Shawangunk Trails

General Description

The first mile of this section is on an old dirt road through the woods. The rest of the section follows paved roads, some quite busy, that pass through rural Ulster County and the Town of Kerhonkson.

Access

Take the New York State Thruway to Exit 18, New Paltz. Continue west on NY Route 299 through the Town of New Paltz. At the T-junction with US Route 44/ NY Route 55, turn right to head uphill. About a mile beyond the Minnewaska State Park parking area on the left and a few hundred yards past a small stream crossing, turn right on a narrow gravel access road. Take the first right to the parking area.

Parking

0.00 Parking area at Jenny Lane. (18T 562229E 4621346N)
1.00 End of Old Minnewaska Trail (limited parking). (18T 561595E 4622338N)
4.10 Street parking in Kerhonkson. (18T 558278E 4625005N)
12.80 DEC parking area at entrance to Catskill Park on Upper Cherrytown Road. (18T 554278E 4634905N)

Trail Description

0.00 From the end of Section 12 (just north of the parking area) proceed north on Jenny Lane.
0.10 A gravel road goes left 0.1 miles to Route 44/55. The Long Path continues straight ahead on a dirt road not open to traffic. The general trend is downhill through the forest. At one point, there is a view of the Catskill Mountains.
1.00 Reach the end of Old Minnewaska Trail, a gravel road. A few cars can be parked here. The trail continues straight ahead and crosses a wooden bridge.

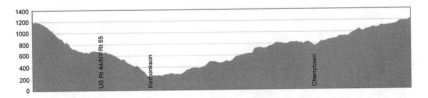

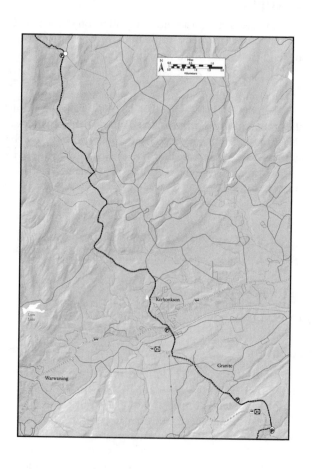

1.30 The road becomes paved and houses become more frequent.

1.80 Old Minnewaska Trail ends at Upper Granite Road (Ulster County Route 27). The trail bears turns onto Upper Granite Road.

2.30 Upper Granite Road ends at US Route 44/55. The trail turns right and follows this busy highway.

2.80 Pass through an intersection and continue downhill.

3.40 Where the road flattens out, take the first right. This road has a double yellow line but no sign.

3.90 Cross Rondout Creek on a steel bridge in Kerhonkson.

4.10 Cross US Route 209 at a traffic light.

4.15 At a split in the road, turn left onto a quiet residential road.

4.40 Cross a small stream.

5.60 Turn left onto Ulster County Route 3, a busy street.

5.90 Take the first left on Cherrytown Road and go uphill.

9.50 Pass Baker Road on the left.

9.60 The trail turns left where the road it has been following ends on another road, Upper Cherrytown Road, that goes straight and left. As it makes the turn, houses are on the left and a garage is on the right.

12.80 The section ends at a DEC parking area on the right side of the road. To continue, turn left and enter the woods on a DEC snowmobile trail.

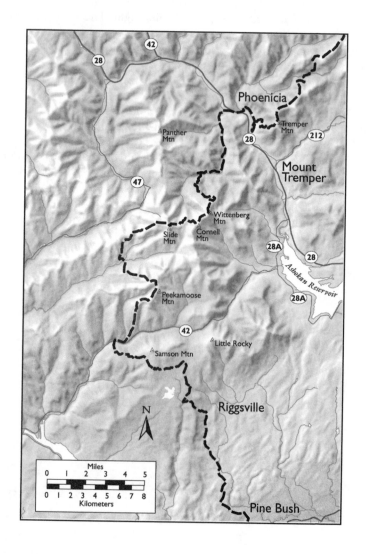

Southern Catskills

These sections of the Long Path mark the beginning of the route through Catskill Park. The Catskill Park has spectacular scenery and considerable rugged terrain. It passes over Slide Mountain, the tallest in the Catskills. Nowhere does the Long Path go higher. Small villages nestled in the valleys provide a break from the traverses through dense forests carpeting most of the Catskill Mountains.

Most of its route follows DEC trails maintained by the Trail Conference. The trails are generally marked with different colored plastic markers. These are usually the only trail identification except at major trail junctions. The Aqua paint blaze is reserved for when the trail crosses private property. As the Long Path changes frequently from one DEC trail to another, the hiker must watch carefully for turns and make sure that they are on the proper trail. Most trail DEC junctions have signs that give the trail names and the direction and distance to important points.[10] At many of these intersections, a plastic Long Path marker indicates the route of the Long Path.

Camping is permitted on State land at elevations below 3,500 feet (this elevation is usually marked by signs along the trails), and at locations at least 150 feet away from trails and water. The Long Path also passes several DEC lean-tos and campgrounds.

---

[10] The distances given on these signs are not always accurate.

The Southern Catskills from High Point, Minnewaska State Park

HERB CHONG

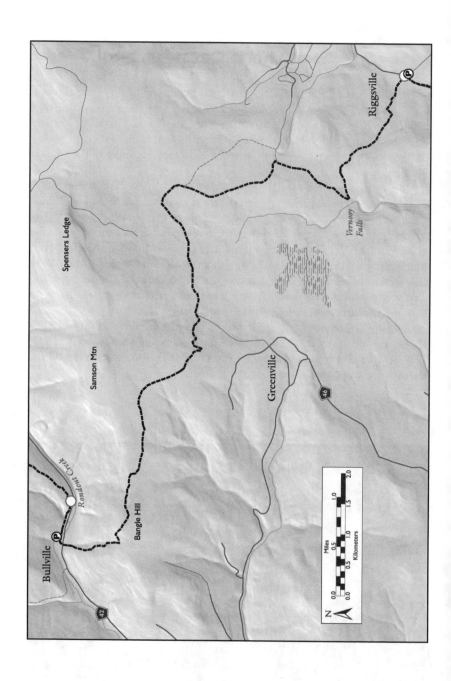

14. Riggsville to Bull Run

Features: Vernooy Falls, Bangle Hill
Distance: 10.10 miles
USGS Map Quads: Kerhonkson, West Shokan, Peekamoose Mountain
Trail Conference Maps: Map 43, Southern Catskill Trails

General Description

The Long Path follows a snowmobile trail to Vernooy Falls, a series of lovely waterfalls. After the cascade, the Long Path leaves the snowmobile trail to follow and cross many dirt roads on gentle grades for the first six miles. The trail becomes narrower and more rugged as it passes the shoulder of Samson Mountain and climbs gently over Bangle Hill. The final descent to Bull Run is steep and long.

Access

Take the New York State Thruway to Exit 19, Kingston. Continue on NY Route 28 west for about three miles, then turn left onto NY Route 28A. At Ulster County Route 3, go west to and through Samsonville. Go right on Sundown Road, then turn left onto Upper Cherrytown Road and follow it to the trailhead.

Parking

0.00 DEC parking area at entrance to Catskill Park on Upper Cherrytown Road. (18T 554278E 4634905N)
9.65 Sundown Primitive Campsite on Peekamoose Road. (18T 546612E 4640690N)
10.10 Parking area on Peekamoose Road (also known as Gulf Road and Ulster County Route 42). (18T 547333E 4640489N)

Camping

9.65 Sundown Primitive Campsite.

Trail Description

0.00 Opposite a DEC parking area on Upper Cherrytown Road, the Long Path enters the woods at a DEC sign with a red marker indicating a snowmobile trail. Follow the blue hiking trail markers and the large yellow snowmobile markers on a wide path. The trail crosses a small stream and begins to ascend.

0.25 Cross a stream on a wooden footbridge and turn right to follow the stream. In another 0.1 miles, pass a piped spring on the left. The trail turns left away from the stream and ascends more sharply as large trees give way to a smaller forest. The trail eventually levels off and crosses several small streams.

1.70 Reach a clearing with Vernooy Falls, a series of lovely cascades in a large stream, on the left. A number of old foundations are in this area, and the hiker can explore several paths. The Long Path makes a sharp right turn on a wide cobble path as it continues to follow the blue trail markers and the yellow markers of the snowmobile trail. After a gradual ascent, the trail levels off. Here, it is often wet.

2.65 The Long Path turns left up a gentle hill as the yellow-marked snowmobile trail continues straight ahead. The Long Path now follows a wide woods road. It reaches a gentle hilltop and becomes fairly level.

3.90 The trail goes left at an intersection of woods roads. It crosses a stream on three metal pipe culverts. Several dirt roads lead away from the trail. A stream approaches from the left and the trail runs alongside it.

4.60 Cross a tributary stream on a wood plank bridge. The trail passes through hemlock forest before rejoining hardwoods. This section of the trail is often wet.

5.30 Cross a stream on a metal pipe culvert. In 500 feet, another dirt road goes off to the left.

5.60 The Long Path goes right on a narrow track, leaving the woods road. The trail climbs, often fairly steeply, until it reaches another woods road. Here it turns left on level ground. (For reverse direction, the turn off this woods road is a few hundred feet before the road curves to the left.)

6.10 At a small crest in the woods road, the Long Path turns right on a footpath, leaving the road. A few hundred yards further on, it makes a sharp left on a well-defined path. The general trend is gently downhill as it crosses several small streams.

7.95 The trail jogs left and runs along a level grade with a sharp drop to the right.

8.65 After reaching the top of Bangle Hill, the trail descends steeply, and then turns left and continues along a nearly level contour.

8.85 Cross a rocky intermittent stream, turn right, and head downhill, parallel to the stream. It is now steep downwards all the way to the base of Bangle Hill. On the way down, the trail crosses the stream two more times. It then crosses the outlet of a spring and continues along the valley of the stream. The trail widens into a woods road and passes several other woods roads on the left.

9.65 Reach Peekamoose Road (Ulster County Route 42) and turn right, passing a parking area for the Sundown Primitive Campsite on the left. Occasional Aqua blazes appear on roadside objects to mark the way.

9.75 The road crosses a bridge over Rondout Creek. In another 600 feet, it crosses a bridge over a tributary stream.

10.10 The Long Path departs from the road by turning left.

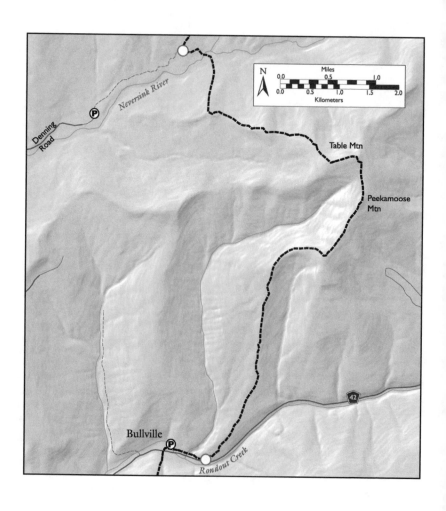

15. Bull Run to Denning Road

Features: Peekamoose and Table Mountains
Distance: 7.60 miles
USGS Map Quads: Peekamoose Mountain
Trail Conference Maps: Map 43, Southern Catskill Trails

General Description

This is a rugged trail section that begins with a three-mile, 2,500-foot ascent of Peekamoose Mountain. Shortly before the top, there is a tremendous view of the Rondout Creek valley. After climbing out of the saddle between Peekamoose and Table Mountains, the trail ascends along the broad, gentle "top" of Table to the summit. From Table, the trail drops to the valley of the East Branch of the Neversink River. The trail then climbs out of the river valley and joins the Phoenicia-East Branch Trail. For the entire length of the section, the Long Path follows the blue-blazed Peekamoose-Table Trail.

Access

Take the New York State Thruway to Exit 19 (Kingston). Continue on NY Route 28 west. In Boiceville, about 17 miles from the Thruway, turn left onto NY Route 28A. (Do not turn left onto Route 28A where it first meets Route 28, about 3 miles west of the Thruway.) In West Shokan, turn right onto Peekamoose Road (Ulster County Route 42, also known as Gulf Road and as Sundown-West Shokan Road). (This turn may not be marked by a street or route sign, but a large sign points to Grahamville and Town Offices.) Follow Peekamoose Road for about 10 miles to a parking area on the right.

Parking

0.00 Parking area on Peekamoose Road. (18T 547333E 4640489N)
7.60 Parking area at end of Denning Road (1.2 miles along the Phoenicia-East Branch Trail from the end of this section). (18T 545364E 4646082N)

Camping

0.00 Sundown Primitive Campsite (on Peekamoose Road, 0.4 miles west of trailhead).
5.20 Bouton Memorial Lean-to.

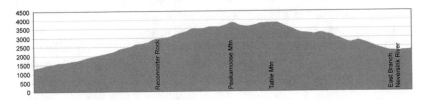

Trail Description

0.00 From the north side of Peekamoose Road, about 250 feet south of the parking area, the Long Path proceeds uphill on a woods road, following the blue-blazed Peekamoose-Table Trail.

0.85 The trail turns right, leaving the woods road, and continues on a footpath. The ascent is steady but varying in pitch as the trail alternates between gentle stretches and sharp, rocky climbs.

2.35 Reach Reconnoiter Rock, a rock outcrop, with a partial view to the northwest. The trail now levels off for some distance.

3.10 Just past the 3,500-foot elevation sign, reach a wide ledge to the right of the trail, with excellent views. In another 250 feet, an unmaintained trail, with some old red paint blazes, goes off to the right and descends to Peekamoose Road.

3.35 Pass a spring that comes from a small cleft in the rock to the left, a source of water. The trail now passes through a dwarf spruce forest.

3.80 Begin to climb steeply.

3.95 Reach the summit of Peekamoose Mountain, marked by a large rock to the left of the trail. Some views to the northeast are possible from the top of the rock. The trail descends steeply into the col between Peekamoose and Table Mountains.

4.20 Reach the base of the col, and begin gentle ascent.

4.40 Begin a steep ascent up Table Mountain. The grade moderates, and then becomes extremely gentle when the nearly flat ridge of Table Mountain is attained. Shortly after attaining the ridge, an unmarked trail to the right leads to an excellent viewpoint over the Burroughs Range and Rocky and Lone Mountains to the northeast.

4.80 Reach the summit of Table Mountain, on the divide between the drainage basins of the Hudson and Delaware Rivers. (The wooded summit affords no views.) Descend, sometimes steeply, as hardwoods replace spruce forest.

5.15 Pass a sign indicating the 3,500-foot elevation. In another 400 feet, a faint side trail leads right, about 50 feet to an unreliable spring, a possible source of water.

5.20 Opposite the spring a trail leads left to the Bouton Memorial Lean-to.

5.55 Begin to climb over a small knoll. The way down includes four sharp drops that are separated by gentler sections.

6.35 The descent is interrupted briefly by a second small knoll.

7.20 The trail drops into the broad, flat flood plain of the East Branch of the Neversink River.

7.30 Pass the flood plain of the East Branch of the Neversink River. At the crossing of Deer Shanty Brook, two new log bridges have been constructed where crossings at times of high water were formerly a problem.

7.45 Climb out of the flood plain and ascend gently.

7.60 Reach the yellow-blazed Phoenicia-East Branch Trail. To continue, turn right and follow the yellow markers. To the left, it is 1.2 miles to the parking area at the end of Denning Road.[11]

---

[11] This junction marks the eastern end of the Finger Lakes Trail, a hiking trial that continues west along the Southern Tier of New York to the Pennsylvania border at Allegheny State Park.

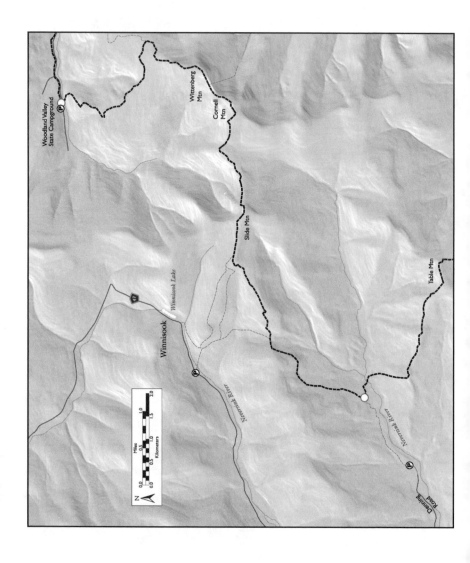

16. Denning Road to Woodland Valley State Campground

Features: Slide, Cornell and Wittenberg Mountains
Distance: 11.15 miles
USGS Map Quads: Peekamoose Mountain, Phoenicia
Trail Conference Maps: Map 43, Southern Catskill Trails, Map 42, Central Catskill Trails

General Description

From the valley of the East Branch of the Neversink River, the Long Path follows the route of the Phoenicia-East Branch Trail. At the Curtis Monument, it turns onto the ridge of the Burroughs Range. Slide Mountain, the first encountered on the ridge, is the highest peak in the Catskills. The trail then passes over Cornell and Wittenberg Mountains before dropping down into Woodland Valley. Since the Long Path in this section follows several DEC trails, the hiker should be careful at trail junctions to choose the correct trail.

Access

From New York City: Take the New York State Thruway to Exit 16 (Harriman). Continue on NY Route 17 west to Exit 100 (Liberty). Turn right at the end of the exit ramp and follow NY Route 55 east for 10 miles to Curry. At a sign on the right for Claryville, turn left onto Sullivan County Route 19 (Claryville Road) and follow it for 13 miles to the trailhead at the end of the road. The name of the road changes to Denning Road upon reaching Claryville. After about 7.5 miles, the designation of the road as a county road ends, and the road narrows. To reach the beginning of this section of the Long Path, follow the Phoenicia-East Branch Trail northeast from the parking area for 1.2 miles.

From the Hudson Valley: Take the New York State Thruway to Exit 18 (New Paltz). Continue west on NY Route 299 through the Town of New Paltz. At the junction with US Route 44/55, go west (right). Follow Route 55 to Curry, and make a right onto Sullivan County Route 19. Continue as described above.

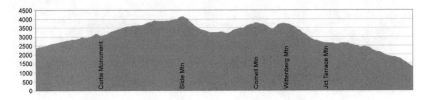

Parking

0.00 Parking area at end of Denning Road (1.2 miles along the Phoenicia-East Branch Trail from the beginning of this section). (18T 545364E 4646082N)

11.20 Woodland Valley State Campground (parking fee charged in season). (18T 553205E 4653970N)

Camping

8.55 Terrace Mountain Lean-to (0.9 miles from the Long Path on yellow-blazed Terrace Mountain Trail; no water).

11.20 Woodland Valley State Campground (fee charged).

Trail Description

0.00 From the intersection of the Peekamoose-Table Trail with the Phoenicia-East Branch Trail proceed north on the yellow-blazed Phoenicia-East Branch Trail (a woods road). The trail rises gently but steadily through hardwood forest, crossing a few small streams.

0.55 Pass spring to the left of the trail.

0.85 Cross a stream on a wooden bridge. The trail runs along the shoulder of a steep slope, with the rushing water of Deer Shanty Brook below to the right.

1.75 Turn right onto the blue-blazed Curtis-Ormsbee Trail. The yellow-blazed Phoenicia-East Branch Trail continues straight ahead, reaching Ulster County

The Ashokan Reservoir from Wittenberg Mountain

HERB CHONG

Wittenberg Mountain

Route 47 in 1.5 miles. Near the junction is a stone monument in memory of William ("Father Bill") Curtis and Allen Ormsbee, both of whom died in a snowstorm on Mt. Washington on June 30, 1900. The trail is named in their memory. The Curtis-Ormsbee Trail leads up the ridge of the Burroughs Range, which comes into view just before the trail junction. The ascent is sometimes steeply up rock ledges, and alternates between hardwood and spruce forest.

2.40 About 500 feet past the sign marking the 3,500-foot elevation, a short side trail leads, right, to a ledge with a spectacular lookout. Table Mountain (with its long, flat top) and Rocky and Lone Mountains are clearly visible. The ascent continues, with level, swampy stretches and steep climbs.

3.40 Turn right onto the red-blazed Wittenberg-Cornell-Slide Trail. The trail ascends gently through dense spruce trees.

4.05 Reach the summit of Slide Mountain (marked by a concrete slab-a remnant of a former fire tower). At 4,180 feet in elevation, this is the highest point in the Catskill Mountains. In another 300 feet, an outcrop on the left side of the trail offers an excellent view to the east, with the Ashokan Reservoir visible in the distance below. The Burroughs Plaque, commemorating John Burroughs, is set into the side of this outcrop. The descent from Slide is steep and rugged, with wooden steps provided in the steepest section. Several good views are possible along the way.

4.30 A sign marks the way to a spring-a dependable source of water-on the left side of the trail. The pitch of the descent becomes more moderate, but several sharp rock faces must be traversed.

5.00 Reach the low spot between Slide and Cornell Mountain. An unmarked trail leads, right, about 300 feet to a spring. This is a popular camping spot for those doing the Wittenberg-Cornell-Slide circular. Beyond the col, the trail levels off and passes around a wet area. In the spring, the hobblebush puts on a spectacular show in this area. The trail begins to ascend Cornell Mountain, passing through a dense spruce-balsam forest. As the trail nears the summit of Cornell, it climbs steeply over a series of rock ledges.

6.25 Reach the top of a rock ledge. To the left of the trail is a rock outcropping with a spectacular view of the great Panther-Slide Wilderness Area-the largest unbroken landmass in the Catskills. Views of Slide Mountain and its slide are directly ahead. To the left, Peekamoose, Table, Lone and Rocky Mountains are visible. To the right of Slide are Giant Ledge and Panther Mountain, with the Devil's Path range in the far distance. From this viewpoint, there is no evidence of civilization in the Catskills.

6.45 To the right, a short yellow-blazed side trail leads to the summit of Cornell Mountain. The view from Cornell is somewhat overgrown, but there are good views eastward to the Ashokan Reservoir. From here, the trail begins to descend.

6.55 The trail reaches the top of a rock ledge, with a view to the northwest toward Wittenberg Mountain. The trail scrambles down a very steep crevice in the rock ledge and onto the "Bruin's Causeway"-the path along the ridge between Cornell and Wittenberg. This is one of the highest cols in the Catskills, with the elevation remaining over 3,500 feet.

6.90 Reach the col between Cornell and Wittenberg Mountains. To the right, a faint old trail leads down extremely steeply to Moon Haw Road in Maltby Hollow. This trail should be avoided by all but the most experienced hikers. The Long Path now begins its climb to the summit of Wittenberg Mountain.

7.25 Reach the summit of Wittenberg Mountain, with a large open rock ledge that affords a tremendous view to the east. The Ashokan Reservoir is visible down below, with Ashokan High Point beyond. On a clear day, the Hudson River may be seen in the distance, with the Taconic Mountains at the Connecticut-Massachusetts border far beyond. To the north, the Devil's Path range is visible. The trail begins a steep descent over a series of rock ledges, continuing through the characteristic spruce-balsam summit forest.

8.15 The Long Path begins to level off and now follows a trail that was constructed by the CCC. It passes through a high elevation deciduous forest.

8.55 The Long Path turns left, following the red-blazed Wittenberg-Cornell-Slide Trail, as the yellow-blazed Terrace Mountain Trail continues straight, reaching the Terrace Mountain Lean-to in 0.9 miles. This trail once continued down to Woodland Valley Road, and was the original route up Wittenberg Mountain from the north, but the part beyond the lean-to was abandoned when the present route of the Wittenberg-Cornell-Slide Trail was constructed from the Woodland Valley State Campground. The Wittenberg-Cornell-Slide Trail dips slightly to cross a small stream and then levels off as it follows the northern shoulder of Wittenberg Mountain.

9.70 The trail passes a spring about 300 feet to the left of the trail, where water flows over a rock ledge. Shortly beyond the spring, the trail begins to descend more steeply. After one steep section, the trail passes through a hemlock grove, with a view from a ledge to the right over Woodland Valley. The trail continues to descend through a series of boulders, levels off for a short distance, and then makes its final descent into Woodland Valley.

11.05 After passing a register box, the trail crosses Woodland Creek on a wooden bridge.

11.15 Reach Woodland Valley Road. To the left, there is a large parking area. The DEC charges a fee to park here (in season). To continue, turn right and follow Woodland Valley Road eastward.

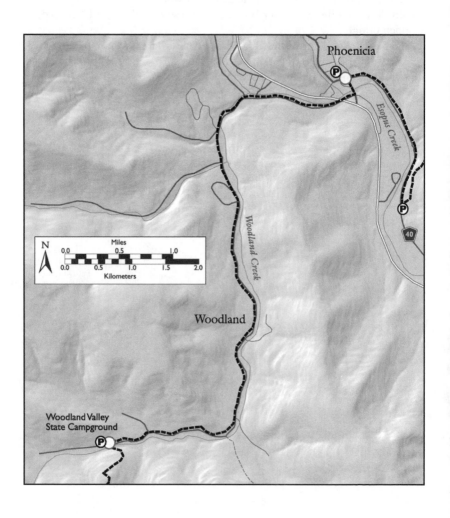

17. Woodland Valley State Campground to Phoenicia

Feature: Road Walking
Distance: 5.75 miles
USGS Map Quad: Phoenicia
Trail Conference Maps: Map 43, Southern Catskill Trails, Map 42, Central Catskill Trails, and Map 43, Northeastern Catskill Trails

General Description

Long Path follows paved roads in this section. The trail runs along Woodland Creek much of the way through a narrow, mountainous corridor. After Woodland Creek intersects Esopus Creek, the trail continues east along Esopus Creek, and crosses the Esopus into the Village of Phoenicia.

Access

Take the New York State Thruway to Exit 19 (Kingston). Follow NY Route 28 west for 23 miles to Phoenicia. Turn right at the second turn to Phoenicia (Bridge Street). Follow Bridge Street to just before the railroad tracks, and turn left onto High Street. Follow High Street and then Woodland Valley Road 5.5 miles to the Woodland Valley State Campground.

Parking

0.00 Woodland Valley State Campground (parking fee charged in season). (18T 553205E 4653970N)
5.75 Village of Phoenicia (parking available on Main Street or behind the Phoenicia Pharmacy on NY Route 214). (18T 556830E 4659268N)

Camping

0.00 Woodland Valley State Campground (fee charged).

Trail Description

0.00 From the Woodland Valley State Campground, proceed eastward on Woodland Valley Road.
1.30 Pass old swinging suspension bridge to the right. This was the original route of the Wittenberg-Cornell-Slide Trail (and Long Path) over Terrace

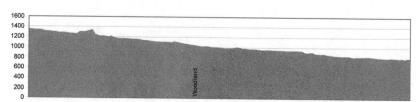

Mountain, but was abandoned some years ago when the private landowner along the creek closed the trail.

2.10 Pass Fawn Hill on the left.

3.85 Cross Panther Kill.

4.20 Cross Woodland Creek.

4.60 Herdman Road comes in from the left. Continue straight ahead.

4.70 To the left, an old bridge, now closed to vehicular traffic, crosses Esopus Creek. The Long Path continues ahead on High Street, which runs parallel to Esopus Creek. It crosses under NY Route 28 and intersects Bridge Street.

5.60 The Long Path turns left on Bridge Street, crosses the railroad tracks and then Esopus Creek, and enters Phoenicia. The railroad tracks-formerly the route of the Ulster and Delaware Railroad-are now operated by a local tourist short-line, the Catskill Mountain Railroad. The Ulster and Delaware once brought trainloads of tourists to this portion of the Catskills. Today, the Catskill Mountain Railroad ferries tubers from Mt. Pleasant to Phoenicia.

5.75 Reach Main Street in Phoenicia (Ulster County Route 40). To the left is the center of Phoenicia. While just two blocks long, it is well worth the detour. It is home of several restaurants and a number of antique shops. There is also a grocery store and general store here for backpackers to resupply. To continue on the Long Path, turn right and proceed eastward on Main Street (Ulster County Route 40).

18. Phoenicia to Silver Hollow Notch

Feature: Tremper Mountain
Distance: 11.50 miles
USGS Map Quads: Phoenicia, Bearsville, Hunter
Trail Conference Maps: Map 41, Northeastern Catskill Trails

General Description

The Long Path leaves Phoenicia on public roads, paralleling the Esopus Creek. The trail then climbs up the south side of Tremper Mountain, following an old tote road to the former state fire tower. From there, it heads toward Carl Mountain and circles it to descend to Warner Creek before going over Edgewood Mountain to Silver Hollow Notch. This section begins a long stretch between supply points. From Phoenicia to Palenville is over 40 miles. Only two roads are crossed in this distance, neither of which have stores within 4 miles of the crossings. There is an unbridged stream crossing at 6.95 (Warner Creek) that is dangerous to impassible at medium to high water.

Access

Take the New York State Thruway to Exit 19 (Kingston). Follow NY Route 28 west for 23 miles to Phoenicia. Turn right at the second turn to Phoenicia (Bridge Street). Follow Bridge Street across the Esopus Creek to Main Street in Phoenicia.

Parking

0.00 Village of Phoenicia (parking available on Main Street or behind the Phoenicia Pharmacy on NY Route 214). (18T 556830E 4659268N)

Camping

3.15 Baldwin Memorial Lean-to.
4.00 Tremper Mountain Lean-to.

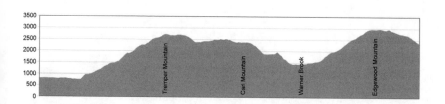

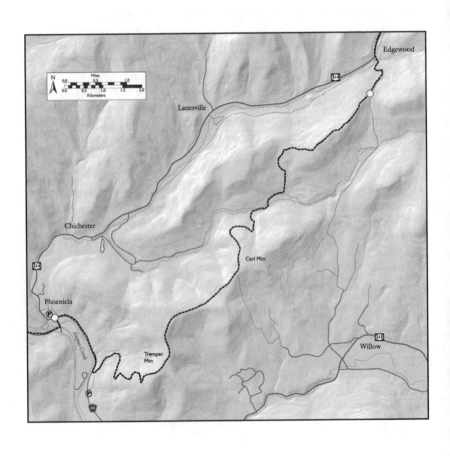

Trail Description

0.00 From the intersection of Bridge Street and Main Street in Phoenicia continue east on Main Street (Ulster County Route 40), following the north side of Esopus Creek. In the spring, the Esopus is filled with white water canoers and kayakers, as well as trout fishermen. The Esopus is one of the most famous trout streams in America. In the summer, the primary recreational use of the creek is by people who ride lazily downstream in inner tubes.

1.30 The Long Path arrives at the unmarked beginning of the old fire warden's road leading up Tremper Mountain on the left. This was the trailhead for the Phoenicia Trail before it was moved 0.3 miles east to a new parking lot in the late 90's. Turn left following the wide road steeply uphill for about 100 yards to a junction with the Phoenicia Trail. Red markers to right lead 0.3 miles to the parking area on Ulster County Route 40. Continue straight ahead on red markers following the fire warden's road to the abandoned state fire tower. The grade varies between steep and gradual. On the steeper sections, the trail is rocky and eroded. For most of the way, the trail passes through a mixed hardwood and hemlock forest.

2.05 Pass rock ledges on the left

2.15 Pass a seasonal spring on left, which is reliable in all but the driest times.

2.20 The trail passes an abandoned bluestone quarry on the left. Bluestone mining was once one of the primary industries in the Catskills. As you pass the quarry, you can see the layering that made bluestone an easy mineral to mine. Past the quarry the trail levels off, crosses several woods roads, and begins a series of switchbacks.

2.95 The trail sidehills through a steep slope with rock walls on the right and a steep drop on the left. After a short level stretch, the trail again begins a steep climb.

3.15 A side trail to the right leads to the Baldwin Memorial Lean-to. In another 250 feet, pass an undependable pipe spring 50 feet to the left of the trail.

3.65 After a switchback, the trail climbs to the top of the ridge, and then follows it the rest of the way to the summit. Here the forest is less mature; consequently, there is more undergrowth.

Frost growing from the rocks

HERB CHONG

4.00 Pass the Tremper Mountain Lean-to on the left.

4.05 Reach the flat, level summit of Tremper Mountain, with an abandoned state fire tower, formerly used by fire observers with two-way radios. These towers were placed on top of selected mountains in the early 1900's after a series of fires devastated the mountains. More recently, the fire towers have been replaced by aircraft patrols. This fire tower has been restored and is open to the public. To the right of the tower is an open area that affords a view of the Devil's Path when the leaves are down. Continuing past the tower, the Long Path passes through a cleared area and then begins to descend, now following the blue-blazed Warner Creek Trail. It passes through a fairly open forest, with a base of blackberry brambles.

4.30 The trail enters a more mature forest, with little undergrowth. It continues to descend along the ridge top towards the col between Tremper Mountain and Carl Mountain. Initially, the trail follows the eastern slope of the ridge, with seasonal views through the trees over the Devil's Path to the north.

4.95 The trail levels out and then begins a gradual climb of the north peak of Tremper Mountain. For the most part, the trail stays about 200 vertical feet below the top of the ridge, following the western slopes.

5.80 After passing through a hemlock grove, the trail descends along the eastern side of the ridge.

6.20 Reach the col between Tremper Mountain and Carl Mountain. Here, the yellow-marked Willow Trail turns right, leaving the ridge, descending steeply 1.8 miles through Hoyt Hollow to Jessop Road and the Willow Post Office. Continue ahead on the blue-marked Warner Creek Trail following an old, gently sloping woods road with little elevation change.

6.60 Bear left leaving the woods road and begin a moderate descent through open hardwoods. When the leaves are down, there are views to Tremper Mountain and the Central Catskills beyond.

7.00 The trail eases onto a wide bench and contours to the right around Carl Mountain, slowly gaining elevation.

7.35 Begin a steep descent to Warner Creek, passing a series of cataracts in the seasonal stream to the right of the trail. There are many switchbacks on the way down.

7.60 The trail descends some stone steps into the bed of seasonal stream. Continue across the streambed to meet terminus of an old quarry road and follow it. In about 0.2 miles, there is a bluestone quarry on the right. Once past the quarry, the trail descends again for a few hundred feet.

8.80 Pass a stone foundation to right. It is in open park-like surroundings. Continue gently downhill towards Warner Creek.

8.25 The trail crosses Warner Creek on a gravel bar in a hemlock grove. There is no bridge for this crossing, making it dangerous at medium or high water.

8.30 Reach a woods road and turn right to follow it. There is a small stream within 500 feet located in a hemlock grove.

8.60 Turn left, leaving the woods road, and begin the climb to the summit of Edgewood Mountain. The ascent is moderate to steep through open hardwoods and an occasional hemlock grove.

9.25 Pass a black birch tree with a large burl in its trunk. Just beyond, the trail joins a faint old quarry road and steepens.

9.55 The trail reaches the broad ridge and turns right to follow it uphill.

10.00 The trail traverses a grassy area.

10.50 Pass large bog on right.

10.70 The trail crosses the broad summit of Edgewood Mountain. There are no views. Shortly beyond, begin a steep descent through rocky ledges toward Silver Hollow Notch.

11.00 Reach a view into Warner Creek Valley with Olderbark Mountain opposite.

11.20 Reach a view to the south over Warner Creek Valley

11.50 Arrive at Silver Hollow Notch and the end of Section 18. To continue on the Long Path, turn left and descend, following Aqua paint blazes along the severely eroded Silver Hollow Road. Turning to the right leads in 0.8 miles to the end of the drivable portion of Silver Hollow Road coming up from Willow.

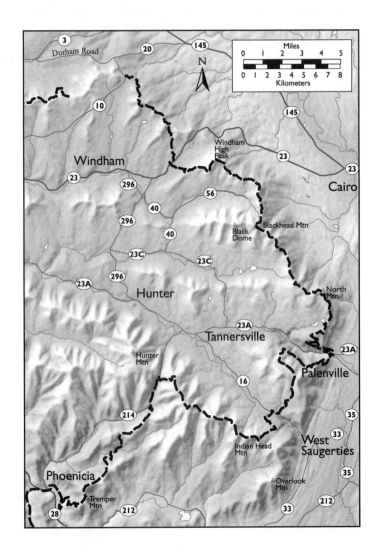

Central Catskills

Once out of the southern parts of the Catskills, the Long Path enters the more well traveled and civilized regions. The trail joins the Devil's Path, one of the most strenuous hiking trails in New York, and passes near the former sites of two large hotels. Both hotels played a huge role in the development and then subsequent protection of the Catskills as an area "forever wild" to be spared from logging and other encroachments of civilization on nature. North/South Lake State Campground now occupies the land owned by both hotels to preserve the landmarks and vistas seen by the rich and famous when the Catskills were "the" place to go to for travel and vacation. The trail also passes a bounty of waterfalls, some directly on the trail and some nearby. Kaaterskill Falls, a short distance from North Lake State Campground has two major drops, each a major waterfall in its own right, that add up to the tallest falls in New York State.

Porcupine

HERB CHONG

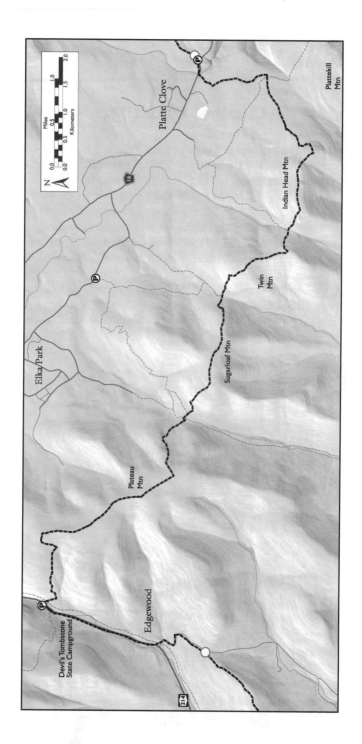

19. Silver Hollow Notch to Platte Clove Road

Features: Sugarloaf and Twin Mountains
Distance: 14.55 miles
USGS Map Quads: Hunter, Bearsville, Woodstock, Kaaterskill
Trail Conference Maps: Map 41, Northeastern Catskill Trails

General Description

This section of the Long Path contains some of the most spectacular and rugged scenery in the Catskills. After descending from Silver Hollow Notch, it follows NY Route 214 to Stony Clove Notch and the Devil's Path. It follows the Devil's Path over Plateau, Sugarloaf, Twin and Indian Head Mountains. This trail ascends and descends in dramatic fashion, clambering over and through large rock ledges. Each mountain offers excellent views. The Devil's Path is the most dramatic trail in the Catskills, going up and over six major peaks. The long Path traverses the 4 eastern peaks. As its name implies, there are tremendous drop-offs between the peaks. The hike of the entire Devil's Path (west to east) involves a gain of over 8,000 feet in total elevation – an elevation gain comparable to that of the Great Range in the Adirondacks!

Access

Take the New York Thruway to Exit 19. Follow NY Route 28 west to Phoenicia and then north on NY Route 214 to Edgewood. The beginning of the southern end of this section is not accessible by car.

Parking

1.25 Parking area on west side of Rt. 214, 0.30 miles north of Silver Hollow Road junction. (18T 565080E 4665688N)
2.25 Notch Lake in Stony Clove Notch (part of Devil's Tombstone State Campground – Fee in season). (18T 565809E 4667842N)
14.55 Steenberg Road. (18T 575825E 4665015N)

Camping

2.10 Devil's Tombstone State Campground (fee)
6.70 Mink Hollow Lean-to
13.40 Devil's Kitchen Lean-to

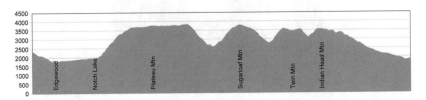

Trail Description

0.00 Silver Hollow Notch – The trail bears left from the col where Silver Hollow Road passes through the notch following the Long Path Aqua blazes. Begin a moderate descent.

0.40 State land stops on the left side (downhill) of road. State land continues along right side.

0.60 Keep right, avoiding a wood road to left.

0.70 There is a private house on left. This is the end of the drivable portion of Silver Hollow Road on the north side of the notch.

0.80 At the bottom of the descent, the trail crosses a wooden deck bridge between stone abutments. This is a part of the old Stony Clove branch of the Ulster & Delaware Railroad that ran from Phoenicia to North Lake.

0.90 Bear right on Route 214.

1.25 There is a parking area on the west side of the highway opposite a large clearing.

1.35 Pass the state land boundary on right. State land continues from here to beyond Stony Clove Notch. Continue ahead on Rt. 214. An alternate bushwhacking route from here to Stony Clove Notch is to turn right, following the yellow blazes of the state land boundary about 250 feet to the old Stony Clove railroad grade, and then left (north) to the Devil's Path. The RR grade is never more then 100 yards away from the highway but provides a pleasant alternative to a mile of road walking. This alternate is not maintained.

1.60 Cross Stony Clove Creek in a beaver meadow. There are good views up to Plateau Mountain in this area.

Rocks on Plateau Mountain

HERB CHONG

View from Sugarloaf Mountain

1.90 Pass the Devil's Tombstone Picnic Area on right. A fee is charged in season.

2.10 The Devil's Tombstone State Campground headquarters is on the left. The campground operates from Memorial Day to Labor day with a fee charged. Camping is not permitted at other times. Purchase a day permit for the Notch Lake parking area from this facility.

2.30 The Long Path meets the Devil's Path at the Notch Lake parking area (fee in season). The Devil's Path continues west (left) to the summit of Hunter Mountain. Notch Lake is on the left just beyond the parking area. Turn right following the red markers. The climb up Plateau is very steep and steady beginning 200 yards from NY Route 214.

3.30 The climb abruptly ends at the open rock of Orchard Point Lookout. Here there are excellent views south through Stony Clove Valley and the southern Catskills. Directly across Stony Clove, Hunter Mountain dominates the view. Begin a pleasant 2-mile walk along the more or less flat summit ridge of Plateau through mature spruce/fir woods. Acid rain and other environmental factors have contributed to the high death rate of the largest trees, some of which exceeded 2 feet in diameter.

3.40 There is a wide view to the north/northeast with the Black Dome Range and mountains of the Northeast Catskills in the distance.

3.60 View northeast.

4.50 Pass an unmarked trail to left – private trail, keep out.

4.80 Cross the summit of Plateau Mountain in dense spruce woods.

5.50 View east. The trail begins a steep descent.

6.30 Spring right of trail.

6.70 Junction with the southern leg of the Mink Hollow Trail – continue ahead on red markers. To the right, the blue-marked Mink Hollow Trail leads 3 miles to the end of Mink Hollow Road 3 miles north of Lake Hill on Rt.

212. Mink Hollow Lean-to is located 200 feet to the right.

6.90 Junction with the northern leg of the Mink Hollow Trail. Left on blue markers leads 2.25 miles to a trail junction with the Pecoy Notch Trail. Continue ahead on red markers to reach the first of a series of 5 rock ledges that the trail climbs over.

7.25 The forest becomes primarily balsam fir and red spruce, with birch mixed in, as the grade begins to moderate.

7.45 Pass the sign indicating the 3,500-foot elevation line. The forest now becomes more open with views to the left of the Blackhead Range to the north. The trail passes a large rock on the right with excellent views of Plateau Mountain and Mink Hollow.

7.65 A yellow-blazed side trail leads to the right to a rock ledge with an outstanding view of the southern Catskills. Visible are the Burroughs Range, Giant Ledge and Panther Mountain, and the mountains along the Pine Hill–West Branch Trail. The Ashokan Reservoir can also be seen with the Shawangunks in the background. On a clear day, you can see all the way to the Hudson River valley.

7.70 Reach the flat, level summit of Sugarloaf Mountain. The trail continues through a mature balsam-spruce forest, beginning to descend in a series of steps, alternating with level sections.

8.30 Reach a viewpoint to the east over Pecoy Notch, with Twin and Overlook Mountains visible beyond and the Ashokan Reservoir and the Shawangunks in the distance. The trail now begins a very steep descent into Pecoy Notch.

8.45 Descend steeply over a series of rock ledges. There are many good views

Bluestone Quarry on Indian Head Mountain

HERB CHONG

View from Overlook Mountain

over Pecoy Notch and towards Twin Mountain.

8.90 Descent ends abruptly shortly before reaching a junction with the Pecoy Notch Trail in the col between Sugarloaf and Twin Mountains. Left on blue markers leads 1.75 miles to the north end of the Mink Hollow Trail. The Long Path continues, beginning a steep climb of the west summit of Twin Mountain and climbing over large rocks and several rock ledges in the process. There are several good views back towards Sugarloaf during the ascent.

9.10 Pass a huge rock on the left that separated from the main ledge.

9.25 The trail goes through a narrow passage and climbs up a rock ledge.

9.45 Reach a rock ledge with a large overhanging rock, a good temporary shelter, on the left. The trail continues through a cleft in the rock ledge. At the top of the ledge, there is a good viewpoint of Sugarloaf Mountain with the fire tower on Hunter Mountain visible to the west, and the Blackhead Range, Stoppel Point and Roundtop visible to the north. The grade now moderates.

9.60 The trail turns left and climbs a small ledge to reach a viewpoint near the north or true summit of Twin Mountain. From this vantage point, one can see Sugarloaf, Plateau and Hunter Mountains to the west, the Burroughs Range to the south, and the Ashokan Reservoir and the Shawangunk Mountains to the southeast, with the Hudson Valley and the Hudson Highlands far in the distance. The actual summit of Twin is slightly beyond this viewpoint. The trail now descends through a mature spruce-balsam forest.

9.90 Reach the col between the two peaks of Twin Mountain. The trail now ascends gradually to the south peak of Twin.

10.25 Reach the south peak of Twin Mountain, with an excellent 180-degree view. To the west, Sugarloaf and Plateau Mountains are visible, and to the south all the major peaks of the southern Catskills may be seen. To the southeast, the Ashokan Reservoir and the Shawangunks are visible, with the Hudson Highlands and the Hudson Valley in the distance. Overlook Mountain may be seen to the east, with the Hudson River and the Taconics in the far distance. This is one of the best views in the Catskills. The Catskill 3500 Club does not consider the south peak of Twin, while over 3,500 feet high, as a separate peak, since the drop between the north and south peaks of Twin is less than the required 200 feet. The trail continues eastward, beginning to descend.

10.35 Reach a viewpoint to the east over Jimmy Dolan Notch and Indian Head Mountain. The trail now begins to descend more steeply.

10.50 Descend over a rock ledge and pass under a large balanced rock to the left.

10.65 The trail reaches Jimmy Dolan Notch, the col between Twin and Indian Head mountains, at a trail junction. This notch has the highest elevation of all the cols along the Devil's Path at 3100'. Left, the blue-marked Jimmy Dolan Notch Trail descends steeply at first, then moderately for two miles north to Prediger Road. Continue ahead following the red markers to begin a moderate to steep climb up Indian Head.

11.20 The ascent becomes gentler as the trail reaches thick spruce woods after a steep scramble up the final ledge to the summit of Indian Head Mountain. This is the highest of the three summits making up the summit ridge.

11.65 Reach a spectacular overlook after going over the second summit. Below is eastern summit with Plattekill Mountain beyond and Overlook Mountain to the right. Below and to the left is Platte Clove with Huckleberry Point prominent above the north side of the Clove. On the far horizon is Vermont to the north, Massachusetts to the northeast and Connecticut to the southeast. In between is the Hudson Valley from just south of Albany to the Highlands beyond Newburgh. A short but very steep descent brings one to the low point between the middle and east summits.

12.15 View to north with Kaaterskill High Peak and Roundtop across the upper Schoharie Valley with the northern Escarpment mountains and Black Dome Range beyond. Begin a steep to moderate descent.

13.40 The trail meets the blue-marked Overlook Trail coming in from the right on a wide woods road. Turn left on the road, continuing to follow the red markers. The Overlook Trail leads in 0.15 miles to the Devil's Kitchen Lean-to.

13.45 Reach another trail junction. The Long Path continues ahead on the road following blue markers while the Devil's Path turns left. There is a large bluestone quarry on right.

13.70 Cross onto Platte Clove Preserve. The blue markers change to green metal Platte Clove Preserve markers. Camping is not permitted within the Platte Clove Preserve, which runs from here to beyond Platte Clove Road.

14.40 Cross Plattekill Creek on bridge at head of Platte Clove. Continue steeply uphill to Platte Clove Road. Turn right following paved Platte Clove Road east.

14.55 The dirt Steenberg Road and a state snowmobile trail lead to the left.

Waterfall at Platte Clove Preserve

This is the end of Section 19. A large parking lot is located 250 feet north on Steenberg Road from this intersection. To continue on the Long Path, turn left on Steenberg Road.

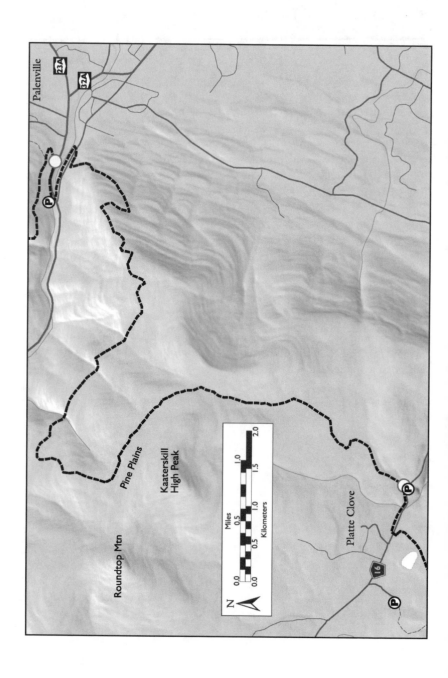

20. Platte Clove Road to Palenville

Features: Buttermilk and Wildcat Falls
Distance: 10.00 miles
USGS Map Quads: Kaaterskill
Trail Conference Maps: Map 41, Northeastern Catskill Trails, Map 40, North Lake Area

General Description

The first part of this section runs along a DEC snowmobile trail that ascends the northern slopes of Kaaterskill High Peak on rather gentle grades. After leaving the snowmobile trail, the Long Path descends gradually at first and then steeply to the old Red Gravel Hill Road, which it follows the rest of the way. For the next two miles it is level, passing a series of dramatic waterfalls with a spectacular view into Kaaterskill Clove. After a brief ascent, it descends continuously into Palenville, passing a number of abandoned bluestone quarries. For most of this section, blue DEC trail markers mark the Long Path. The last part of the section, which crosses private property, is marked by Aqua paint blazes.

Access

Take the New York State Thruway to Exit 20 (Saugerties). Continue on NY Route 212 west to the small town of Centerville. As Route 212 curves to the left, bear right onto Ulster County Route 35 and stay on it for the next 1.6 miles. Shortly after passing the Blue Mountain Campground, Route 35 makes a sharp left turn. Turn left here, but afterwards continue straight ahead on Ulster County Route 33, as Route 35 turns right. In about two miles, the road (now known as Platte Clove Road or Greene County Route 16) turns into a dramatic mountain road that climbs over 1,000 feet in less than three miles. At the top of the climb, four miles after leaving Route 35, the road crosses a small brook; the trailhead is immediately beyond the brook on the right at the intersection with Steenberg Road.

Winter Access

Take the New York State Thruway to Exit 20 (Saugerties). Take NY Route 32 north to NY Route 32A. Continue on Route 32A north to Palenville. Turn left (west) onto Route 23A, and follow it through Kaaterskill Clove and past Haines Falls to Tannersville. In Tannersville, turn left at the traffic light and

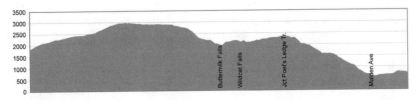

continue along Greene County Route 16 (known for most of the way as Platte Clove Road) to the top of Platte Clove. The trailhead is on the left at the intersection with Steenberg Road.

Parking

0.00 On Steenberg road about 250 feet north of the trailhead. (18T 575825E 4665015N)

9.45 On the north side of Malden Avenue, about 100 feet beyond where NY Route 23A joins this road (the road is barricaded to vehicular traffic beyond this point). (18T 579529E 4669860N)

Trail Description

0.00 From Platte Clove Road take the snowmobile trail to the north, following the old Steenberg Road uphill. The snowmobile trail is blazed with large orange or yellow DEC plastic snowmobile markers in addition to blue DEC markers for the Long Path.

0.70 Turn right onto another dirt road.

0.95 Turn right, leaving the old Steenberg Road, and follow another old woods road northward.

1.05 To the right, an unofficial trail, with yellow markers, leads to Huckleberry Point, an excellent viewpoint. The Long Path continues straight ahead on nearly level grades.

1.35 Cross bridges over a pair of streams in a swampy area. After the second bridge, the ascent resumes, as the trail climbs to the 3,000-foot elevation on the north flank of Kaaterskill High Peak.

2.25 Reach the highest point on the trail in this section in an area known as the "Pine Plains." The trail continues through nearly level–though swampy–terrain. For the next 0.75 miles, the forest is typical of that found at higher elevations, with considerable spruce, hemlock and birch.

3.50 The snowmobile trail turns left, uphill, while the Long Path, blazed with blue DEC markers, continues straight ahead. To climb Kaaterskill High Peak, turn left with the snowmobile trail, turn right in 0.1 miles onto the snowmobile loop trail, and then turn left onto an unofficial blue-blazed trail that leads to the summit of High Peak. The Long Path now goes through drier terrain.

3.70 The Long Path turns right (north) onto an old trail that formerly ran from the private community of Twilight Park to High Peak, and begins to descend off the ridge. The descent is often steep and contains many small switchbacks.

4.15 Leave the old Twilight Park Trail and begin to descend over a series of sharp slopes and narrow flat ledges.

4.80 The trail reaches another narrow ledge, turns right on the old Red Gravel Hill Road, and begins to run parallel to the edge of the great drop to Kaaterskill Clove on the left.

5.00 Reach Buttermilk Falls just to the left of the trail, a spectacular two-step waterfall. Cross the stream and continue along level ledge.

Buttermilk Falls during the dry season

5.50 Reach Wildcat Falls, another spectacular waterfall. The ledge to the west of the falls affords an excellent view of Kaaterskill Clove and the Hudson Valley to the east. Cross the stream and continue along the level trail. You will descend a small ledge to the left, pass a large boulder, and bear right along the slope edge again.

6.00 Cross the two streams of Hillyer Ravine, which provide the last sure source of water in this section. The trail now ascends slightly and crosses several intermittent streams.

6.95 Reach the crest of the rise and begin to descend. The trail continues downhill–at times, steeply–until reaching Malden Avenue. The trail uses several long switchbacks in its descent, and an old bluestone quarry is passed to the right of the trail.

8.50 Cross the state land boundary. Since the Long Path now runs over private property, the trail markers change from blue DEC plastic markers to Aqua paint blazes.

8.95 Reach Malden Avenue in Palenville and turn left along the road.

9.45 After going around a barricade which blocks vehicular traffic, turn right onto NY Route 23A.

10.00 The section ends where a woods road leaves to the left, just east of an "Entering Catskill Park" sign. To continue, turn left onto the old road.

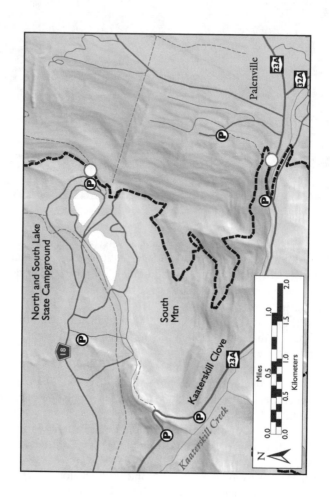

21. Palenville to North Lake State Campground

Features: Kaaterskill Clove and North Lake
Distance: 4.80 miles
USGS Map Quads: Kaaterskill
Trail Conference Maps: Map 41, Northeastern Catskill Trails, Map 40, North Lake Area

General Description

For most of this section, the Long Path follows the Sleepy Hollow Horse Trail, the route of the old Harding Road that led from Palenville to the Hotel Kaaterskill. There are a number of views along this route, which is blazed with the yellow markers of the horse trail. The Kaaterskill Clove Lookout provides a dramatic open view of the clove, and there are continuous views of the clove through the trees when the leaves are down. Upon reaching the Escarpment, the Long Path follows the blue-blazed Escarpment Trail, passing the sites of the two most famous nineteenth century hotels in the Catskills–the Hotel Kaaterskill and the Catskill Mountain House. Along the way, there are several spectacular views of Kaaterskill Clove and the Hudson Valley. The section ends at North Lake, once used for recreation by guests of the Catskill Mountain House. Today, it is the site of a large state campground, complete with a beach and a boat rental facility.

Access

Take the New York State Thruway to Exit 20 (Saugerties). Take NY Route 32 north to NY Route 32A. Continue on Route 32A north to Palenville. Turn left (west) onto NY Route 23A, and pass through the Village of Palenville. The section begins a short distance beyond the village, about 100 feet east of an "Entering Catskill Park" sign, where the Long Path enters the woods on the Sleepy Hollow Horse Trail.

Parking

0.00 On NY Route 23A, about 0.4 miles west of the "Entering Catskill Park" sign, there is a small parking area on the north side of the road, just before the bridge over Kaaterskill Creek. (18T 579529E 4669860N)
4.80 North Lake State Campground, at North Lake Beach (parking fee charged in season). (18T 579614E 4672230N)

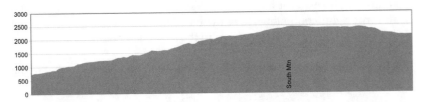

Camping

4.80 North Lake State Campground (fee charged).

Trail Description

0.00 From Route 23A, about 100 feet east of the "Entering Catskill Park" sign, the Long Path proceeds north, following the red markers–the route of the old Harding Road from Palenville to the Hotel Kaaterskill. Shortly after leaving Route 23A, the trail switchbacks to the left and begins a long climb up Kaaterskill Clove. The trail parallels the clove most of the way, climbing 1,400 feet in three miles.

0.25 A woods road goes off to the right. The Long Path continues ahead on old Harding Road.

0.95 Reach a trail register. Here the trail turns right and follows a deep side gorge formed by a stream. Just past the register, the trail reaches Kaaterskill Clove Lookout, which affords a spectacular view to the left into Kaaterskill Clove. Kaaterskill High Peak towers over the clove on the south side. On the right side of the trail, there is a stone fireplace below a small rock ledge. This is a great place for a picnic. Beyond the viewpoint, the trail continues to parallel the gorge, now often lined with hemlock trees.

1.20 The trail reaches the head of the gorge and turns left to cross the stream that formed the gorge. There is a small waterfall here. The trail continues uphill, once again paralleling the clove. When the leaves are down, there are continuous views through the trees of Kaaterskill Clove and Kaaterskill High Peak.

1.90 The trail makes a switchback to the right and begins to move away from Kaaterskill Clove. The Long Path now parallels the Escarpment Trail, which runs to the north, about 300 feet above the level of the Long Path. Again, there are views of Kaaterskill Clove through the trees, now with the Hudson River valley beyond.

2.45 Reach a viewpoint to the east, down Kaaterskill Clove, with the Hudson Valley, the Hudson River and the Taconics visible beyond.

2.65 The Long Path turns left, following the red markers, as a horse trail goes off to the right to the Palenville Lookout and Rip Van Winkle Hollow.

2.85 Turn right onto the blue-blazed Escarpment Trail. To the left, the Escarpment Trail leads to Inspiration Point and the Layman Monument.

3.25 Reach the top of South Mountain. This was the site of the famous Hotel Kaaterskill, built in 1881 by George Harding, an influential guest at the Catskill Mountain House, who became upset when the Mountain House refused to accommodate the special dietary needs of his daughter. As a result, he left and built his own hotel. That building was destroyed in a fire in 1924. The Long Path turns right, continuing along the blue-blazed Escarpment Trail, as the red-blazed Schutt Road Trail goes off to the left. The Long Path now follows a wide and level trail.

3.85 A red-blazed trail continues straight ahead and provides a shortcut to the Catskill Mountain House, as the Long Path turns right, following the blue-

HERB CHONG

Kaaterskill Falls

blazed Escarpment Trail, which begins to descend.

4.05 Reach Split Rock and Boulder Rock, which afford a fine view of Kaaterskill Clove and the Hudson Valley. Boulder Rock–a large glacier erratic that is perched atop the ledge–makes a fine scramble for those who enjoy bouldering.

4.15 The red-blazed shortcut trail rejoins from the left as the Long Path, still following the blue-blazed Escarpment Trail, continues north along the ledges. The trail passes an area known as "Puddingstone Hall"–named for the conglomerate rock in the area–and descends to the Catskill Mountain House site.

4.55 Reach the site of the former Catskill Mountain House. Built in 1824, it was the earliest and most famous of the old Catskill hotels, and was frequented by Presidents and famous artists. Just east of the hotel site, an inclined railway brought guests up from the Hudson Valley. The Mountain House fell into disrepair in the early twentieth century, when travelers chose the American West and Europe, rather than the Catskills, as the destinations for their summer vacations. It was burned in 1963 by the DEC, since it had become a hazard. The area around the hotel is well-worth exploring. From the hotel site, the trail continues along a former hotel access road towards North Lake and then turns right, along the Escarpment, and follows a chain-link fence.

4.80 The trail passes through a picnic area, where a short side trail leads left to the North Lake parking lot. To continue, proceed straight ahead on the blue-blazed Escarpment Trail.

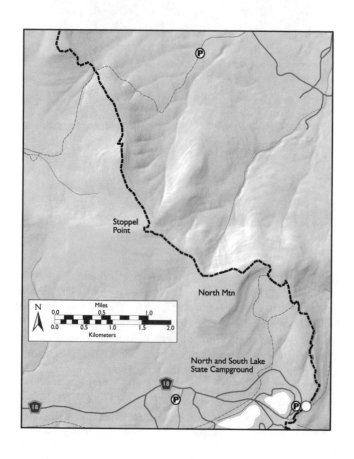

22. North Lake State Campground to Batavia Kill

Features: Catskill Escarpment, Blackhead Mountain
Distance: 9.80 miles
USGS Map Quads: Kaaterskill, Freehold
Trail Conference Maps: Map 41, Northeastern Catskill Trails, Map 40, North Lake Area

General Description

This section of the Long Path offers dramatic scenery. From North Lake, the trail proceeds north along the Catskill Escarpment (also known as the "Great Wall of Manitou"), with many spectacular views of the Hudson River valley over 2,000 feet below. Thomas Cole of the Hudson River School of Painting made this area famous. After a steep climb to North Point, the trail becomes more rugged, descending from Stoppel Point to Dutcher Notch and then climbing Blackhead Mountain. The summit of Blackhead is the second highest point on the Long Path. North of Blackhead, the trail descends to the Batavia Kill Trail along one of the steepest trail sections in the Catskills. For the entire length of this section, the Long Path follows the Escarpment Trail, blazed with blue DEC trail markers.

Access

Take the New York State Thruway to Exit 20 (Saugerties). Take NY Route 32 north to NY Route 32A. Continue on Route 32A north to Palenville. Turn left (west) onto NY Route 23A, and continue through Kaaterskill Clove to Haines Falls. In Haines Falls, turn right onto Greene County Route 18 and follow the signs to North Lake State Campground 3 miles ahead. Pass through the gate (a fee is charged in season) and continue ahead to the parking area at North Lake.

Parking

0.00 North Lake State Campground, at North Lake Beach (parking fee charged in season). (18T 579614E 4672230N)
9.80 Parking area at end of Big Hollow Road. This is 1.4 miles along the red-blazed Black Dome Range Trail and the yellow-blazed Batavia Kill Trail from the beginning of this section). (18T 572932E 4682265N)

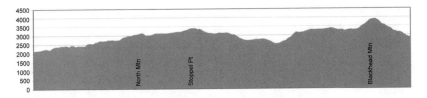

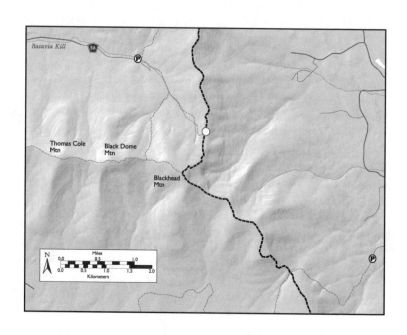

Camping

0.00 North Lake State Campground (fee charged).
9.80 Batavia Kill Lean-to (0.25 miles from the Long Path along the yellow-blazed Batavia Kill Trail).
Camping is prohibited between North Lake and North Point.

Trail Description

0.00 From the end of a short side trail that begins at the east end of the parking lot, the Long Path proceeds north along the blue-blazed Escarpment Trail, passing through a picnic area. The trail passes a register box and begins to ascend.
0.30 After a short, steep climb over a rock ledge, the trail reaches Artist Rock, which provides a good view of the Hudson River valley. Artist Rock was made famous by Thomas Cole, the founder of the Hudson River School of Painting. Beyond Artist Rock, the trail climbs a series of small ledges and passes through an area of hemlock, white pine, pitch pine, red spruce and balsam fir. The trail passes a large rock ledge on the right. This was the site of "Jacob's Ladder," which allowed Catskill Mountain House visitors to climb up to Sunset Rock above.
0.80 To the right, a yellow-blazed side trail leads to the top of Sunset Rock, which offers a dramatic view of North and South Lakes and the site of the Catskill Mountain House, with Kaaterskill High Peak visible directly behind the lakes. This was the site of one of Thomas Cole's most famous paintings.
1.00 Reach Newman's Ledge, a large overhanging rock outcropping with a spectacular view north over the Hudson River valley. On a clear day, the tall buildings of Albany are visible in the distance, with the Taconics and Green Mountains of Vermont beyond. The trail now climbs about 140 feet and emerges in an open area, with an interesting mountaintop swamp that is well worth exploring.
1.55 The yellow-blazed Rock Shelter Trail leaves to the left. This trail drops into Mary's Glen and continues to the gatehouse at the entrance to the North Lake area. From Mary's Glen, the red-blazed Mary's Glen Trail can be followed back to North Lake. The Rock Shelter Trail is named for a large overhang known as Badman's Cave, which was reputed to be a hideout for outlaws in the 1700's. The Long Path continues to the right and climbs through a rocky area in a spruce-balsam forest.
2.20 The red-blazed Mary's Glen Trail leaves to the left. This trail descends through a beautiful wooded area and provides an alternate return route to North Lake. The Long Path continues ahead and begins a very steep ascent to North Point.
2.35 Reach North Point, an open rocky ledge, which provides a spectacular 360- degree view. To the south, directly below, are North and South Lakes, with Kaaterskill High Peak and Roundtop in the background. To the east is the ridge of the Escarpment that we have been following, with the Hudson Valley precipitously below. To the west and immediately ahead is North Moun-

ED WALSH

Ledge on the Escarpment Trail

tain, with Blackhead Mountain behind to the right (northwest). The City of Albany is visible in the distance to the northeast. From here the trail continues to climb North Mountain.

2.80 Reach the summit of North Mountain. While only slightly over 3,000 feet high, North Mountain has a spruce-balsam forest that is characteristic of the higher elevations. The trail continues up, at times steeply, through brushy, rocky areas.

4.05 Reach Stoppel Point, which provides a view northeast over the Hudson Valley, with Albany and the Taconics in the distance. Stoppel Point was the site of a recent plane crash, and parts of the wreckage may still be seen. From Stoppel Point, the trail begins to descend towards Dutcher Notch, with occasional views of the Blackhead Range through the trees and then levels off.

5.15 The trail curves to the north and resumes its descent. Just before the descent, there is an excellent view back to the southeast. From here, it is evident that you have already descended a substantial distance from Stoppel Point. After a short, steep descent, the trail levels off again.

6.30 After another short, steep descent, the trail reaches Dutcher Notch, the lowest point on the Escarpment Trail since just beyond North Lake. To the right, the yellow-blazed Dutcher Notch Trail drops 1,700 feet in 2.4 miles to Floyd Hawver Road. There is a reliable spring on the Dutcher Notch Trail 0.35 miles and about 500 vertical feet below this point–the only reliable water in this section. To the left, the yellow-blazed Colgate Lake Trail descends to Colgate Lake, first passing around an unnamed lake and skirting private Lake Capra. The Long Path continues straight ahead, beginning a steep ascent to a level area sometimes known as Arizona Plateau.

7.15 After an 800-foot climb, the trail reaches the Arizona plateau and begins to level off. To the left, a short side trail leads to a viewpoint back towards Stoppel Point and Lakes Capra and Colgate. The trail follows this level plateau for about a mile, with increasingly spectacular views of Blackhead Mountain straight ahead.

8.30 The trail begins its final 600-foot ascent to the summit of Blackhead Mountain. Near the summit, there is a spectacular view to the east over the Escarpment below, with Albany and the Taconics visible to the north.

8.80 Reach the summit of Blackhead Mountain, the second highest point on the Long Path and the fourth highest mountain in the Catskills. The view from the summit is overgrown, but views to the south are possible by heading into the scrub vegetation just left of the trail. Here, the Long Path, following the blue-blazed Escarpment Trail, turns right, as the yellow-blazed Blackhead Mountain Trail goes straight ahead and descends to Lockwood Gap between Blackhead and Black Dome Mountains. (It is worth the 0.2-miles detour down this trail to a spectacular view to the south and west). The Long Path drops precipitously down the north face of Blackhead, plunging over ledges in one of the steepest descents in the Catskills. Near the base of the descent, there are two fine views of the Hudson Valley to the east.

9.80 Reach the base of the descent from Blackhead Mountain. Here, the yellow-blazed Batavia Kill Trail descends to the left, passing the Batavia Kill Lean-to in 0.25 miles, and ending at the red-blazed Black Dome Range Trail in 0.9 miles. From this point, the Black Dome Range Trail continues straight ahead to the parking area at the end of Big Hollow Road in another 0.5 miles. To continue on the Long Path, proceed straight ahead on the blue-blazed Escarpment Trail.

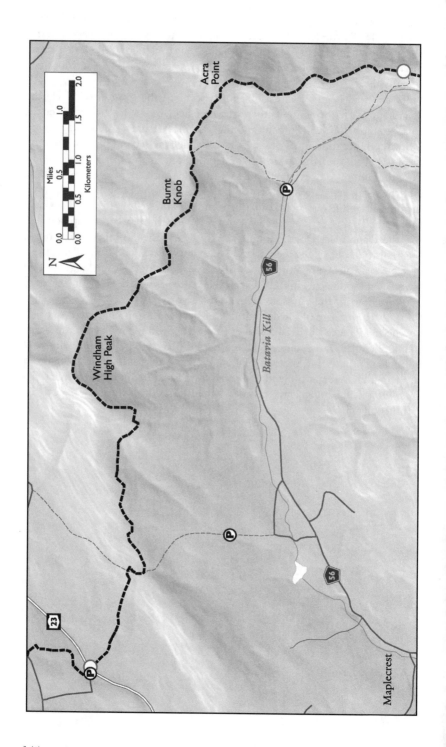

Acra
Point

Burnt
Knob

Windham
High Peak

Batavia Kill

56

56

23

Maplecrest

N

Miles

0.0 0.5 1.0 1.5 2.0

0.0 0.5 1.0

Kilometers

23. Batavia Kill to NY Route 23

Features: Northern Catskill Escarpment, Windham High Peak
Distance: 8.55 miles
USGS Map Quads: Freehold, Hensonville
Trail Conference Maps: Map 41, Northeastern Catskill Trails

General Description

The Long Path continues along the blue-blazed Escarpment Trail to NY Route 23 in East Windham. The trail crosses several 3,000-foot peaks before making the final climb over Windham High Peak. There are many views along the way over the Blackhead Range to the south and the Catskill and Mohawk valleys to the north. On a clear day, one can see all the way to the southern Adirondacks. From Windham High Peak, the trail descends to NY Route 23, at the northern edge of the Catskill Park, passing through two groves of Norway spruce planted by the CCC in the 1930's. For the entire length of this section, the Long Path follows the Escarpment Trail, blazed with blue DEC trail markers.

Access

Take the New York State Thruway to Exit 21 (Catskill). Continue on Route 23 west about 22 miles to Brooksburg. At a sign for Hensonville, turn left and proceed south on Greene County Route 65. In Hensonville, turn left onto Greene County Route 40 and follow it to Maplecrest. In Maplecrest, bear left onto Big Hollow Road, passing the Sugar Maples Resort, and continue about 5 miles to a parking area at the end of the road. To reach the beginning of this section of the Long Path, follow the red-blazed Black Dome Range Trail straight ahead for 0.5 miles to the intersection with the yellow-blazed Batavia Kill Trail. Continue ahead on the Batavia Kill Trail 0.9 miles to the Escarpment Trail.

Parking

0.00 Parking area at end of Big Hollow Road This is 1.4 miles along the red-blazed Black Dome Range Trail and the yellow-blazed Batavia Kill Trail from the beginning of this section. (18T 572932E 4682265N)
8.55 Parking area on Route 23 in East Windham, at intersection with Cross Road. (18T 566761E 4684806N)

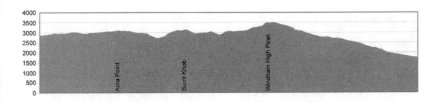

The Devil's Path from Blackhead Mountain

Camping

0.00 Batavia Kill Lean-to at 0.25 miles from the Long Path along the yellow-blazed Batavia Kill Trail.

7.45 Elm Ridge Lean-to.

Trail Description

0.00 From the intersection of the blue-blazed Escarpment Trail with the yellow-blazed Batavia Kill trail, the Long Path proceeds north along the Escarpment Trail, ascending an unnamed knob with a fine viewpoint over the Hudson Valley. Although the trail runs close to the edge of the Escarpment, there are

no other views on this section of the trail. The trail begins a gradual climb up to Acra Point.

1.80 Reach the open rock summit of Acra Point. The view here is somewhat obscured by low growth and is confined to the north. However, a short distance down the trail there is an open view to the west towards Big Hollow, with the Blackhead Range towering behind. As the trail begins to descend, a short side trail to the left leads to an open rock with another view toward Big Hollow and the Blackhead Range. There is also a view northwest along the ridge towards Burnt Knob and Windham High Peak. A little further down the trail there is a view to the north. The trail continues to descend to the col between Acra Point and Burnt Knob.

Windham High Peak from Burnt Knob

2.50 The trail reaches the col. Here, the red-blazed Black Dome Range Trail descends to the left to Big Hollow Road. Water is available from a stream 0.7 miles down this trail. The Long Path continues ahead to the west, beginning a steep climb up Burnt Knob.

2.80 At the top of the climb, the trail curves to the left and reaches the southern side of Burnt Knob, where a short yellow-blazed side trail to the left leads to a beautiful viewpoint over Big Hollow and the Blackhead Range.

3.45 After descending from Burnt Knob, the trail passes by a viewpoint to the north.

3.80 The trail reaches the summit of another unnamed knob, where a short side trail to the left leads to a viewpoint to the southwest over Big Hollow.

3.95 After descending from the knob, the trail begins its ascent of Windham High Peak.

4.35 The trail passes through an open area, with views of Windham High Peak directly ahead, and begins to ascend steadily.

5.05 The Trail reaches the summit of Windham High Peak. Just before the summit, there is a large rock outcropping to the right, with an open view to the north. Sometimes called the "Great Northern Viewpoint," this is the last spectacular view from the Escarpment Trail. To the north, the lesser peaks of Ginseng, Hayden, Pisgah and Huntersfield–followed by the Long Path to the north–are visible. In the far distance, the Helderbergs and the southern Adirondacks may be seen on a clear day. The Hudson River valley is visible to the northeast and, on a clear day, the City of Albany, the Taconics and the Green Mountains of Vermont may also be seen. The trail bears left and continues along the level summit, with a partial view over the Blackhead Range to the southeast, and another partial view northwest at the west end of the summit, then begins a steady descent.

6.75 The trail enters the first of two groves of Norway spruce trees planted by the Civilian Conservation Corps in the 1930's. The trail climbs over the tangled roots of these trees. Between the two groves, the trail passes through a small open area.

7.40 Shortly after passing a short yellow-blazed side trail to a rock ledge (the view from this point is obscured by overgrown vegetation), the trail passes the Elm Ridge Lean-to, to the left of the trail.

7.45 The Long Path turns right at a junction, continuing along the blue-blazed Escarpment Trail, as the yellow-blazed Elm Ridge Trail descends to the left for 0.85 miles to the parking area at the end of Peck Road. The Long Path now follows a wide snowmobile trail-the route of an old turnpike across the mountains.

7.60 Turn left, leaving the old road, and continue to descend on a narrower path.

7.70 Turn sharply to the right and descend steeply.

8.55 After passing a trail register, the trail crosses a bridge over a stream and reaches NY Route 23 near East Windham. To continue, go across Route 23 and follow Cross Road to the northwest.

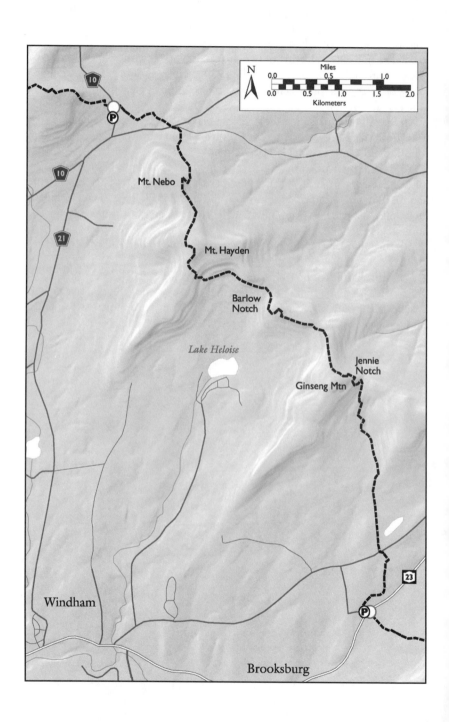

24. NY Route 23 to Greene County Route 10

Features: Ginseng Mountain, Mt. Hayden
Distance: 7.20 miles
USGS Map Quads: Hensonville
Trail Conference Maps: Map 41, Northeastern Catskill Trails

General Description

In this section, the Long Path leaves the Catskill Park after a journey of 94 miles and continues to the north. The terrain is similar to that found in Catskills, but on a smaller scale. The primary ridge followed by the trail in this section is a continuation of the Catskill Escarpment. For much of the distance along the ridge, the trail follows logging roads. The area is still alive with logging activity, but forest recovers quickly, as there has not been any clear cutting. There are no great open views, but there are many good views along the way when the leaves are down. The trail crosses two notches, Jenne and Barlow, which are bisected by the remnants of old mountain turnpikes that connected the mountains to the valley to the east. The first 0.75 miles of the section goes through state land and is marked with blue DEC trail markers, while the rest of the section is on private land and is marked with Aqua Long Path paint blazes. On these private lands, crossed with the permission of the owners, no camping and no fires of any kind are permitted. This section of the trail is closed during deer hunting season.

Access

Take the New York State Thruway to Exit 21 (Catskill). Continue on NY Route 23 west approximately 20 miles to East Windham. About 0.5 miles past the "Entering Catskill Park" sign, turn right at Cross Road. There is a DEC parking area just south of the intersection of Route 23 and Cross Road.

Parking

0.00 Parking area on NY Route 23 in East Windham, at intersection with Cross Road. (18T 566761E 4684806N)
6.55 Intersection of Sutton Road and Cunningham Road. (18T 563930E 4691498N)
7.20 Greene County Route 10 about 100 feet south of the trail intersection. (18T 563182E 4691621N)

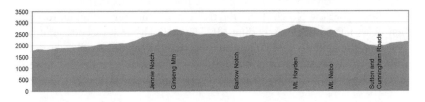

Trail Description

0.00 From the intersection of NY Route 23 and Cross Road proceed north on Cross Road for about 150 feet-just beyond the DEC parking area. The Long Path, blazed with blue DEC trail markers, then turns right, crosses a small field and enters the woods. The trail continues east, parallel to Route 23, crosses a stone wall, passes through a swampy area and then crosses another stone wall.

0.30 Here we leave the Catskill Park, which the Long Path has traversed for the last 94 miles. The trail turns left, away from Route 23, and ascends gradually to an old spruce and hemlock forest. From here, the trail descends gradually to the left.

0.75 Cross Old Road and continue north on paved Jenne Notch Road. The Long Path now leaves state land, and for the remainder of the section it is marked with Aqua paint blazes. Jenne Notch Road becomes a gravel road.

1.30 After passing several houses, Jenne Notch Road officially ends at an old red brick house. The trail passes through an iron gate and continues along a newly constructed gravel road uphill to Jenne Notch. This road follows the route of an old 19th century mountain turnpike.

2.10 Reach another iron gate. Not long afterwards, the trail turns left off of the logging road onto a faint woods road.

2.35 At the height of land, the trail turns sharply to the left and begins a steep climb up Ginseng Mountain on an old logging road. Many logging roads cross the ridge in the next 4 miles and the hiker may encounter active logging areas. At the top of the steep rise, the trail turns right, leaving the logging road. The trail goes to the east of and below the summit of Ginseng Mountain and emerges on an old logging road just north of the summit.

2.85 The trail turns onto a newer logging road and descends to the north off Ginseng Mountain. Along this section, there are good views ahead to Mt. Hayden on the ridge and to Mt. Pisgah and Huntersfield Mountain in the distance. Huntersfield Mountain is the highest mountain in the Catskills north of Route 23.

3.20 The logging road that has been followed by the trail turns left and descends steeply to Lake Heloise (where there is a private campground) as the Long Path continues ahead along the western edge of the ridge, skirting a recently logged area. There are views back towards Ginseng Mountain to the south, and west through the trees to Lake Heloise and Cave Mountain, home of the Windham Ski Resort. The trail turns back toward the center of the ridge. It then turns very sharply left and climbs an unnamed knob.

3.70 Reach the top of the knob, which is grassy and logged. The trail now descends, first to the west and then to the north, towards Barlow Notch.

4.00 Reach Barlow Notch. Here the trail crosses another mountain turnpike then bears left to begin ascending Mt. Hayden. The trail ascends gradually, levels out, then climbs gradually again following the top of a small escarpment.

4.60 The trail crosses a faint woods road that descends to the left towards Lake Heloise then climbs steeply through a rock ledge and crosses another

Frozen mud on the trail

wood road. After crossing the second wood road, the trail ascends very steeply through a series of switchbacks.

4.85 The grade moderates as the trail bears to the left. It reaches an eroded logging road, turns right and follows it through the woods as it ascends Mt. Hayden along the southwestern ridge.

5.10 The trail reaches a private property boundary just below the summit of Mt. Hayden and bears left and stays just west and below the summit. The trail begins to descend towards Mt. Nebo, again on the west side of the ridge.

5.50 The Long Path bears left on a faint road, descending gradually to the col between Mt. Hayden and Mt. Nebo.

5.80 Reach the summit of Mt. Nebo, which is really a shoulder of Mt. Hayden. Here the trail turns right and descends to the east, gradually at first and then steeply via a series of switchbacks, with views through the trees to the farms and fields of the Hudson Valley below. At the bottom of the steep section, the trail joins an old road that parallels the ridge and descends, passing the ruins of an abandoned house just before Sutton Road.

6.55 Turn left onto dirt Sutton Road close to its fork with Cunningham Road (no sign). Cross both roads and re-enter the woods. The trail continues westward, parallel to Cunningham Road, descending gradually.

7.20 After a brief climb, reach Greene County Route 10. The parking area is about 100 feet south on Route 10. To continue, cross Route 10 and proceed uphill on a quarry road.

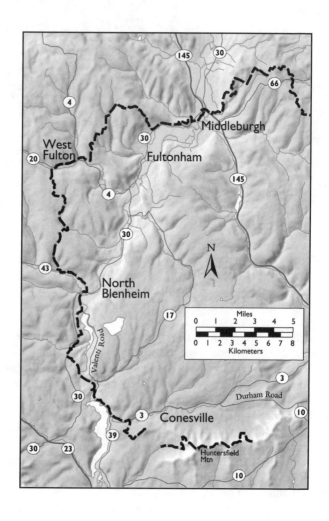

Northern Catskills

The tall mountains of the Catskills are left behind as the Long Path heads west and then northwards, becoming lower and lower until they are mere hills standing above the plain. Much of the route parallels the Schoharie Valley, an important route into the Catskills from points north. Early Dutch settlers made their homes here and there are many reminders of their past in the names of the places one passes. A major feature of the area is the reservoir complex maintained by the New York State Power Authority. In addition to hydroelectric power, the Schoharie Reservoir is a member of the great Catskill water reservoirs that supply far-away New York City with clean drinking water.

Wildflowers by the trailside

ED WALSH

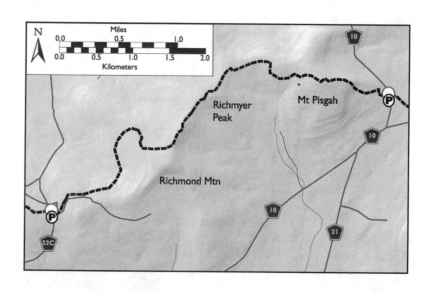

25. Greene County Route 10 to Greene County Route 32C

Features: Mt. Pisgah, Richtmyer Peak, Richmond Mountain
Distance: 4.50 miles
USGS Map Quads: Hensonville, Durham, Livingstonville, Ashland
Trail Conference Maps: none

General Description

After a short section on private land, this section of the Long Path enters the first of many state reforestation areas between the Catskills and the Mohawk River. The trail climbs steeply up Mt. Pisgah and follows the ridgetop for the rest of the way, passing through both mixed deciduous forests and plantations of red pine and Norway spruce. There are several good views, both north towards the southern Adirondacks, and south towards the Blackhead Range and the Devil's Path. The first 0.55 miles of the section goes through private land and is marked with Aqua Long Path paint blazes, while the rest of the section is on state land and is blazed with blue DEC trail markers.

Access

Take the New York State Thruway to Exit 21 (Catskill). Continue on NY Route 23 west approximately 20 miles to the Town of Windham. In Windham, turn right on Mitchell Hollow Road (Greene County Route 21) and go north about 5 miles to Greene County Route 10. Turn right on Route 10, which continues east for a very short distance and then curves left. Cunningham Road continues straight ahead here; stay on Route 10. About 0.6 miles past the curve, the Long Path begins where a woods road goes off to the left.

Parking

0.00 Greene County Route 10 about 100 feet south of the trailhead. (18T 563182E 4691621N18T 563182E 4691621N)
4.20 Intersection of CCC Road and woods road on left. (Unlocated)
4.50 Intersection of CCC Road and Greene County Route 32C. There is room to park several cars on the shoulder of CCC Road. In winter, Route 32C is plowed only up to 0.3 miles from the trailhead and no parking is allowed at the end of the road. It is a snowplow turnaround. (18T 558523E 4690176N)

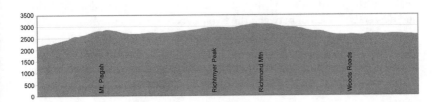

Trail Description

0.00 From Greene County Route 10, the Long Path proceeds uphill on a quarry road that is blocked by a metal chain to prevent vehicle access. The trail-marked with Aqua paint blazes–follows the quarry road for about 250 feet, turns left and passes through a red pine plantation, then turns right and skirts the south side of the quarry. The trail reaches an interesting rock wall, follows it to the right, then makes a sharp switchback to the left and passes through a cleft in the cliff. It continues gradually uphill through the woods.

0.25 The trail turns right onto an eroded woods road and continues uphill.

0.35 The Long Path turns right onto another woods road and then immediately turns left and begins climbing steeply. The trail crosses a rock wall and begins an extremely steep climb. Mt. Hayden can be seen from here when there are no leaves on the trees.

0.55 The trail crosses the state land boundary and enters the Mt. Pisgah Reforestation Area. The trail blazing now changes to blue DEC trail markers. The trail continues uphill, intersects a woods road and finally turns left for the final ascent to the summit of Mt. Pisgah.

0.85 Reach the summit of Mt. Pisgah. This was formerly the site of a summit observatory. Remnants of the well that supplied water to the site may still be seen. To the south is the old carriage road that provided access from the valley. The summit was once cleared of vegetation, but today it is covered with a mature Norway spruce and red pine grove. There is a view to the north of the Helderbergs and the Adirondacks in the distance. From the summit, the Long Path descends through the forest. It approaches the state land boundary, where it turns left and continues to descend on state land. There is an interesting contrast here between the deep greens of the spruce and pine grove and the lighter greens of the deciduous forest to the right. After a while, the trail leaves the evergreen grove and continues to descend.

1.25 Reach the col between Mt. Pisgah and Richtmyer Peak. The trail now begins a gradual ascent, skirting below private land to the north. It turns right, ascends to the top of the ridge and then turns left to follow the ridge. After a level stretch, the trail continues to ascend to Richtmyer Peak.

2.20 The Long Path reaches the flat summit of Richtmyer Peak. To the left, there is a seasonal view through the trees towards the Blackhead Range. The trail then turns right and makes a very short descent to the col between Richtmyer Peak and Richmond Mountain. The trail continues along the ridge and climbs to the east summit of Richmond Mountain.

2.60 Reach the east summit of Richmond Mountain. To the left, a short side trail leads to a view to the south, with the Blackhead Range, Kaaterskill High Peak and the Devil's Path visible. The Long Path continues along the ridge and descends to the col between the two peaks of Richmond Mountain. Here it levels off and follows the north shoulder of the main peak of Richmond Mountain, avoiding private land, then begins a steep descent.

3.35 Turn right, onto a woods road, and continue to descend. Another woods road joins from the right. The trail continues ahead to the left.

The Blackhead Range from Richmond Mountain

3.50 The trail levels off and turns left onto another woods road. This road was used by the state to log adjacent lands.

4.20 Turn right onto CCC Road, a dirt road marked as a state motor vehicle trail, and descend gradually.

4.50 Reach an intersection with Greene County Route 32C. To the left, Route 32C descends to Windham. To the right, CCC Road leads to Conesville in Schoharie County. To continue, cross Route 32C and continue along the ridge.

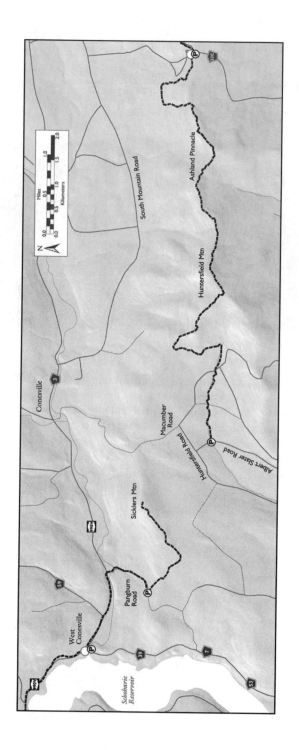

26. Greene County Route 32C to West Conesville

Feature: Huntersfield Ridge
Distance: 12.60 miles
USGS Map Quads: Ashland, Prattsville, Gilboa
Trail Conference Maps: none

General Description

This section of the Long Path is mostly pleasant ridge walking. While there are few good viewpoints, there are many views through the trees when the leaves are down. In this section, the trail traverses some of the highest peaks in the Catskills outside the "Blue Line," with Huntersfield Mountain being the highest point on the Long Path outside the Catskill Park. The trail passes through three State reforestation areas–Mt. Pisgah State Forest, Ashland State Forest and Huntersfield State Forest. As the state forests are not connected, the Long Path also crosses private land. Between Mt. Pisgah State Forest and Ashland State Forest, the trail must descend off the ridge to avoid private property. In this section, the trail traverses land that was recently acquired by the New York–New Jersey Trail Conference to allow access between the two reforestation areas. Beyond Huntersmark Macumber Road, the trail crosses state land then traverses Sickler Mountain before the section ends with 1.75 miles of road walk.

Access

Take the New York State Thruway to Exit 21 (Catskill). Continue west on NY Route 23 for about 20 miles to the Town of Windham. About 3 miles west of Windham, turn right onto North Settlement Road (Greene County Route 19). In another mile and a half, turn left onto Steinmetz Road. Follow Steinmetz Road to the stop sign at Greene County Route 10, and then continue ahead across Route 10. Steinmetz Road becomes Greene County Route 32C at this point. Continue on Route 32C to the top of the ridge. There is a parking area on the left side of the road at the top of the ridge.

Parking

0.00 Route 32C at top of ridge on west side. (18T 558523E 4690176N)
6.55 On Huntersmark Macumber Road. (Unlocated)
10.90 Pangman Road (limited). (18T 547972E 4690958N)
12.60 NY Route 990V and Prattsville Road. (18T 546855E 4692197N)

Camping

Camping is available to backpackers in the reforestation areas. You may camp anywhere in the reforestation areas, so long as you are 150 feet off the trail and away from water.

Trail Description

0.00 The Long Path crosses CCC Road and heads west along a woods road, which passes through a mature forest of Norway spruce.

0.15 Turn right, leaving the woods road, and begin to descend to avoid private property. At the higher elevations, the trail continues through the spruce plantation.

0.40 The trail nears the private property boundary and begins to descend more steeply through a hardwood forest.

0.80 After descending almost 500 feet, the trail turns left, levels off and leaves the reforestation area, entering land acquired by the New York-New Jersey Trail Conference to provide a protected corridor for the Long Path in this area.

1.00 The Long Path reaches the far end of the private property and turns left to steeply ascend the ridge, following a narrow strip of land between two private tracts.

1.15 Cross a boundary and enter Ashland State Forest. The trail begins to veer away from the private property as it heads uphill to the ridge, entering a reforestation area of spruce and pine. As the trail continues uphill, the grade moderates, but remains steep. There is ample evidence of logging here, with many old logging roads crisscrossing the area.

1.40 At the top of the ridge at the broad logging road, the trail turns left, follows the road downhill for a short distance, then turns sharp right to a short, steep climb to regain the ridgeline, then left. After a short distance in a spruce-pine forest, the trail enters a hardwood forest. When the leaves are down, there are views through the trees towards the Catskills to the south. After turning right on another old logging road, the trail stays on the north side of the ridge. If heading south, take care to follow the Long Path blazes straight ahead as the logging road descends off the ridge.

1.80 The trail descends gradually. The Long Path turns left and follows a woods road that stays on the north side of the ridge, ascending toward Ashland Pinnacle. There are views through the woods toward the valley of West Conesville and to the north toward Albany and Schoharie Counties.

2.20 Reach a height of land just below the flat, level summit of Ashland Pinnacle, and begin to descend along the woods road. When the leaves are down, there are views through the trees to the north, as well as west toward Huntersfield Mountain.

2.35 Reach a col at the base of the descent. At a Y-intersection, the Long Path turns right, and begins to ascend the first of two unnamed knobs. Cross the boundary of Ashland State Forest and enter private property. Camping, fires, etc., prohibited.

Upper Rapids of Manor Kill Falls

2.75 The trail reaches the top of the first knob and begins to descend. The trail follows the west side of the ridge, which is narrow at this point, with steep drop-offs on both sides. The trail descends below several rock ledges and continues west, just below the ridgetop.

3.05 Reach a col and begin to ascend the second knob.

3.25 The trail reaches the top of the second knob, and then begins a short descent, continuing to follow the ridge.

3.65 The Long Path levels off, with views south along the logging road toward the Catskills. The trail now begins to ascend Huntersfield Mountain, with the grade alternating between steep and moderate.

4.35 The trail leaves private property, crosses into Huntersfield State Forest and continues to climb.

4.40 About 100 yards before the summit of Huntersfield a yellow-blazed side trail leads left for 0.10 miles to the Huntersfield Lean-to. Just before the lean-to there is a view to the east along the ridge toward Mt. Pisgah. At the lean-to there is a view south of Hunter and Slide Mountains.

Continuing on the yellow trail for another 0.10 miles there is a view to the west and north of the Schoharie Valley and the reservoirs. The yellow trail continues for another 0.10 miles to rejoin the Long Path just west of Huntersfield's summit. Following the Long Path you reach the summit of Huntersfield Mountain and turn right. Although the summit is wooded, Huntersfield Mountain is the highest point on the Long Path outside the Catskill Park. It is the last of the high Catskill peaks; north of here, the Long Path does not reach any summits higher than 2,500 feet in elevation. The trail now begins to descend, sometimes steeply, along the west side of the ridge, with rock ledges and steep drop-offs to the west.

5.25 Reach a spectacular viewpoint from a rock ledge, about 75 feet to the left of the trail, toward the Schoharie Reservoir. The ridge that the Long Path will follow to the edge of the Schoharie Reservoir is visible in the foreground. West and north of the Schoharie Reservoir, you can see the mountains of Eminence State Forest that the Long Path follows through Schoharie County. Just past the viewpoint, the trail descends to a rock shelter on the left. There are a series of small caves in this area.

5.40 The trail crosses into private property as it continues to descend along the ridge.

5.50 Cross a stone wall and re-enter Huntersfield State Forest, passing through a mature pine forest.

5.60 The Long Path intersects an old logging road, turns left and follows the road through the pine plantation.

6.10 The Long Path continues along the gravel logging road.

6.25 The trail crosses a stream, then turns right, leaving the road, and follows the stream downhill.

6.55 Reach Huntersmark and Macumber Road. There is room to park several cars at this point. The Long Path crosses Huntersmark and Macumber Road and enters the woods by a "Huntersfield State Forest" sign. It descents to Huntersfield Creek and follows the bank of Huntersfield Creek through a reforestation area. The other side of the creek is private property and is a hardwood forest.

7.05 The trail crosses a wood road and reaches the western boundary of Huntersfield State Forest. The Long Path continues along Huntersfield Creek now in private property. The forest has changed to a hardwood forest. The trail follows an old wood road along the creek that emerges on to an open field.

7.55 The Long Path reaches paved Albert Slater Road, turns right and follows the road.

7.85 to 8.80 Trail closed.

8.80 The trail turns left and ascends Sickler Mountain. There are two short steep sections followed by more gradual climbs. At the end of the second steep section, the trail follows a wood road uphill.

9.25 Reach the level wooded summit of Sickler Mountain. When the leaves are down it is possible to see through the trees across the valley to the north. The Long Path turns left and begins to descend along the wood road, eventually crossing a barbed wire fence to continue on the road.

9.50 The trail turns right and follows another woods road, continuing to descend.

10.60 The trail makes a right jog, leaves the wood road to go through some dense brush before turning left onto another wood road. Shortly there is a view to the right to a farmhouse below as the trail crosses a power line. The trail continues downhill along the road through a hemlock forest.

10.90 The Long Path reaches gravel Pangman Road. Pangman Road, which is closed in the winter, is sometimes known locally as Dog Hill Road. The trail turns right and descends along Pangman Road.

11.50 Cross the Manor Kill.

11.60 Pangman Road ends. The trail turns left on NY Route 990V. The trail continues along 990V paralleling the Manor Kill. The trail passes through the hamlet of West Conesville.

12.60 The Long Path reaches the intersection of Schoharie County Route 39, Prattsville Road, and NY Route 990V. To the left several hundred feet is Manor Kill Falls. To continue, follow 990V north along the Schoharie Reservoir.

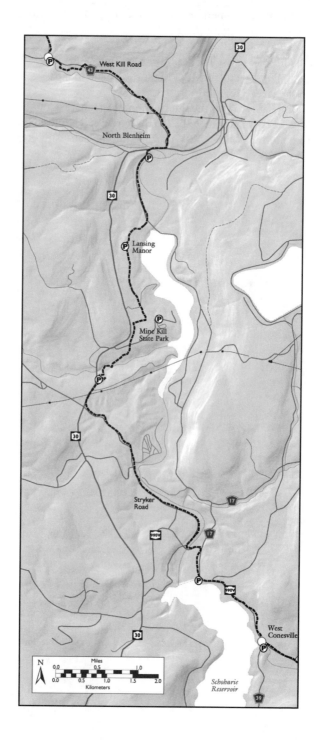

27. West Conesville to Doney Hollow

Features: Mine Kill State Park and Lansing Manor
Distance: 10.75 miles
USGS Map Quads: Gilboa
Trail Conference Maps: none

General Description

In this section, the Long Path leaves the rugged terrain of the Catskills and descends into the Schoharie Valley. After passing the Schoharie Reservoir, which is the northernmost outpost of the New York City water supply system, the Long Path begins a 30-mile journey along the Schoharie Valley and the hills surrounding Schoharie Creek. The trail passes through Mine Kill State Park, whose primary attraction is Mine Kill Falls. The Long Path passes both the top and the bottom of the falls, which plummet out of a spectacular gorge. Between the falls and the main part of the park, the trail follows a beautiful pine and hemlock forest. In the north end of the park are spectacular open views of the Schoharie Valley. Beyond Mine Kill State Park, the trail passes through the Lansing Manor Visitors Center of the Power Authority's Blenheim–Gilboa pumped storage complex. There are expansive views up the Schoharie Valley from both Mine Kill State Park and Lansing Manor. From Lansing Manor, the Long Path follows roads most of the way to Doney Hollow.

Access

Take the New York State Thruway to Exit 21 (Catskill). Continue west on NY Route 23 for about 30 miles to the Village of Prattsville. At the end of Prattsville, NY Route 23 crosses a steel bridge that goes over Schoharie Creek. Just before the bridge, turn right on Prattsville Road, and follow it for about 5 miles to the intersection of Prattsville Road and Route 990V.

Parking

0.00 Intersection of NY Route 990V and Prattsville Road. (18T 546855E 4692197N)
1.20 Gilboa Dam overlook. (Unlocated)
4.50 Mine Kill Falls overlook. (18T 543431E 4697369N)
5.90 At north end of swimming pool, when park is open. (18T 544745E 4698543N)
6.65 Lansing Manor Visitors Center. (18T 544034E 4699753N)

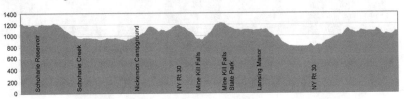

7.50 On North Access Road near turnoff for fishing access to Schoharie Creek. (Unlocated)

10.75 West Kill Road at Doney Hollow. (18T 542369E 4703777N)

Camping

3.30 Campsites available at Nickerson Park Campground (fee charged).

Trail Description

0.00 At the intersection of Prattsville Road and NY Route 990V, the Long Path turns left and follows NY Route 990V downhill toward Gilboa. On the left side of the trail is the Schoharie Reservoir, part of the New York City water supply system.

0.90 On the left is the former site of the Gilboa Settlement. From 1840 to 1869, a cotton mill, tannery, church and cemetery stood on the ground that is now covered by the Schoharie Reservoir. On the right is the Gilboa–Conesville Central School.

1.05 Pass Wyckoff Road on the right. The trail continues on NY Route 990V.

1.20 The Gilboa Dam of the Schoharie Reservoir is to the left. There is an overlook here, with views west over the reservoir. The trail continues to descend.

1.50 Flat Creek Road goes off to the right, near the Gilboa Town Hall and Post Office. On the right a few yards past the town hall is an exhibit of fossilized trees. They were discovered while constructing the Schoharie Reservoir. The Long Path continues ahead along NY Route 990V, which curves left and goes downhill.

1.75 The Long Path crosses Schoharie Creek on a bridge. The trail turns right

Lansing Manor Visitor Center

MICHAEL WARREN

Lansing Manor

on an abandoned road north along the creek.

2.50 The Long Path intersects paved Stryker Road (Schoharie County Route 13) and turns right. Pass a large farm on the left with views of Schoharie Creek to the right.

3.00 Here, there is a large overhanging rock that extends over Schoharie Creek.

3.30 To the right, the trail passes Nickerson Park Campground, a privately operated campground. The Long Path continues along Stryker Road, which turns left, leaves Schoharie Creek and begins climbing up a hill. As the trail crests the hill, there is an expansive view up the Schoharie Valley across an open field.

4.20 The Long Path intersects NY Route 30 and turns right (north) to follow Route 30.

4.50 The trail turns right at the entrance to the Mine Kill Falls overlook and continues to the overlook parking area. Past the overlook parking area, the trail descends to the top of the falls. There are park benches along the trail and picnic tables with charcoal pits to the side of the trail. The trail is in an open field here.

4.65 Ahead is a path that leads 100 feet to the Mine Kill Falls overlook. The path is protected with a fence, as there is a sharp drop-off here. It is worth the detour to the overlook. The Long Path turns right on a trail marked as a hiking trail and descends through a series of switchbacks to the bottom of the falls through a forest of pine and then hemlock.

4.90 Mine Kill Falls is to the left. The falls come out of a deep gorge and plummet into a pool where swimming is restricted. The trail turns right and follows the Mine Kill downstream. Across the Mine Kill are steep cliffs that were cut by water.

Mine Kill Falls

5.05 The trail turns left and crosses the Mine Kill, then begins ascending north away from the Mine Kill. In times of high water it is necessary to follow NY Route 30 at mile 4.50 to the main park entrance, then follow the entrance road to where the trail crosses (mile 5.50), then turn left.

5.20 The trail crosses another stream. To the left is a beautiful cascading waterfall. The trail climbs continuously from here to the park entrance road. Part way up, the trail passes several rock piles on the right. Near the top, two trails lead right; the Long Path continues straight ahead.

5.50 The trail emerges on an open field and crosses the main park entrance road. It continues on the western edge of an open field to reach the park administration building.

5.60 To the right is the park administration building, where there are restroom facilities. The trail bears left and follows a grassy road at the western end of an open field. From this path, there is a spectacular view up and down the Schoharie Valley.

5.80 The trail turns right and descends along the northern boundary of the soccer field, then passes a small playground that is just north of the swimming pool.

5.95 Turn left and follow a cross-country ski and snowmobile trail that leads from Mine Kill State Park to Lansing Manor. Here, there is a spectacular view north along the Schoharie Valley and across the Blenheim–Gilboa Reservoir. Soon, a blue-blazed cross-country ski trail leaves to the right. The Long Path continues ahead on a red-blazed cross-country ski trail that is also marked with Long Path Aqua blazes.

6.30 The trail crosses an open field, leaving Mine Kill State Park and entering the New York State Power Authority Lansing Manor Blenheim–Gilboa complex. The boundary is not marked. Note the small cedar trees with fences around them. These trees are pruned so as to provide the deer with a source of browse. The fences prevent the deer from killing the trees. There are also a number of bluebird feeders. Be sure to watch for the Long Path blazes on top of the fence posts by the cedar trees.

6.65 The Long Path enters a picnic area and then crosses the parking lot of the Lansing Manor Visitors Center. At the far end of the parking lot, the trail follows a walkway through the Visitors Center, where brochures on the historic Lansing Manor and the Blenheim–Gilboa pumped storage power plant are available. Brochures are also available at the nearby museum. There are picnic tables at the Visitor Center, making this an ideal lunch stop in the warm months.

6.80 Take the left fork in the walkway and pass the entrance to the museum. The Long Path now heads diagonally across a field, and then turns right and skirts the edge of a ravine. There is another deer feeding area here. At the end of the ravine, the trail continues straight ahead across the field to enter the woods.

7.05 After a rather steep descent, reach the bottom of a ravine. The trail now ascends gradually to reach a power-line right-of-way. At the power line, the trail turns right and follows the right-of-way for a short distance to a microwave tower, where it turns left and ascends.

7.35 Reach the top of a hill, with a view down to the dam of the Blenheim–Gilboa Reservoir. During periods of low electrical demand, water is pumped up the hill to the reservoir. During periods of high demand, the water is released, thus generating electricity. The Long Path turns left and descends, passing between two rows of white pines.

7.50 Turn left onto Baldwin Road, also known as North Access Road. In a few hundred feet, a road to the right leads to a parking area, used by fishermen for access to Schoharie Creek below the dam.

8.35 Reach NY Route 30. The Long Path turns right and follows Route 30 through the Village of North Blenheim. Originally named Patchin Hollow for Freeman Patchin, who was a fifer for the Albany Militia in the Revolutionary War, North Blenheim was the site of a gristmill at the confluence of the West Kill and Schoharie Creek.

8.65 The Long Path turns left onto West Kill Road, which was a main Iroquois route from the Susquehanna River to the Delaware River via the Schoharie Valley.

9.05 Burnt Hill Road leaves to the right. The Long Path bears left and continues along West Kill Road.

9.95 Pass a small pond on the right.

10.20 The trail turns left and descends to West Kill Creek. The trail continues west along West Kill Creek. After about a half a mile, the trail climbs back up to West Kill Road at a parking lot for Doney Hollow.

10.75 The trail emerges at a parking lot where there is room to park several cars. This section ends just across Doney Hollow where the trail turns right to follow Doney Hollow.

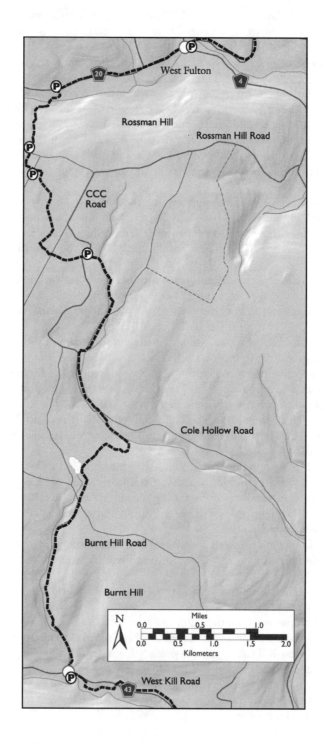

West Fulton

Rossman Hill

Rossman Hill Road

CCC
Road

Cole Hollow Road

Burnt Hill Road

Burnt Hill

West Kill Road

N

Miles
0.0   0.5   1.0

0.0   0.5   1.0   1.5   2.0
Kilometers

28. Doney Hollow to West Fulton

Feature: Eminence State Forest
Distance: 8.40 miles
USGS Map Quads: Gilboa, Breakabeen
Trail Conference Maps: none

General Description

In this section, the Long Path passes from Doney Hollow to the highlands of Eminance State Forest. While there are no great views in this section, the trail is full of glimpses of the area's historic past. Along the way, the trail passes through sites of abandoned sawmills, gristmills and cemeteries–evidence that this area was once settled. In the early to mid-1800s, this area was home to some of the earliest settlements in the Schoharie region. During the depression in the 1930s, the State purchased many of the marginal farms in this area and established state reforestation areas, and the CCC built some primitive roads on this newly acquired state land.

This section of the Long Path gradually ascends from Doney Hollow to the highlands of the Burnt Hill Reforestation Area. It then descends to Cole Hollow before again climbing to the level highlands of Rossman Hill. From there, the trail descends steeply to Sawyer Hollow and the Village of West Fulton. For part of the way, the Long Path follows the Schoharie Trail, which was constructed in the early 1980s by the SUNY Cobleskill Outing Club. In areas where the Schoharie Trail follows drivable roads, the Long Path follows newly constructed trail.

Access

Take the New York State Thruway to Exit 21 (Catskill). Continue on NY Route 23 west for 35 miles to Grand Gorge. In Grand Gorge, turn right, and follow NY Route 30 north for about 8 miles to North Blenheim. Turn left on West Kill Road, which is the second left after Route 30 crosses the West Kill, and follow Westkill Road for 2 miles to Doney Hollow.

Parking

0.00 At West Kill Road in Doney Hollow. 18T 542369E 4703777N)
4.85 On Duck Pond Road by the brook. (18T 542525E 4709628N)
6.30 Along Morey Road. (18T 541816E 4710817N)
6.50 Near Looking Glass Pond. (18T 541761E 4711109N)

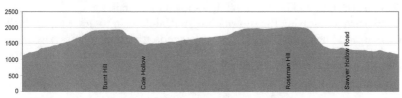

8.10 Sawyer Hollow Road where Long Path enters the road. (18T 542160E 4711979N)

8.70 Village of West Fulton picnic area. (18T 544086E 4712582N)

Camping

Camping is allowed in the state reforestation areas 150 feet away from the trail and water.

5.80 Rossman Hill Lean-to.

Trail Description

0.00 The Long Path turns right off West Kill Road and follows an old road up Doney Hollow. This section of the Long Path follows the Schoharie Trail, which was constructed in the early 1980s by the Cobleskill Outing Club (COC), and its beginning is designated by an COC trail marker. The trail, which is marked with Long Path Aqua blazes as well as occasional blue DEC trail markers, heads uphill on the left side of the stream.

0.40 The trail crosses Doney Hollow on a bridge and continues uphill on the right side of the stream.

0.90 Cross a state forest boundary and enter the Burnt Hill Reforestation Area of Eminence State Forest. Burnt Hill got its name from the many wildfires that spread through this area in the early 1900s, improving the huckleberry crop. One part of the area was known as Huckleberry Kingdom. Today, the area has become a mature forest, and the state periodically harvests the timber here. Just past the boundary, the trail passes through a small open field.

1.05 To the left is a large man-made structure, constructed of local rock. This is the site of one of the two water-powered sawmills that operated along Doney Hollow in the mid 1800s. The rock structure was part of an impoundment of the stream.

1.30 An old road comes in from the left across Doney Hollow. The Long Path continues straight ahead on this woods road. The trail passes through a stand of red pines and begins to level off.

1.70 The old woods road ends at the gravel Burnt Hill Road. The Long Path crosses Burnt Hill Road and continues north through the woods.

2.00 An opening to the left leads to a large unnamed pond off Burnt Hill Road. Camping is allowed in the state reforestation areas 150 feet away from the trail or water. The trail continues ahead through the woods to the right of the pond.

2.25 The trail reaches the crest of Burnt Hill, turns left, and begins a steep descent to Cole Hollow.

2.35 Turn right and begin to follow a snowmobile trail.

2.45 Turn left, leaving the snowmobile trail, and begin to descend, gradually at first and then very steeply. As it descends, the trail follows a series of switchbacks, eventually descending west on an old woods road to the bottom of Cole Hollow.

3.00 Turn right and cross Cole Hollow Brook on a bridge, skirting private property. After crossing the brook, the trail turns left, passes an illegal campsite, and then continues along a dirt road.

3.15 Turn left on gravel Cole Hollow Road, cross a bridge over the brook, and continue uphill on the road.

3.70 Just after crossing into the Town of Fulton, Cole Hollow Road turns left. The Long Path turns right and follows gravel Huckleberry Kingdom Road.

4.05 On the right is the site of the childhood home of Henry Conklin. Author of *Through Poverty's Vale*, he wrote of the difficulty of eking out a living in these hills in the 1840s. This book, an interesting early history of the Schoharie Valley, is available at the Old Stone Fort in Schoharie. The trail goes back into state land, and crosses a small stream. Just after the stream crossing, the trail leaves the road, turns left, and follows the stream uphill, crossing a number of stone walls.

4.25 Turn left on an old logging road that parallels the stream and continue uphill.

4.55 The trail leaves the logging road to skirt private property, crosses the stream on a bridge, and continues uphill, following the left bank of the stream.

4.70 Cross a tributary stream on a bridge and turn left, following the tributary uphill. Near the top of the hill, the trail turns right and leaves the stream. Here, to the left, there is a series of cascading waterfalls along the stream.

4.85 The Long Path turns left onto the first of a series of CCC-constructed roads. Just before Duck Pond Road crosses the stream, there is a small parking area. At a concrete abutment along the stream, the trail turns right, makes a short, steep climb to pass a small old cemetery, and then descends to the left to cross the stream. After the stream crossing, the trail switchbacks to the left and then turns back to the right, following the stream. It leaves the stream and continues uphill.

5.20 Turn right and continue between two stone walls.

5.30 Cross a Burnt Hill Road and continue west through the woods. There is room to park several cars here.

5.45 The trail swings to the right, makes a short gradual decent, crosses a stream, and enters a flat area of Rossman Hill.

5.80 The Long Path passes the Rossman Hill Lean-to. Water is available from a well located 100 yards in front of the lean-to. It may be dry in summer.

5.85 Pass through some hemlocks and enter a pine forest. The trail continues in a generally northwesterly direction.

6.30 Reach Morey Road. Here, the trail bears left and crosses the road. One hundred feet to the right is the historic Rossman Hill Cemetery. Its large size is a good indication of how many people lived in these hills prior to reforestation. Past the cemetery on the right was the site of the Rossman Hill Methodist Church, which was abandoned in the 1930s. There is no evidence of the church today.

6.50 The trail continues west for a short distance then turns right at the edge of Looking Glass Pond. The West Fulton Rod and Gun Club constructed this 20-acre pond. The trail intersects a yellow-blazed mountain bike trail that circles the pond. At the dam the Long Path turns right and follows the pond's outlet stream downhill.

6.55 Cross Rossman Hill Road and continue to follow the stream downhill, passing a series of cascades. At the bottom of the cascades there is an old stone foundation, which was once the site of a gristmill. Please help protect what is remaining. The stonework is very fragile.

7.00 The trail follows the stream steeply down to Sawyer Hollow passing several waterfalls along the way. Near the bottom of the hillside the trail crosses a stream on a wooden bridge, then heads east to a new bridge over Panther Creek. This 40' long bridge is over a structure called a "pool digger" which helps put oxygen in the water and provides a pool for trout to survive dry spells. There are several of these up and down the creek. Men of the Civilian Conservation Corps built them back in the 1940's. During the 60's the Camp Summit inmates rehabbed them and last year the West Fulton Rod and Gun Club did further repairs.

7.10 From the bridge, turn left and follow along the creek bed downstream to an old logging road that crosses an open field up to Sawyer Hollow Road. If traveling from the opposite direction, this point is just uphill from a DEC fisherman's parking sign.

7.20 Turn right onto paved Sawyer Hollow Road and follow it into West Fulton. This road closely follows the route of an old Native American trail that was used during the Revolution by the British in October 1780. On the left the hiker passes the Peter Smith Church. Peter Smith, the founder of West Fulton, built it in 1831. At one time it was featured in Ripley's "Believe It or Not," as the steeple and bell were located on the hill behind the church. Since then, the church was turned around and the steeple and bell were put in place. It is currently a private residence.

8.40 Reach the Village of West Fulton at an intersection with West Fulton Road. To the right on West Fulton Road and across the stream there is a picnic area on the left side of the road, with room to park several cars. To continue, proceed straight ahead on Patria Road.

29. West Fulton to Middleburgh

Features: Patria State Forest and Vroman's Nose
Distance: 12.00 miles
USGS Map Quads: Breakabeen, Middleburgh
Trail Conference Maps: none

General Description

Leaving West Fulton, the Long Path regains the highlands west of Schoharie Creek. The trail continues through pleasant reforestation areas and passes through stands of mature pine and spruce, with occasional evidence of the early settlement in this area. After descending steeply to cross Pleasant Valley, the Long Path climbs over the top of a hill, and then descends to Hardscrabble Road near NY Route 30, with dramatic views of the Schoharie Valley. The Long Path follows NY Route 30 north through Vroomansland, the flat floodplain of Schoharie Creek. The trail ascends Vroman's Nose on the steep red trail. A sentinel over the Schoharie Valley, Vroman's Nose is one of the most spectacular natural features in New York. The Long Path descends off Vroman's Nose to the north on the blue trail, crosses Vroomansland, and follows the edge of Schoharie Creek to the Village of Middleburgh.

Access

Take the New York State Thruway to Exit 21 in Catskill. Continue on NY Route 23 west about 8 miles to NY Route 145, then go west on Route 145 west about 30 miles to the Village of Middleburgh. In Middleburgh, take NY Route 30 south about 8 miles to West Fulton Road (Schoharie County Route 4), then turn right on West Fulton Road and follow it for 3 miles to West Fulton.

Parking

0.00 West Fulton town Picnic Area (18T 544079E 4712555N).
1.95 On Patria Road (18T 545025E 4712835N).
2.95 On Mallon Road (18T 546041E 4714883N).
10.40 Church Street and the blue trailhead on Vroman's Nose (18T 553295E 47158631N)
12.00 In the Village of Middleburgh along NY Route 145 (18T 554551E 4716419N).

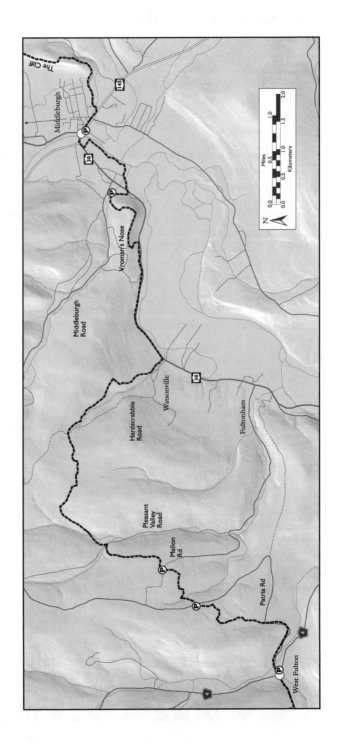

Camping

1.10 Camping is allowed in the state reforestation areas 150 feet away from the trail and water.

9.45 Near the summit of Vroman's Nose to the left of the trail

Trail Description

0.00 The Long Path leaves West Fulton on Patria Road, which it follows through a residential area, and heads uphill.

0.90 Patria Road makes a sharp right turn. Here, the Long Path turns left, leaving Patria Road, and heads into a small field. Look carefully for the blazes, as there are some missing. The trail follows a hedgerow on the right side of the field, then turns right, passes through the hedgerow, crosses a stream and emerges on a larger field. The trail begins ascending as it crosses the field to the left, passing the tallest tree in the field.

1.05 The trail reaches the top of the field, crosses into state land, and continues uphill through the forest.

1.20 Turn right on an old woods road for 150 feet, then turn left, leaving the woods road. The trail continues uphill, with a break in the slope to the left.

1.65 The trail levels off, turns right, and crosses the ridge. After the ridge, turn left and descend on an old woods road toward Patria Road.

1.95 Cross Patria Road and descend through the woods to a stream. The trail

Vroman's Nose

HERB CHONG

View from Vroman's Nose

turns left and heads uphill along the stream in a deep hemlock forest.

2.35 Turn right, cross the stream, and continue through a plantation of spruce and pine. After a short level stretch, the trail turns left and climbs steeply up the ridge. When the grade levels off, the trail turns right and crosses the ridge, following the edge of the reforestation area. At the east end of the ridge, the trail turns left and follows the east side of the ridge.

2.85 On the right is an open area, with a view across Mallon Road.

2.95 Cross Mallon Road and re-enter the reforestation area. The trail follows a woods road, crosses under a power line, and then turns right, leaving the road. The trail turns left and begins a gradual descent toward Pleasant Valley.

3.35 Cross a seasonal stream and parallel a rock wall, an old property boundary, skirting private land.

3.80 The trail switchbacks to the right as it continues downhill on a moderate grade.

3.95 Turn left and descend very steeply on a series of switchbacks to Pleasant Valley Road. A snowmobile trail comes in from the right.

4.10 Turn left on Pleasant Valley Road and follow it past private property. After crossing Pleasant Valley Stream on a bridge, the trail turns right on an old woods road and follows the state land boundary, ascending along a tributary stream.

4.35 Cross the stream on a bridge and ascend moderately, leaving the stream, and continue to follow the woods road through a pleasant hemlock forest.

5.15 The Long Path turn right to follow another woods road. As the trail reaches the crest of the hill, a woods road comes in from the right. The Long Path continues ahead, over the crest of the hill, to reach a logging road, then turns left to follow the logging road through a flat area.

5.55 Turn right, leaving the logging road and snowmobile trail, and begin to descend through the woods, paralleling a rock wall. There is a small parking area here.

5.95 Turn right and follow the abandoned Hardscrabble Road, continuing to descend. On the left is a reliable spring. In a few hundred feet, another abandoned road, now a snowmobile trail, comes in from the left near the site of an abandoned farm. The Long Path continues downhill along Hardscrabble Road.

6.00 The Long Path turns left off abandoned Hardscrabble Road and rejoins the snowmobile trail as it heads downhill.

6.05 The trail crosses a stream and continues to follow the snowmobile trail downhill along a rock wall. As the trail leaves State land, the snowmobile markers change from the round DEC discs to orange diamond-shaped markers.

6.65 Cross under a power line, then turn left uphill away from the stream onto a logging road.

6.85 The trail leaves the logging road on the right and turns downhill.

7.45 At the edge of an open field the Long Path turns left to briefly leave the snowmobile trail to cross a barbed wire fence on a wooden stile. The trail continues across the field with views of the Schoharie Valley.

7.60 Turn right to cross another fence on a stile to Hardscrabble Road. Across the road is a large gray barn. Turn left on the road.

7.65 Reach NY Route 30 near highway marker 30/9502/1179. Turn left on Route 30 and follow it north.

9.15 Just before a NY Route 30 sign on the right near highway marker 30/9502/1195 on the left, the Long Path turns left and follows a red-blazed trail up Vroman's Nose on a very steep grade. As there is loose dirt and scree here, it is suggested that you have very sturdy boots and carry a walking stick or ski pole for balance.

9.35 The trail reaches the top of the extreme grade, having gained 400 vertical feet in the last 0.2 miles. At this point the trail turns right and continues to climb the ridge at a more moderate grade. As the trail begins to level off, views of the Schoharie Valley open up through the trees.

9.45 The red trail ends at an intersection with the green trail. The Long Path turns right and follows the green trail up to the summit of Vroman's Nose. There is a view to the right, across the Schoharie Valley to the Catskills. To the left of the view is a campsite.

9.60 The trail reaches the summit of Vroman's Nose, with a spectacular view across the Schoharie Valley and Vroomansland south to the Catskills. This is a wonderful place to rest and take in the sun or to have lunch. Locals have been taking the hike up here for over a hundred years, as is evidenced by the initials in the rock. The mountain is owned by the Vroman's Nose Preservation Corp., which has preserved it as forever wild. Although the route followed by the Long Path up the mountain is quite steep, the summit can also be reached by an easy 600-foot climb from the maintained parking lot at the base of the green trail on West Middleburgh Road. A very informative book on the history of Vroman's Nose and its environs, written by Dr. Vincent Schaefer, the founder of the Long Path, is available at the Old Stone Fort in Schoharie. The Long Path continues along the green trail, following the cliffs, with spectacular views along the edge of the escarpment.

9.80 Reach an overhanging promontory, with views both up and down the Schoharie Valley. You can see north to the Village of Middleburgh and the cliffs of Middleburgh, where the Long Path continues north and east toward Albany County. Here the green trail ends and the Long Path continues on the blue trail that descends, sometimes steeply, through the woods.

10.10 The yellow trail, which leads to a parking area on Mill Valley Road, begins to the left. The Long Path turns right and continues to follow the blue trail downhill on an old road.

10.40 The blue trail ends at Church Street, just past a church and a house. The Long Path turns right on Church Street and follows it to Route 30.

10.60 Turn left on NY Route 30 and then immediately right onto Old Route 30 Number 3.

10.85 West Middleburgh Road, also known as Old Route 30 Number 3, ends at Line Creek. Cross a new snowmobile bridge to the other side of the stream. Then turn right and follow the hedgerow at the edge of a field to Schoharie Creek.

10.95 Turn left and follow the hedgerow along Schoharie Creek. As you walk north along the hedgerow, there are occasional views along the creek. There are also views west across the fields to the ridges west and south and to Vroman's Nose.

11.50 Reach the Middleburgh Rotary Pavilion and picnic area along Schoharie Creek. There is a large parking area here. The Long Path continues along the hedgerow until it reaches the NY Route 30 Bridge.

11.65 Turn right and cross Schoharie Creek on the NY Route 30 bridge.

11.75 Reach the intersection of NY Routes 145 and 30 in the Village of Middleburgh. To continue on the Long Path, follow Route 145 east.

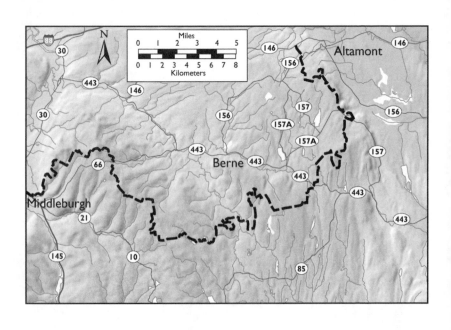

Capital District

These northernmost sections of the Long Path slope down from the edge of the Catskills into the edges of the Mohawk River Valley. The hills of the western sections give way to gentle rises and falls shaped by glaciers and water punctuated by sharp cliffs of escarpments formed by tilted rock layers. Most of the lands have been settled for a long time and have remained productive farm or forest. Much of the trail passes through nature that has been coerced by civilization to behave in certain ways, whether by being farmed for generations, or used as a managed forest for the supply of lumber.

Field near East Berne

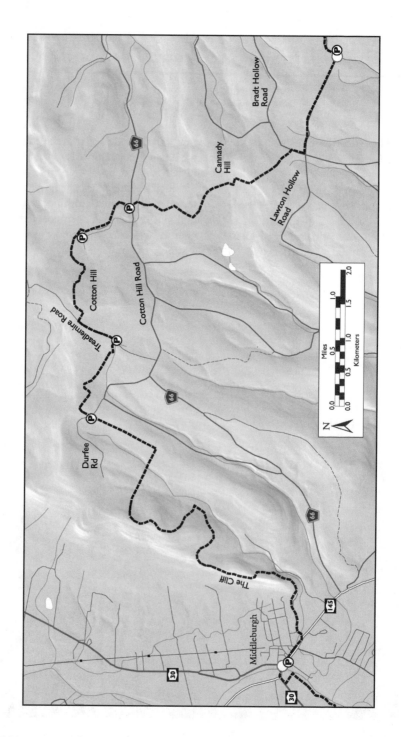

30. Middleburgh to Albany County Line

Features: The Cliffs of Middleburgh, Cotton Hill, Canady Hill
Distance: 12.10 miles
USGS Map Quads: Middleburgh, Schoharie, Renssellaerville
Trail Conference Maps: none

General Description

After leaving Middleburgh, the Long Path ascends the cliffs. The trail route meanders from the eastern slopes, looking down into "The Gorge," to the western slopes, which follow the edge of the cliffs. When along the cliffside, there are spectacular views across and down the Schoharie Valley. Caution is required at all viewpoints, as they drop right off. Beyond the cliffs, the trail crosses the head of "The Gorge," then traverses three sections of Cotton Hill State Forest. The hike through Cotton Hill is a pleasant variety of trail and old woods roads. The forest varies from hemlock to red and white pine. As you enter each section of the forest, a climb to a high point is required. The Cotton Hill sections revolve around the northeast corner of Schoharie County. The section ends spectacularly, as after the trail crosses Canady Hill; there are great open views to the Catskills and Partridge Run and Cole Hill in Albany County. The last mile of this section to the Albany county line is on Lawton Hollow Road. The eastern and western ends of this section follow private property, while the middle 5 miles are on state land.

Access

Take the New York State Thruway to Exit 21 (Catskill). Take NY Route 23 west about 8 miles to NY Route 145. Take NY Route 145 west about 30 miles to the Village of Middleburgh. The trail section begins at the intersection of NY Route 145 and NY Route 30 in the Village of Middleburgh.

Parking

0.00 Village of Middleburgh. (18T 554551E 4716419N)
5.10 Durfee Road. (18T 558339E 4719698N)
6.55 Treadlemire Road. (18T 559554E 4719264N)
7.80 At the end of the access road north of Cotton Hill Road. (Unlocated)
8.45 Cotton Hill Road. (18T 561596E 4719032N)
11.90 On Lawton Hollow Road at the Albany county line. (18T 564048E 4715801N)

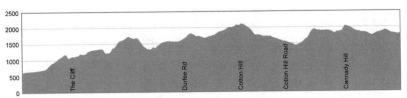

Camping

6.95 Cotton Hill Lean-to.
Camping is allowed in the Cotton Hill State Forest 150 feet away from the trail and water.

Trail Description

0.00 The trail turns east on NY Route 145 through the village of Middleburgh.
0.35 The trail follows Straub Lane past the Cliffside Senior Apartments to a hedgerow. Follow a hedgerow to the base of the cliffs.
0.75 The trail turns right to follow the base of the cliffs for 200 feet and then turns left to follow a steep and rocky trail up the cliffs.
1.10 A logging road leads right to the bottom of "The Gorge." Just past the logging road there is a view right across "The Gorge" to Cotton Hill State Forest. As the trail continues to climb it intersects several logging roads. The Long Path follows the leftmost road as it ascends.
1.40 A fork to the left leads to southern cliffs. After 200 feet the Long Path intersects the main north-south trail along the cliff edge and turns right. If you are making a short loop from Middleburgh, turn left and follow the cliff trail down into Middleburgh. Be careful on this trail, as it is steep and rocky. If you are continuing on the Long Path northern extension, it is worth a detour left several hundred feet to a spectacular view across the Schoharie Valley to Vroman's Nose. To continue north on the Long Path here, turn right and follow the cliffs. Please be careful here as the cliff trail, to the left, is also blazed in Long Path Aqua.
1.65 Reach a spectacular view across the Schoharie Valley. There is a view south across the Village of Middleburgh to Vroman's Nose and Vroomansland. Looking west across lands of the Middleburgh Rod and Gun Club are the hills that lead to Cobleskill. As the trail continues along the cliffs there are occasional views across the valley. The forest is red and white pine.
2.05 The trail intersects a series of logging roads and turns right to cross the ridge to the east, passing through a recently logged area. As the trail swings to "The Gorge" side of the ridge it intersects several logging roads. The Long Path stays to the right above "The Gorge."
2.35 A logging road leads right to the bottom of "The Gorge." Just beyond, a faint old road leads left back to the cliff. The Long Path continues straight ahead.
2.45 The Long Path turns right, leaving the logging road to descend steeply toward "The Gorge."
2.60 The trail turns left and ascends steeply back to the ridge.
2.75 Rejoin the logging road and turn right as it continues uphill.
3.00 Pass a logging road that leads left. Fifty feet past the logging road the Long Path turns left and ascends back to the cliffs, passing through a recently logged area.
3.15 The trail turns right on a woods road paralleling the cliff. Shortly, the trail crosses another logging road and ascends to a 1,700-foot hill that is the

ED WALSH

Cotton Hill lean-to

highest on the cliffs. As it descends from the high point, the trail crosses two logging roads; the first heads right, the second left.

3.70 The trail turns right, leaves the woods road, and descends to the head of "The Gorge." At this point the trail climbs less steeply then makes a right jog on an old woods road and continues to descend, joining a stream in a hemlock forest.

4.05 The trail crosses three streams at the head of "The Gorge." Between the streams, there are views north through an open field. On the right past the second stream is a dense Norway spruce forest.

4.30 Cross the third stream and ascend to Cotton Hill State Forest.

4.50 The trail crosses the boundary into Cotton Hill and turns left to follow a narrow strip of state land along the ridge.

4.70 Cross power lines with a view left toward the cliffs. The trail continues north through hemlocks.

5.30 The trail crosses Durfee Road. There are parking areas both to the left and right. The trail continues uphill through red and white pine.

5.40 The trail reaches the top of the hill and bears right, intersecting a woods road, and descends.

5.60 The trail turns left on another woods road. To the right is an old well that was once used by firefighters in the 1930s to fill their "Indian Fire pumps" that they carried on their backs.

5.70 The trail turns right and descends to another woods road, following an old stone wall.

5.90 The trail turns left on another woods road and gradually ascends to the state forest boundary.

6.00 The trail turns right, leaves the woods road and descends to a gorge. At the gorge the trail turns left and follows the gorge through hemlocks to Treadlemire Road.

6.35 The trail turns left and follows Treadlemire Road uphill, passing some houses. There are views to the Catskills back along the road.

6.75 A small parking area is here. The trail turns right and re-enters Cotton Hill State Forest. Shortly the trail turns left and passes underneath a small rock ledge as it ascends.

6.85 The trail turns left and follows a western escarpment to the top of Cotton Hill.

6.95 The trail passes the Cotton Hill Lean-to.

7.00 Turn right and cross Cotton Hill, which at 2,114 feet is the highest point on this section. A radio tower may be visible through the woods to the left. Begin descending following the north border.

7.45 The trail turns left, levels off and crosses a stone wall at a corner boundary of Cotton Hill. The trail bears right, makes a short descent, and then levels again.

7.95 The Long Path turns right on a logging road and emerges at an open field that was the site of an abandoned farm. It is possible to drive in to this point, though the road is in barely passable condition. The trail continues along this access road, which is the boundary between state land on the left and private land on the right.

8.35 Another road comes in from the left. Continue ahead.

8.65 The trail crosses Cotton Hill Road and descends to cross a bridge across the stream. It then begins to ascend.

8.75 The trail turns right on an old woods road and continues to ascend.

9.00 Left is a faint old road. The Long Path bears right and ascends more steeply, crossing another old road.

9.15 The trail turns right, leaving the woods road, and climbs very steeply to a shoulder of Canady Hill. At the top of the hill, the trail continues south along Cotton Hill's eastern boundary. The trail begins to descend.

9.45 Just before reaching another boundary corner, the trail crosses a logging road. At the boundary corner, the trail turns east, staying inside state land.

9.65 The Long Path leaves state land and turns right to follow a logging road through a recently logged are. Camping, fires, etc. are prohibited beyond this point. This area is confusing as many logging roads crisscross it. The Long Path stays to the rightmost road.

9.95 The logging road turns right and descends. The Long Path turns left on an older road, bears left again uphill through the woods, then turns right on a woods road 100 feet below Canady Hill.

10.25 The trail turns left and climbs very steeply over Canady Hill.

10.40 Over the top of Canady Hill, the trail emerges on an open field with a spectacular view. From the right, you see the Blackhead Range in the Catskills, Partridge Run and Cole Hill. In the far left is the Albany Doppler Radar Tower in Berne on the Long Path. Continue downhill, following the right side of a hedgerow. The trail crosses the hedgerow and descends on a grassy road.

10.95 The Long Path turns right on Canady Hill Road.

11.05 Go left on Lawton Hollow Road. There are views to the Catskills and Green Mountains of Vermont along the way.

12.10 Cross into Albany County. To continue, stay on Lawton Hollow Road.

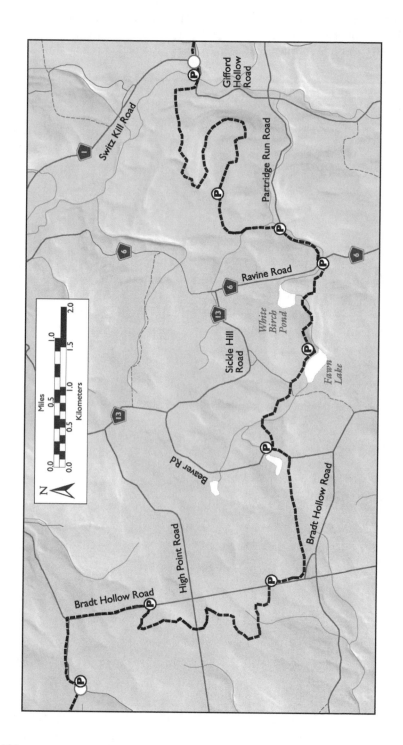

31. Albany County Line to Switz Kill

Feature Partridge Run Wildlife Management Area
Distance 11.85 miles
USGS Map Quads Rensselaerville, Westerlo
Trail Conference Maps: none

General Description

Section 31 of the Long Path mostly follows old ski trails and snowmobile trails through the Partridge Run Wildlife Management Area. The walking is not difficult and there is little elevation gain, just small ups and downs. The exceptions are at the beginning and end of the section, where the Long Path must climb up to the plateau of Partridge Run. The first 1.2 miles and the last 0.2 miles are on paved roads. The one foot-only trail section is at the very eastern part of Partridge Run. Some of the park trails are also accessible by vehicle, but see little use. The trail passes through many reforestation areas, primarily of Norway spruce and red pine. There are also several ponds and lakes along the way. Views are limited, but more numerous when the leaves are down. As skiers and snowmobilers share the trails in the winter, there are a number of wet areas, particularly in the beginning.

Access

Take the New York State Thruway to Exit 22 in Selkirk. Turn right on NY Route 144 and go south to NY Route 396. Turn right on Route 396 and follow it 6 miles to South Bethlehem, where Route 396 ends. The road becomes Albany County Route 301 here. Follow Route 301 west another 6 miles to its terminus at NY Route 443 in Clarksville. Turn left on Route 443 and follow it 11 miles to the village of Berne. Continue on Route 443 another 3 miles to West Berne. In West Berne, turn left on Albany County Route 9. Follow Route 9 for about a mile until it makes a sharp left. Continue straight ahead on Bradt Hollow Road. Follow Bradt Hollow Road for about 3 miles, where it intersects Lawton Hollow Road. Turn right on Lawton Hollow Road and follow it for 0.5 miles to the Albany/Schoharie county line.

Parking

0.00 Albany county line. (18T 564048E 4715801N)
1.20 Off Bradt Hollow Road. (18T 565136E 4714776N)
5.55 Tubbs Pond. (18T 567199E 4713091N)

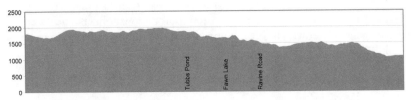

6.30 Fawn Lake. (18T 568505E 4712498N)

7.30 Partridge Run Road and Ravine Road (Albany County Route 6). (18T 569696E 4712436N)

7.80 End of Partridge Run Road. (Unlocated)

8.90 Ravine Road (Albany County Route 6). (Unlocated)

11.85 Switz Kill Road and Gifford Hollow Road. (18T 572337E 4714236N)

Camping

Camping is allowed in Partridge Run only in the reforestation areas 150 feet away from the trail or water, not in the Wildlife Management Areas.

Trail Description

0.00 There is a shale bank on the left, with room to park a couple of cars. This is the Albany county line. The trail heads east on Lawton Hollow Road.

0.50 The trail turns right on gravel Bradt Hollow Road and turns uphill. After about half a mile, the trail passes the Partridge Run boundary.

1.20 The Long Path turns right and enters Partridge Run Wildlife Management Area. There is room to park several cars here, but the parking area is accessible only during dry season. Just past the parking area, the Long Path follows a snowmobile trail. Ironically, this area was recently logged, so the reforestation project must start all over again. The trail goes right through the clear-cut area. At the top of the hill, there are views south toward the Catskills. The trail then descends into the woods following Partridge Run's northern boundary.

1.50 The trail turns left on the Nordic ski trail, continuing straight ahead bordering an area that was clear-cut several years ago. Reach an intersecting trail and bear right. In a short distance another ski trail connects from the right. The LP leaves the ski trail on the left through a brushy area and into fairly open woods following stone walls and logging roads. The trail emerges back on the ski trail at the iron gate on High Point Road.

2.25 The trail crosses High Point Road, and then reenters the forest following another Nordic ski trail. Shortly, the trail enters a Norway spruce reforestation area, swings east into a second reforestation area and then back south again.

2.75 The trail reaches a fork. The left fork heads uphill in the woods, while the Long Path continues to the right, following level ground. There is beaver pond on the right in the distance. Shortly, the trail turns right, crosses the outlet of the beaver pond and enters a hemlock grove. The trail parallels the beaver pond through the hemlocks and then turns left, away from the beaver pond. The trail leaves the hemlocks and enters another spruce grove.

3.15 The trail leaves the spruce forest, crosses an open field, and then turns left on a gravel road that is marked jointly for snowmobilers and skiers. It heads generally downhill to the remnants of an old beaver pond, then heads uphill again.

3.40 The trail turns right on a snowmobile trail, continuing south along a stone wall that marks the boundary of a red pine forest on the left with a

Tubbs Pond

spruce forest on the right.

3.60 Intersect another snowmobile trail, turn left and follow the trail to Bradt Hollow Road.

3.70 The trail turns right, follows Bradt Hollow Road, crosses the road, and then continues on a gravel road.

3.80 Turn right on a snowmobile trail. The trail parallels Bradt Hollow Road for about a quarter of a mile, and then swings away toward the east, passing through a pine forest.

4.55 A snowmobile trail comes in from the right. The Long Path continues straight ahead.

5.05 The trail turns left on gravel Beaver Road.

5.25 Turn right and follow a snowmobile trail downhill through a mature stand of spruce and pine.

5.55 Reach Tubbs Pond, turn right, cross the outlet of the pond and reach the Tubbs Pond parking area. The trail follows the cinder Tubbs Pond access road.

5.95 Intersect Fawn Lake Road, turn right and follow it as it parallels Fawn Lake on the right.

6.30 Reach the end of the road and Fawn Lake parking. The trail turns left on a woods road and descends along a gorge following Fawn Lake's outlet stream. To the left are the remnants of a 1930s deer management area.

6.75 Reach a trail intersection. The trail to the left leads to White Birch Pond. The Long Path turns right, crosses a stream, the bridge is out, and heads east toward Partridge Run Road.

7.00 Reach Partridge Run Road and turn right.

7.20 The trail jogs left on Ravine Road (Albany County Route 6), then continues on Partridge Run Road. On the right is room to park several cars.

7.50 A path leads right about 100 feet to a waterfall along the stream.

7.75 Partridge Run Road bears right and crosses the stream. The Long Path bears left away from the stream, reaches a parking area and picnic area at the end of the road, then continues straight ahead though a gate on a gravel road. The trail passes a small pond on the right.

8.15 Intersect a snowmobile trail that goes left. Continue right on the gravel road, intersecting another trail in 500 feet. The trail left leads to Wood Duck Pond. The Long Path bears right.

8.55 Reach Ravine Road (Albany County Route 6) and turn right.

8.90 Turn left, reach a parking area and continue on a snowmobile trail.

9.10 Reach the crest of the hill and turn right to descend. There are views of the Blackhead Range here when the leaves are down. The trail swings left to reach the eastern escarpment, then left again to follow it.

9.45 Following Partridge Run's eastern escarpment north, there is a view across Gifford Hollow to Cole Hill.

9.75 The trail bears left, switchbacks uphill beneath a rock ledge, then continues north on the escarpment.

10.00 Reach an old woods road and turn right.

10.30 The trail turns right on another woods road and descends down to a level area before climbing again. There has been recent logging in this area and the trail may be hard to follow again until it reaches the field before Gifford Hollow Road.

10.50 Reach the bottom of the hill, turn right and enter a hemlock grove, gently climbing again.

10.65 Turn left on another faint woods road, leave Partridge Run and begin descending to the Switz Kill. The trail enters private property. The landowner of this section has allowed all-terrain vehicles (ATVs) to ride on his property. Please be courteous to any ATV users on this section.

10.80 The trail turns right and descends through the woods. This area was recently logged, so watch carefully for the Long Path blazes. It emerges on an open field and continues east, following a hedgerow. Watch for the blazes to be sure you are in the correct field. At the end of the first field, cross a stream in a hedgerow and follow the hedgerow across a second field.

11.45 The trail reaches the edge of a field and turns right onto a farm road.

11.65 Reach Gifford Hollow Road and turn left..

11.85 Gifford Hollow Road intersects Switz Kill Road (Albany County Route 1), where this section ends. Turn right on Switz Kill Road to continue.

32. Switz Kill to East Berne

Feature: Cole Hill State Forest
Distance: 9.00 miles
USGS Map Quads: Westerlo
Trail Conference Maps: none

General Description

This section of the Long Path is a pleasant blend of ski trails in the state forest, road walking and woodland trails. The Long Path leaves the valley of the Switz Kill and goes along Willsie Road to the top of Cole Hill, where it follows a series of recently constructed ski trails through a mature forest. There are views from Cole Hill, and the trail passes several beaver ponds that have the feeling of the Adirondacks. Past Cole Hill, the Long Path goes along public roads, with a view of the Catskills in the distance. Upon reaching the Doppler weather tower for the Albany region, the trail reenters the woods and begins a gradual descent through land that was once farmed. The Long Path passes through a field, crosses Joslyn Schoolhouse Road, and descends through a pine forest. It then crosses Fox Creek and finally emerges on NY Route 443.

Access

Take the New York State Thruway to Exit 22 (Selkirk). Turn right on NY Route 144, and continue south to NY Route 396. Turn right on Route 396 and follow it for 6 miles to South Bethlehem, where Route 396 ends and the road becomes Albany County Route 301. Continue on Route 301 west another 6 miles to its end at NY Route 443 in Clarksville. Turn left on Route 443 and follow it 11 miles to the village of Berne. About a mile west of Berne, turn left on Albany County Route 1 and follow it south about 4 miles to Gifford Hollow Road.

Parking

0.00 Switz Kill Road (County Route 1) and Gifford Hollow Road. (18T 572286E 4714217N)
3.10 Turnoff on right side of Irish Hill Road. (18T 572927E 4716469N)
4.15 Willsie Road. (18T 573346E 4716061N)
5.10 Cole Hill Road. (18T 574226E 4716190N)
7.00 Woodstock Road at weather station. (18T 576839E 4715372N)
8.50 Joslyn Schoolhouse Road (Albany County Route 14). (18T 577782E

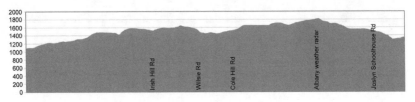

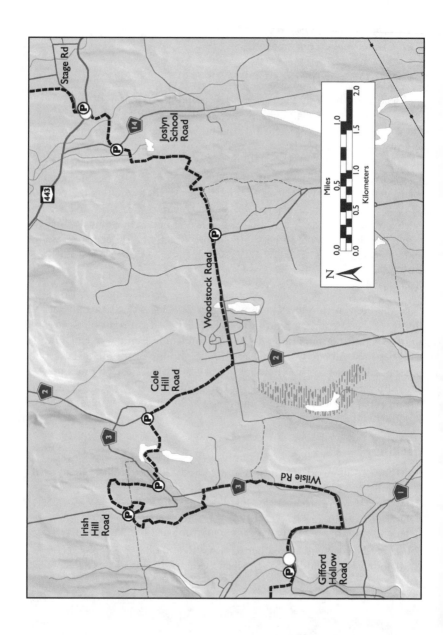

4716630N)

9.05 Intersection of NY Route 443 and Stage Road. (18T 578250E 4717069N)

Camping

2.75 Camping is allowed in Cole Hill State Forest 150 feet away from the trail and from water.

Trail Description

0.00 The Long Path leaves the Switz Kill Valley at the intersection of Switz Kill Road and Gifford Hollow Road and begins to climb following Switz Kill Road.

0.65 Reach Willsie Road, turn left and head uphill, following paved Willsie Road. Near the top of the hill, there is a view back to Partridge Run and the Catskills.

2.10 The trail reaches the southern boundary of Cole Hill State Forest and enters the woods on the left across from a small parking area. It proceeds westward, descending to a small stream and crosses it on a bridge. Beyond the stream, the trail ascends, gradually swinging towards the northwest and then turning to the north at the top of the slope. It then enters a reforested area and passes through alternate fields of pine and spruce, each one separated by mixed hardwoods and stone walls. After the fourth stone wall, the trail turns right (east) on a fire access road to join a cross country ski trail.

3.10 The trail crosses Irish Hill Road. There is a parking area at the north side of this crossing. The trail is mostly marked in the standard Aqua paint blazes,

Bridge in Cole Hill State Forest

Avenue of the Pines

but there are also DEC ski trail markers and red trail markers.

3.25 The Long Path reaches an open area and turns left on an intersecting trail. After a short distance, it turns right, crosses a stone wall, and follows the top of an escarpment.

3.45 Reach an overlook over the escarpment, with views west over the Switz Kill Valley to Partridge Run. Just past the overlook, cross another stone wall and turn left on an old woods road.

3.75 Reach the boundary of the state forest, where the trail turns right. Remain within the forest, as a woods road to the left leads into private property.

4.05 Begin to descend. Turn left on yet another ski trail, then turn right and continue to descend to Willsie Road.

4.15 Cross Willsie Road and re-enter the woods. In another 500 feet, the trail turns left, and then turns right to begin a series of corduroy and stepping stone bridges. Beyond the bridges, the trail begins a gradual ascent and turns left.

4.50 The Long Path passes through a deep forest known locally as the "Avenue of the Pines." At the far end of this forest, there is an opening in the woods, with a view to an abandoned beaver pond. This old pond is now a wetland filled with marsh grass.

4.70 Reach another beaver pond in a beautiful pine forest-a wonderful lunch spot. Here, the Long Path turns left and crosses a substantial bridge. The scene here is quite reminiscent of the Adirondacks. Beyond the beaver pond, the trail climbs steeply to a hemlock grove, briefly turns left on an old woods road, and then descends to Cole Hill Road.

5.05 Turn right and continue uphill on paved Cole Hill Road. There is a parking area here. In the future, it is anticipated that the Long Path will be rerouted through the woods in this area, but for the present, it follows public roads for about 2 miles.

5.45 Reach the crest of Cole Hill Road, with views south toward the Blackhead Range and Windham High Peak in the Catskills. As you continue on Cole Hill Road, the view opens up to include Mt. Hayden, Mt. Pisgah, Richmond Mountain, Ashland Pinnacle and Huntersfield Mountain–the route of the Long Path as it heads northwest from the Catskills to Schoharie County.

5.90 Turn left on Woodstock Road, with Woodstock Park, part of Camp Woodstock, a large private campground and RV park, to the right.

6.35 Pass the entrance to Camp Woodstock and Woodstock Lake on the right.

6.85 Filkins Hill Road goes off to the left. Continue straight ahead on Woodstock Road.

7.00 As Woodstock Road turns right, the Long Path continues straight ahead on a gravel road that leads to a weather station.

7.05 The trail passes the National Weather Service's Albany Region Doppler radar tower on the right. This tower tracks and warns of severe storms. Vehicles may not be driven beyond this point. The Long Path descends from Stafford Hill on a narrow woods road, with a rock ledge on the left at the bottom of the hill.

7.35 Continue straight ahead on an older woods road, as the road that the Long Path has been following turns left. In 500 feet, bear right at a fork, and begin a gradual descent through dense foliage.

7.60 Reach an intersection, with a gravel road to the right, and a level ATV track to the extreme left. The Long Path crosses both roads and descends slightly to the left. If you are going in the opposite direction, continue straight ahead across the gravel roads. You will know that you are following the correct route if you pass between the "Posted" signs of two different landowners. After a slight descent, the trail bears right, following an old woods road.

7.75 The Long Path crosses a seasonal wet area on stepping-stones, and then turns left across level terrain. In 0.2 miles, the trail begins a gradual descent, and then intersects a stone wall that it follows downhill, descending more steeply.

8.30 Turn right on a gravel road that leads to the edge of a field. Cross the field and turn right, by an abandoned farmhouse, to reach Joslyn Schoolhouse Road.

8.50 Cross Joslyn Schoolhouse Road (Albany County Route 14) and reenter the woods just below an open field. The Long Path sidehills through an old red pine forest, then turns left and descends sharply on an ATV trail. At the bottom of the hill, the trail bears left off the ATV trail and descends through a brushy forest to Fox Creek.

8.85 Cross Fox Creek and begin a gradual ascent. In another 500 feet, turn left on a woods road.

9.00 Reach NY Route 443. To continue, cross Route 443 and follow Stage Road.

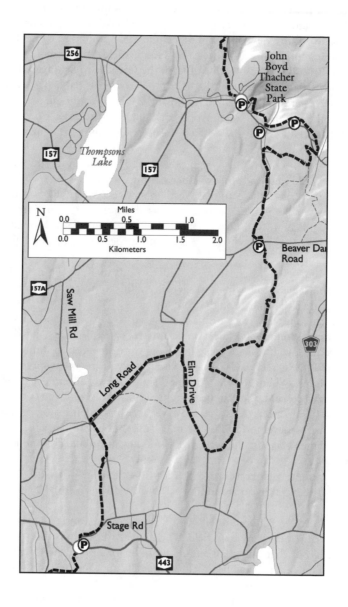

33. East Berne to John Boyd Thacher State Park

Features: Helderberg Escarpment and John Boyd Thacher State Park
Distance: 9.05 miles
USGS Map Quads: Westerlo, Altamont
Trail Conference Maps: none

General Description

This section of the Long Path starts pleasantly as it passes through farm country and then builds into a crescendo as it ends with spectacular views and dramatic cliffs. The section begins where the Long Path leaves NY Route 443 and follows Stage Road past a local farm, and then follows several open areas before climbing over a small, steep ridge. On the far side of the ridge, the trail descends to Elm Drive and continues across another field, then goes down to a stream that empties into Helderberg Lake. The Long Path then heads north along the stream and ascends to a ridgetop that has a dramatic 270-degree view of the Catskills to the south and the Adirondacks to the north. It then descends along a ravine into John Boyd Thacher State Park, where it continues to descend along a ski slope to Beaver Dam Road. After crossing Beaver Dam Road, the Long Path follows a series of trails through the park, emerging on the cliffs of the Helderberg Escarpment at the overlook on the north side of NY Route 157. Here, there are spectacular views northeast into Vermont. This ridge is made up of a core of limestone in which were found many fossils during the early days of geology in the 1800s. These fossils are known worldwide for their sequence from the Silurian to the Devonian eras. Early studies in this area helped lay the foundations for modern paleontology and geology. The Long Path then turns north and descends on the historic Indian Ladder Trail under the base of the cliffs. The section ends at the north end of the Indian Ladder Trail.

Access

Take the New York State Thruway to Exit 22 (Selkirk). Turn right on NY Route 144 and continue south to NY Route 396. Turn right on Route 396 and follow it 6 miles to South Bethlehem, where Route 396 ends and the road becomes Albany County Route 301. Follow Route 301 west another 6 miles to its end at NY Route 443 in Clarksville. Turn left on Route 443 and follow it west about 5 miles to the second intersection with Stage Road, 1.5 miles from the intersection of NY 443/85.

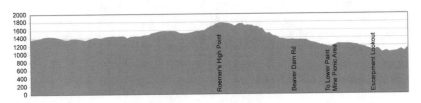

Panorama from Thacher Park lookout

Parking

0.00 Stage Road and Route 443. (18T 578250E 4717069N)

6.35 John Boyd Thacher State Park Ski Area on Beaver Dam Road. (18T 580743E 4721116N)

7.25 Lower Paint Mine Picnic Area (about 0.2 miles off the trail). (18T 580631E 4722541N)

8.05 Helderberg Escarpment Overlook parking area. (18T 580980E 4722697N)

9.05 North end of Indian Ladder Trail. (18T 580499E 4722951N)

Trail Description

0.00 The Long Path crosses Route 443 and heads uphill parallel to Stage Road on its west side to a farmhouse. Here Stage Road turns right; the trail continues to the north side.

0.35 The trail turns left away from the road and descends gradually north along the west side of a hedgerow. Along this leg there is an expansive view west, across open fields, toward Cole Hill and the Schoharie Valley.

0.75 Bearing right through a gap in the hedgerow, the trail enters a young hardwood forest and turns gradually east (right). At a logging trail, it turns north (left).

0.95 The trail reaches Sawmill Road and turns north (left) near the intersection with Stempel Road.

1.30 At the intersection with Long Road, the trail turns right and follows Long Road east.

2.35 At Elm Drive, the trail turns right again and follows Elm Drive south.

3.25 The trail reaches the south boundary of the Roemer Property. It enters the property on the left and continues east along the north side of a hedgerow. After crossing a pipeline, the trail reenters the woods and descends to a stream.

3.95 Reach a larger stream, turn left, and follow alongside the stream through the woods. The trail crosses several seasonal streams and a small spruce plantation before emerging in a larger spruce plantation.

4.35 Turn left at the spruce plantation, leaving the stream, and begin to ascend. The trail crosses a woods road and ascends more steeply.

4.65 The trail reaches Roemer's High Point, one of the most spectacular places on the entire Long Path. To the east, you can see over the edge of the Helderberg Escarpment to the Berkshires and Taconics. To the south you can see the Great Wall of Manitou in the Catskills with the Blackhead Range looming ahead. To the west you look over Cole Hill and Partridge Run. This row of mountains is known as the Hamilton Escarpment or the Endless Mountains, as they head south as far as Binghamton. To the north are the peaks of the southern Adirondacks. The trail turns right and follows the ridgetop. Shortly, the trail reenters the woods and begins a gradual descent to again cross the woods road.

5.15 Shortly after crossing the woods road, the trail ascends a small hill from where there is a view of a beaver pond when the leaves are down. After crossing the top of this hill, the trail takes a right switchback to descend to a ravine.

5.30 The trail intersects an unmarked trail that leads right to the head of the ravine. The Long Path turns left and follows this trail north along the ravine. It crosses a woods road and continues along the ravine.

5.70 The trail reaches the edge of John Boyd Thacher State Park and descends right through a series of switchbacks to the bottom of the ravine.

5.85 As the trail enters the main park, it emerges on a ski slope that it follows downhill. To the left is a lean-to that serves as a warming hut for the Helderberg Ski Club. Upon reaching an intersection, the Long Path stays to the left and follows the ski slope downhill and crosses a small stream. Beyond the stream crossing, the ski slope levels out as it emerges on Beaver Dam Road.

6.35 The trail crosses Beaver Dam Road, and then turns left on a trail that parallels Beaver Dam Road.

Mine Lot Falls in the winter

HERB CHONG

Base of the Indian Ladder Trail

6.50 The trail turns right and follows a gravel park road.

6.95 A nature trail comes in from the right at the head of a ravine. The Long Path continues ahead, gradually descending on the left side of the ravine.

7.25 Straight ahead, the Lower Paint Mine Picnic Area and pavilion are 0.2 miles ahead. The Long Path turns right, crosses the ravine on a bridge and follows the lower part of the nature trail. In 0.1 miles the nature trail forks to the right; the Long Path forks to the left and passes through a dense hemlock forest.

7.70 The Long Path turns left and follows a wood road that leads into the Upper Knowles Flat Picnic Area. The trail follows the north edge of the picnic area, and then descends right on a gravel path to the paved access road. The trail then turns right on the access road to intersect Route 157.

8.05 The Long Path crosses NY Route 157 and reaches the overlook parking area. The trail turns left and follows the overlook along the edge of the Escarpment. There is a spectacular view across the upper Hudson Valley to the Green Mountains of Vermont and the Adirondacks of New York. At the end of the

Ferns growing in the back of Mine Lot Falls

parking area, the trail continues to follow the escarpment fence through the woods.

8.50 The trail reaches a viewpoint over Mine Lot Falls, which plunges over the escarpment. Just past this viewpoint, the Indian Ladder Trail descends to the bottom of the cliff. It follows the escarpment north under the cliffs and passes under Mine Lot Falls. The Indian Ladder Trail is only open from mid-May to late fall; as it is dangerous when there is ice and rock fall. The Long Path follows the Indian Ladder Trail when it is open. If you follow the trail on top of the escarpment, the trail will pass another overlook and then pass over the head of the falls.

9.05 The Long Path reaches the northern end of the Indian Ladder Trail.

34. John Boyd Thacher State Park to NY Route 146

Features: Helderberg Escarpment and Thacher Park
Distance: 7.50 miles
USGS Map Quads: Altamont
Trail Conference Maps: none

General Description

This section begins at the parking area at the north end of the Indian Ladder Trail and follows the western boundary of John Boyd Thacher State Park northward. It then continues north through the park along a newly constructed ski trail, with the Helderberg Escarpment to the right. After leaving the park, the Long Path climbs to the top of the escarpment and heads in a generally northwest direction through the woods on lands recently acquired by the Open Space Institute and currently being managed as a nature preserve. West of the preserve, the Long Path follows old gravel roads and then paved roads to its current end on NY Route 146, a short distance west of the village of Altamont. Plans are underway to extend the Long Path north to the Mohawk River and beyond.

Access

Take the New York State Thruway to Exit 22 (Selkirk). Turn right on NY Route 144 and continue south to NY Route 396. Turn right on Route 396 and follow it six miles to South Bethlehem, where Route 396 ends and the road becomes Albany County Route 301. Follow Route 301 west another six miles to its end at NY Route 443 in Clarksville. Turn left on NY Route 443 and follow it west 1.9 miles to its intersection with NY Route 85. Turn right on Route 85 and follow it east for 2.1 miles. Turn left and follow NY Route 157 3.9 miles to the main entrance to John Boyd Thacher State Park. Parking is available at the northern entrance to the Indian Ladder Trail and other nearby parking lots.

Parking

0.00 North end of Indian Ladder Trail (fee in season). (18T 580499E 4722951N)
5.45 Intersection of Carrick Road and Old Stage Road (limited). (18T 577456E 4725362N)

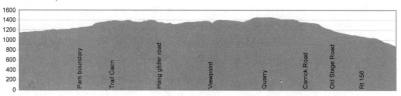

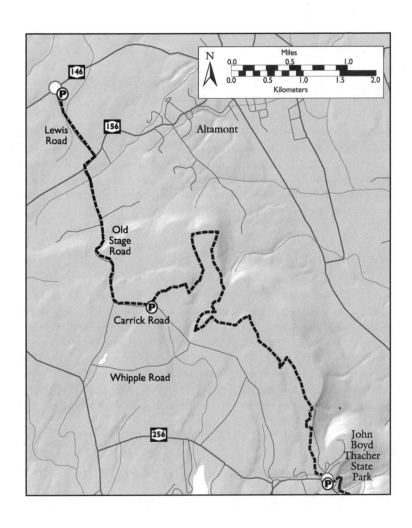

7.50 Lewis Road and NY Route 146 (limited). (18T 576639E 4728200N)

Trail Description

0.00 This section starts at the "Indian Ladder" sign in the parking area, near the restrooms, and goes along the edge of the parking area to the park entrance gate, where it crosses the guardrail and goes through a field behind the administration building.

0.15 The trail enters the woods and follows a newly constructed ski trail, which parallels the park road heading north. The Helderberg Escarpment is visible to the east of the park road.

0.70 The trail crosses a ball field, with several picnic tables along the edge, and a pavilion near the edge of the escarpment. The trail reenters the woods near a group of red pines, and turns right onto a gravel road to the Hailes Cave Picnic area overlooking the escarpment. At two stone pillars, it turns left onto a grassy road, with the escarpment to the right, then again turns left and follows a ski trail along the edge of two fields.

1.00 Halfway northwards along the edge of the second field, the trail turns right into the woods. Many narrow fissures, some very deep, crisscrossing the woods mark this section of trail. The trail parallels and then crosses a stone wall to reach an old woods road, the end of Park property.

Wildflowers growing near the ranger station

LOREN DOBERT

Quarry rocks piled high

1.25 The trail turns right on the old road and enters the OSI Thacher Park Nature preserve.

1.45 Turn left off of the woods road to climb along a switchback to the top of the ridge and a junction with another woods road.

1.55 The yellow-blazed woods road leads left in 0.3 miles to Ryan Road and a small parking area. The trail turns right and follows the crest of the ridge through a mixed forest of pine, hardwoods and low-growing juniper.

1.95 After reaching a cairn that marks the highest point on this trail section, about 1,410 feet, the Long Path descends gradually from the escarpment, staying near its edge.

2.75 The Long Path reaches a gravel road used by hang glider enthusiasts to access a takeoff pad at the edge of the escarpment. Turn right on the road and head toward the takeoff pad.

2.90 Bear right where the road divides into two.

3.00 The trail turns left off of the road and circles a depression in the escarpment. To reach the hang-glider launch site, continue straight on the road and take a left after going through a well-defined stone wall. The point with wonderful far-reaching views is about 0.5 miles further to the east.

3.20 Cross the other branch of the woods road. This road also leads to the hang glider takeoff pad. In another 0.1 miles, the trail crosses an old stone wall.

3.40 Reach the middle of an old juniper stand and turn right. The turn is obscured and not yet well marked. The forest along the trail is laced with fascinating fissures caused by acidity eating away the escarpment's limestone. Cross the head of one of the escarpment ravines and turn left up a small bluff to the Preserve's boundary corner.

3.85 The trail reaches the end of OSI property. Just ahead of you, on private property, is an open viewpoint. To the right Mt. Everett in southern Massachusetts is seen peeking over the shoulder of the hang-glider opening. Panning north you will see Albany, Mt. Greylock, the Town of Altamont, Vermont's Green Mountains with Killington and Pico Peak prominent. Turn left along the Preserve's boundary as it parallels the woods road.

4.10 Meet the woods road as it turns south to enter the Preserve. Turn left to follow the woods road back south.

4.45 Cross a woods road and begin a moderate climb up a rise. At the top of the rise, the trail turns right and winds through some brushy fields before entering the grounds of an old quarry. The path goes through the quarry with its bizarre formations.

4.95 Reach the center of the quarry. You may want to spend some time looking for the abundant fossils of ancient sea life in the limestone before coming out to Carrick Road. As this is being written, there are plans for an interpretive kiosk and a large parking lot that will take advantage of the smooth layer of limestone. Continue across the quarry to Carrick Road.

5.10 Meet Carrick Road and turn right. (Turning left on Carrick Road to follow its yellow blazes will complete the Ryan Road loop.)

5.30 Reach the end of the maintained portion of Carrick Road. Parking is available alongside the road without obstructing traffic. In the wintertime, this parking location marks the limit of snow plowing on Carrick Road.

5.45 Turn right onto paved Old Stage Road. Descend gradually, with views across the valley of Altamont towards the hills just south of the Mohawk River.

6.70 Immediately after passing on old cemetery, turn right onto NY Route 156.

6.85 Turn left onto Lewis Road.

7.50 Reach NY Route 146, the current official terminus of the Long Path. It is possible to follow Route 146 a short distance into the village of Altamont and to continue on local roads through Schoharie County to the Mohawk River. The Schenectady Trail Committee of the Long Path North Hiking Club has marked a temporary route that can be followed to the river until a more permanent off-road route is developed.

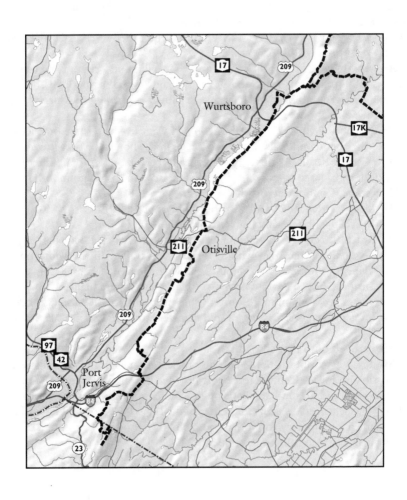

Shawangunk Ridge Trail

The Shawangunk Ridge Trail was originally conceived as a relocation of the Long Path from Harriman State Park to Minnewaska State Park. Now part of the Long Path system, the Shawangunk Ridge Trail provides a woodland alternative to the Orange County route of the Long Path that is mostly a road walk. Aside from being more in wooded and isolated from civilization, the trail provides a more varied experience as it wanders up and down, sometimes on the top of the ridge and sometimes beside it.

Along the Shawangunk Ridge Trail near NY Rt. 211 and Mt. Hope

JAKOB FRANKE

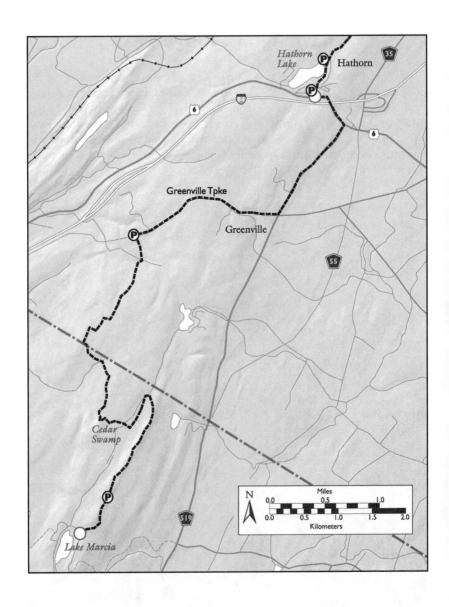

G1. High Point State Park to US Route 6

Features: High Point, Cedar Swamp
Distance: 7.40 miles
USGS Map Quads: Port Jervis South, Unionville, Otisville
Trail Conference Maps: none

General Description

The Shawangunk Ridge Trail begins where the Appalachian Trail heads east from the Kittatinny Ridge in High Point State Park in New Jersey. After leaving the Appalachian Trail, the Shawangunk Ridge Trail passes the highest point in New Jersey, where there is a spectacular view. The trail then continues through High Point State Park. A highlight of the trail is Cedar Swamp, which is a mountaintop cedar bog. In High Point there are three separate ridges; the trail uses all three. Past Cedar Swamp the trail ascends and crosses the border into New York, where it attains the westernmost ridge. The trail then follows the western ridge to Greenville Turnpike. From Greenville Turnpike to Route 6, the trail follows public roads.

Access

Take Interstate 80 west to NJ Route 23 in Wayne. Take NJ Route 23 west to High Point State Park in northwestern New Jersey. Follow the park roads to the High Point Monument.

Parking

0.30 High Point Monument parking lot. (Unlocated)
4.55 Greenville Turnpike (limited). (18T 528895E 4578397N)
7.40 Hathorn Boulevard and US Route 6 (limited parking here; more parking available 0.35 miles into next section at end of Lake Shore Drive). (18T 531563E 4580348N)

Trail Description

0.00 The Shawangunk Ridge Trail begins in High Point State Park, where the Appalachian Trail intersects the Monument Trail. The Appalachian Trail turns right at this point and descends east off the Kittatinny Ridge. The Shawangunk Ridge Trail follows the Monument Trail north through the park and is marked with white rectangular markers with a red-over-green circular blaze. Additionally, the section from the AT to the High Point monument is also blazed in light blue, which signifies an AT side trail. After leaving the AT, the Shawangunk Ridge Trail ascends through the woods, passing through a rocky area. The trail crosses the High Point Monument Road, turns right and climbs steeply on a gravel path to the High Point Monument.

0.25 The trail reaches the High Point Monument, the highest point in New Jersey. From this vantage point there is a spectacular 360-degree view. To the south you can see down the Kittatinnies across the Delaware Water Gap into Pennsylvania. To the west you can see across the Delaware River into the Poconos. To the northwest is the city of Port Jervis, with the Delaware River beyond. The Catskill Mountains are visible to the north, 70 miles distant, and to the northeast is a view all the way up the Shawangunks to Mohonk. To the east you can see into the Wallkill Valley, with the Taconics and the Hudson Highlands in the distance. The highlands of western New Jersey are visible to the southeast. You can take a trip up to the top of the High Point Monument, but it is not necessary for the view. Past the monument, the trail descends gradually to the parking lot. As it descends, the trail passes a park bench with a view across the escarpment to Port Jervis and the Delaware River. The trail passes a concession area with picnic tables. Beyond the picnic area is a public restroom with water fountains. After the restrooms, the trail reaches the parking lot and follows the western edge of the lot in a grassy area.

0.45 The trail reaches the end of the parking lot, goes around the end of the barricade, passes a picnic table and enters the woods between two boulders. The trail follows the ridge north through the woods.

0.95 A side path leads left where there is a view west toward Port Jervis and the Delaware River. Shortly, there is a path to the right to a rock outcropping with a view southeast toward northwestern New Jersey. The trail passes another view to the right and then begins a gradual descent to Cedar Swamp.

1.50 The trail reaches the northeast corner of Cedar Swamp. The Monument Trail continues straight ahead, crossing the outlet of Cedar Swamp. The Shawangunk Ridge Trail turns left and parallels the eastern edge of Cedar Swamp on a woods road. The Aqua Long Path blazes begin here.

1.85 The trail turns right and crosses Cedar Swamp on a boardwalk. Cedar Swamp is a magnificent mountaintop bog that is filled with cedar, wild rhododendron and hemlock. Part of the Dryden Kuser Natural Area, Cedar Swamp is the most inland example of Atlantic white cedar, normally a coastal plain evergreen tree. It was named for New Jersey State Senator Dryden Kuser, a leading conservationist and the son of Colonel Anthony Kuser, who donated the land for High Point State Park to New Jersey in 1923. In New Jersey, a

High Point Monument

natural area has the same protection as a wilderness area in New York. Normally a natural area is designated only in an ecologically significant area. After crossing Cedar Swamp, the trail continues along a woods road on the western side of the swamp.

2.05 The trail turns right off the gravel road at a park bench and ascends to the Monument Trail on the western side of Cedar Swamp. It then turns left onto the Monument Trail, which it follows to the top of a small knob. Atop the knob, the trail turns right, leaves the Monument Trail, then passes a view toward the Delaware River and descends off the knob. The trail continues north along the central of three ridges of Kittatinny Mountain through an understory of blueberry.

2.70 The trail turns left and descends on an old woods road toward a stream crossing in a col. After the stream crossing the trail makes a gradual ascent toward the New York border.

3.10 The trail leaves High Point State Park and crosses into New York by a border monument. After crossing into New York the trail climbs up to the westernmost ridge and heads north along the ridge. Once into New York, the name of the mountain range changes from Kittatinny to Shawangunk.

3.25 The trail reaches a viewpoint west over Port Jervis and the Delaware River. The trail then heads north along the slab with a view north toward the Catskills. Shortly, the trail descends into the woods and then follows the ridge north. It climbs back up to an area of scrub oak and pitch pine, and then turns back north.

3.75 To the left is a view through the trees of the Delaware River and Port Jervis. The trail then begins a gradual descent off the ridge and crosses a woods road, descends to a small stream and levels out.

4.55 The trail reaches Greenville Turnpike and turns right and heads uphill.

5.35 The trail reaches the height of land along Greenville Turnpike and begins to descend. To the left is another mountaintop bog called Mud Pond. Mud Pond in the summer is filled with cattail and purple loosestrife. From Mud Pond there is a view of a radio tower on the ridge. On the right is a small old cemetery called the Seeley Cemetery, which was established in 1840.

6.00 The trail turns left onto Old Mountain Road and parallels the ridge on the east side.

6.90 The trail turns left on US Route 6 and crosses under Interstate 84.

7.40 The trail reaches Hathorn Boulevard, where this section ends. To continue, turn right on Hathorn Boulevard.

G2. US Route 6 to NY Route 211

Feature: Southern Shawangunk Ridge
Distance: 10.20 miles
USGS Map Quads: Otisville
Trail Conference Maps: none

General Description

This section is a mixed bag of ridgetop hiking, abandoned rail beds, an active rail line, and woods roads. This section begins with the trail passing through the Hathorn Lake (Hawthorne Lake on some maps) development to a dead end, where it heads north along the ridge. After a short distance it then descends to the active Conrail Port Jervis line, which it follows north for a half a mile. There is one good view across Shin Hollow in this section. Where Shin Hollow Road crosses the Port Jervis line, the trail leaves the rail bed and follows an abandoned section of Shin Hollow Road, which is a nice woods walking section. After about a half a mile, the trail leaves Shin Hollow Road and begins a gradual descent to Guymard Turnpike, paralleling the Conrail Port Jervis line in the woods. After crossing Guymard Turnpike at a bridge over the railroad, the trail descends to the abandoned Erie Port Jervis line. It continues north on the rail bed for 0.7 miles, and then climbs back to the ridgetop where it stays for the next 2.7 miles. In this section there are a couple of good views to the north and west across the Neversink Valley. The trail then descends again to the abandoned rail bed, which it follows to NY Route 211, where this section ends.

Access

Take the New York State Thruway to Exit 16 (Harriman). Take NY Route 17/future Interstate 86 west to Interstate 84 in Middletown. Take Interstate 84 west to exit 2, Mountain Road. Turn left on Mountain Road and continue a short distance to US Route 6. Turn right on Route 6 west, cross under Interstate 84 and turn right on Hathorn Boulevard.

Parking

0.00 Hathorn Boulevard and US Route 6 (limited parking). (18T 531563E 4580348N)
0.35 End of Lake Shore Drive. (Unlocated)
3.10 End of paved Shin Hollow Road. (18T 532117E 4583717N)

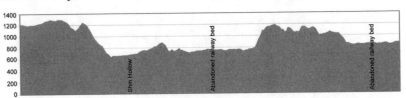

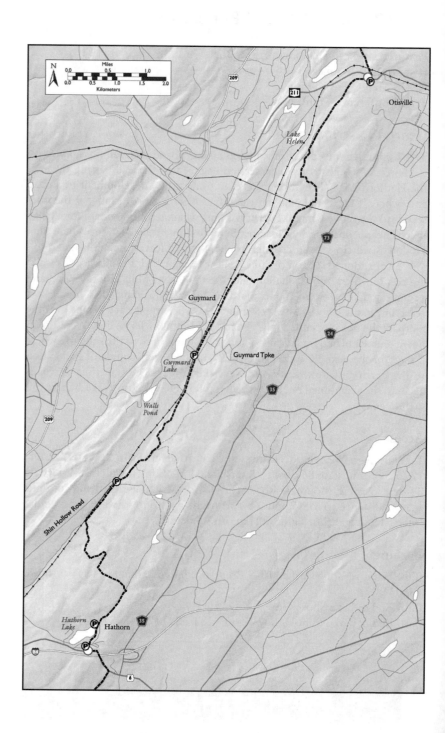

4.90 Guymard Turnpike and rail bridge. (Unlocated)
10.20 NY Route 211 and Otisville Road. (18T 537219E 4591738N)

Trail Description

0.00 The Shawangunk Ridge Trail turns right onto paved Hathorn Boulevard.

0.10 Hathorn Boulevard veers left, but the trail continues straight ahead along the eastern shore of the lake on Lake Shore Drive. On the right is Lookout Drive.

0.35 The trail reaches the end of the road, where there is a cul-de-sac. There is room to park several cars here. The trail heads into the woods on an old woods road. Near a house the trail turns left, passes some old cars and trucks, and continues north through the woods along the ridge. The trail is just to the right of a stream valley that separates the eastern and western sides of the ridge, and crosses several stone walls.

0.95 The trail turns left and crosses the stream valley, which is marshy in the springtime, then turns right and climbs up a small rock wall to the western side of the ridge. The trail continues to the west across the level ridgetop, where it begins to descend toward Shin Hollow.

1.25 The trail crosses a seasonal stream that comes in from the left and continues down. As it descends, the trail crosses the stream several times.

1.40 The trail crosses the stream for the last time, turns right and then begins to climb to the top of a knob that is west of the main ridge.

1.65 The trail reaches the top of the knob and then makes a sharp left. From the top of the knob there are seasonal views to the west. The trail then begins

Conrail tracks at Shin Hollow

JAKOB FRANKE

Hathorn Lake

a steep descent, heading back to the stream valley.

1.90 The trail reaches the stream valley and turns right to follow an old tote (logging) road. The trail continues to descend more gradually on the tote road.

2.15 To the left of the trail is open slab where there are 180-degree views across the valley. Occasional pitch pines just barely cling to the slab. From this vantage you can see south to Port Jervis and the Delaware River with Pennsylvania beyond, west across Shin Hollow directly below and northwest across the Neversink Valley toward the Sullivan County Catskills. Just past the view the trail turns left and leaves the tote road, which is overgrown with blueberries at this point, and continues to descend through a switchback. It then heads north, gradually descending off the ridge.

2.45 After passing through a grassy area, the trail emerges on the Port Jervis line of Conrail. This line still sees daily passenger service to Hoboken. The trail turns right and follows the service road of the railroad north. This service road was once the second track of this line. This is the bottom of Shin Hollow, with a parallel north-south ridge to the west. The trail passes a milepost that states "JC 82." This signifies that it is 82 miles to Jersey City, where the Erie

Railroad terminated prior to its merger with the Lackawanna in the early 1960s.
3.10 The trail turns right, leaves the rail bed and climbs the steep embankment where Shin Hollow Road crosses the rail line. Shin Hollow Road is paved across the tracks and leads back to Port Jervis. To the north, Shin Hollow Road is a woods road that is passable to jeeps heading to hunting camps along the ridge. The trail follows Shin Hollow Road north through the woods as it ascends.

3.60 A gravel road leads right uphill. The Long Path continues on Shin Hollow Road for another 150 feet, when it turns left into the woods and parallels Shin Hollow Road. After another 300 feet, the trail descends gradually on a faint old logging road. The trail turns right and parallels the ridge north.

3.95 The trail crosses a stream at the head of a beautiful waterfall. Above the waterfall, it is a nice place for lunch in a deep hemlock grove. The trail continues north through the hemlocks, gradually descending to just above the railroad tracks.

4.50 The trail crosses a stream above a second waterfall and continues north in the woods, just above the railroad tracks.

4.90 The trail crosses Guymard Turnpike near a bridge and follows the tracks just inside the woods. After about 0.1 miles, the trail descends into a hollow, which was formerly a passing track for heavy freight trains. After crossing the hollow, the trail climbs up to an abandoned rail bed and continues north along it.

5.30 To the right is a short gravel road that connects to Guymard Turnpike and was once the tunnel portal for the freight siding. The trail continues north along the original Erie Railroad Port Jervis line, which was the original route through Otisville Notch. When the Otisville Tunnel was constructed, a new line was constructed at a lower elevation and the original line, which the trail follows, was abandoned. The original line intersects the new line just south of the Guymard Turnpike bridge. The trail continues north along the rail bed, which is passable to passenger cars, and is lined with trees on both sides.

6.15 The trail turns right, passes through some hemlocks, and climbs steeply to the ridgetop, which it reaches in 0.25 miles. Once on the ridge, the trail turns north, crosses a small stream and passes through a white pine forest.

6.65 At the end of the white pine forest, the trail crosses an old road that led to a mountaintop quarry or mine. To the right, there are piles of rock along the edge of the road. The trail continues north along the ridgetop through the woods. After about 0.2 miles, the trail turns left toward the northwest and descends toward a knob that is the western extension to the ridge.

7.00 The trail reaches the top of the knob and turns right. There are views through the pitch pine across the Neversink Valley to the west. After a short distance, the trail turns right and heads along the ridge away from the knob. It then begins a gradual descent, crossing a woods road, passing through some white pines and then some hemlocks. The trail turns left, crosses a seasonal stream and ascends another knob, turns right and then heads north along the knob.

7.70 The trail passes through a grassy area, where from some rocks there is a view west across the Neversink Valley and northwest toward the Sullivan County Catskills. The trail continues north through the woods.

7.90 The trail emerges in the open where the Marcy–South power lines cross the ridge. There are views west across the Neversink Valley, northwest to the high peaks of the Catskills and north along the ridge. The Marcy–South power lines, which were controversial, were constructed recently to bring cheap hydroelectric power from Canada to the New York power grid. After passing under the power lines, the trail crosses a grassy area and descends sharply off the knob.

8.05 The trail crosses over several dry streambeds in a recently logged area, turns left and begins to descend off the ridge. As the trail descends, it goes up and down over several ridges before finally descending to the rail bed. Just before reaching the rail bed, the trail turns left and continues north through the woods.

8.85 The trail again reaches the abandoned rail bed and turns right. Shortly the Marcy–South power lines follow the rail bed north. Where the power lines intersect the rail bed, there are views across the Neversink Valley.

9.45 The Marcy–South power lines turn left and descend off the ridge. The trail continues along the rail bed as it continues north through the woods.

10.20 The rail bed reaches NY Route 211 in Otisville Notch, where this section ends. The trail turns left, crosses Route 211, and continues on Otisville Road (Orange County Route 61).

G3. NY Route 211 to Old NY Route 17

Feature: Basha Kill[12]
Distance: 9.25 miles
USGS Map Quads: Otisville, Yankee Lake, Wurtsboro
Trail Conference Maps: none

General Description

This section begins at the intersection of Orange County Route 61 (Otisville Road) and NY Route 211. It heads north on Route 61, descending below steep cliffs on the right. The road passes over the top of the western portal of the Otisville tunnel of the Conrail Port Jervis line, and after 1.6 miles it reaches Indian Orchard Road. The trail turns right on Indian Orchard Road, which becomes South Road when it enters Sullivan County, and in a few hundred yards it turns left into the woods and reaches the Basha Kill Rail Trail. The trail follows the abandoned "Kingston Line" of the New York, Ontario & Western (O&W) Railroad.

While the 5.5-mile walk along the Basha Kill is straight and level, it is a wonderful area, with many fine views across the Basha Kill–one of the largest wetlands in southern New York. In the springtime the Basha Kill fills with runoff from the nearby Catskills and Shawangunks to form a giant lake. At this time sections of the trail may be flooded. If this is the case, South Road, which parallels the Basha Kill Rail Trail nearby, can be followed to bypass flooded areas. In the summer the Basha Kill is a large wetland with many channels that are perfect for canoeing, and because it is a stop-off point on the Shawangunk migration routes, it is a splendid area for bird watching.

After leaving the Basha Kill the trail follows roads for about 2 miles through the Village of Wurtsboro en route to the Wurtsboro Ridge section.

Access

Take the New York State Thruway to Exit 16 (Harriman). Take NY Route 17/future Interstate 86 west 20 miles to Exit 120, NY Route 211. Take Route 211 west through Middletown and then west 11 miles to the Village of Otisville. In Otisville, take NY Route 211 west past the ridge crest to Otisville Road (Orange County Route 61), where this section begins. Alternatively, take Route 17 west 31 miles to Exit 113, US Route 209 south. Take US Route 209 south

---

[12] The Basha Kill is also variously spelled Basher Kill, Bashakill, and other variants of approximately the same pronunciation.

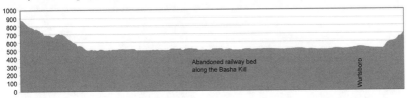

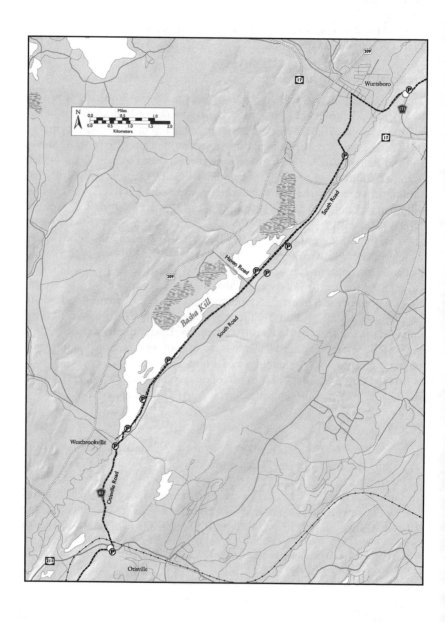

5 miles to Westbrookville. Turn left on Otisville Road and follow it for 3 miles to the intersection with Route 211, where the trail begins.

Parking

0.00 NY Route 211 and Otisville Road (limited). (18T 537237E 4591746N)
1.70 DEC parking area, Otisville Road and Indian Orchard Road. (18T 537384E 4594290N)
1.95 DEC parking area. (18T 537632E 4594639N)
2.45 DEC parking area. (18T 538019E 4595332N)
3.10 DEC boat launch parking area. (18T 538539E 4596224N)
5.10 Main Basha Kill parking lot. (18T 540869E 4598279N)
5.65 DEC parking area; side trail 0.1 miles to Basha Kill. (18T 541574E 4599031N)
6.00 Another DEC parking area; side trail 0.1 miles to Basha Kill. (18T 541876E 4599445N)
7.35 South Road, just to the right of the trail. (18T 542956E 4601268N)
9.25 Old Wurtsboro High Line O&W Rail Station. (18T 544473E 4602729N)

Trail Description

0.00 At the intersection of NY Route 211 and Otisville Road (Orange County Route 61) the Shawangunk Ridge Trail crosses Route 211, and follows Otisville Road, descending below steep cliffs on the right. The trail passes over the top of the western portal of the former Erie Railroad's Otisville Tunnel. This line is still used daily for both passenger and freight service.

1.60 The trail turns right on Indian Orchard Road, which will become South Road in Sullivan County, and passes a parking and fishing area on the left side of the road.

1.75 The trail turns left into the woods just past the parking area, and reaches the Basha Kill Rail Trail in about 0.1 miles.

1.85 The trail turns right on the Basha Kill Rail Trail. The rail-trail is the remnants of the Port Jervis to Kingston branch of the New York, Ontario & Western Railroad (O&W). Built in direct competition to the D&H Canal, which was on the western side of the Basha Kill, it was abandoned when the O&W went bankrupt in the early 1950s. The trail is unmarked except for occasional Long Path Aqua blazes or Long Path discs. There are also a few yellow DEC discs. The Basha Kill Wildlife Management Area is a huge wetland in the floodplain of the Basha Kill stream. The walk along the Basha Kill is a beautiful one. While the trail is level, there is much to see along the way. There are views across the Basha Kill toward the Catskills and east to the Shawangunks. The Basha Kill is home to many migratory birds and there are bird-feeding stations along the way. One can put down a canoe in one of the many channels for a lazy trip through the wetland, or to find a location to fish. In the springtime, the Basha Kill fills up with the runoff from the mountains and becomes a large, shallow lake. In the summer, it is a green wetland, a rich home to aquatic life.

1.95 The trail passes a DEC parking area on the right.

2.45 The trail reaches another larger DEC parking area across a bridge to the right. To the left are several short nature trails that lead to a point in the Basha Kill. The trail continues ahead. It passes a house on the right, and then passes another nature trail that heads left. The trail crosses a small bridge where there are views across the Basha Kill. Beyond here, the trail passes through a white birch forest.

3.10 The trail crosses a large parking area with a boat-launching site to the left. From here one can launch a canoe or other nonmotorized boat in a side channel of the Basha Kill. From the side channel there are many interesting routes to either canoe or fish. The trail continues ahead along the edge of the Basha Kill. In this section there are many views across the open expanse of water and marshlands, as well as many bird feeding stations on the Basha Kill, making it a good area for bird-watching.

4.85 The trail crosses Haven Road. Haven Road crosses the Basha Kill on a causeway and is the only road crossing along the Basha Kill Wildlife Management Area. You will see many people fishing along the causeway. The trail continues straight ahead on the rail bed, which for this section is a gravel road that leads to the main parking area in the Basha Kill.

5.10 Reach the main parking area. The trail passes through a gate and reverts to the abandoned rail bed.

5.50 A nature trail leads left 0.1 miles to a raised platform with a spectacular view across the Basha Kill and the mountains beyond. Along this nature trail, markers identify the different trees along the way. Near the platform are several signboards that show pictures of various flora and fauna found at this location. Unfortunately, they have been vandalized.

Basha Kill railway bed

JAKOB FRANKE

Basha Kill railway bed

5.60 The trail passes the north end of the nature trail. In another 300 feet, a side trail leads right 0.1 miles to a parking area.

6.00 The trail passes another side trail that leads 0.1 miles to a parking lot.

6.30 The trail passes a resort (Paradise II) on the right along South Road. There are views to the Shawangunks from here. Beyond this point, the Basha Kill changes from open marshland to a stream with multiple channels that run through the forest. The trail crosses some of these channels on a series of bridges.

6.80 The trail crosses under NY Route 17 (Quickway) in a culvert and continues north.

7.35 The abandoned rail bed turns into a dead-end street with houses on both sides. The Shawangunk Ridge Trail turns left off the rail-trail onto South Road. South Road becomes Pennsylvania Avenue, which the trail follows into the Village of Wurtsboro. On the left is the Mamakating Little League Field, a charming small-town baseball stadium.

8.30 The trail turns right on Sullivan Street in Wurtsboro by the firehouse. To the left is the Village of Wurtsboro, with several stores and restaurants in this section. Sullivan Street was part of the original NY Route 17 before the Quickway was constructed.

8.70 On the right is the Wurtsboro train station on the Port Jervis–Kingston O&W branch. The train station is now a private house and the owner has turned it into a private O&W museum, complete with old signs, a caboose and other railroad memorabilia. The trail continues uphill on Old Route 17 (Sullivan County Route 171).

9.25 The trail turns left here. The trail reaches the abandoned O&W High Line right-of-way, where this section ends.

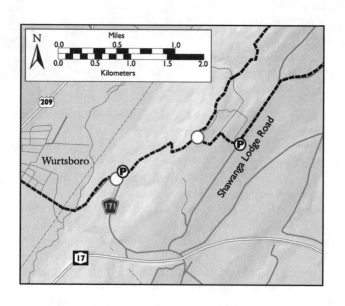

G4. Old NY Route 17 to Long Path

Feature: Wurtsboro Ridge
Distance: 1.00 mile
USGS Map Quads: Wurtsboro
Trail Conference Maps: Map 9, Southern Shawangunk Trails

General Description

Upon leaving Old Route 17, the Shawangunk Ridge Trail quickly gains the ridgetop. From there it follows the ridgetop to its intersection with the Long Path. This ridgetop trail section is one of the most dramatic in southern New York, with many spectacular views in all directions. With the forest primarily scrub oak, blueberry and occasional pitch pine; the hiker is frequently above the trees with unlimited visibility. There are also sections of Shawangunk slab, though not as frequently as found in the northern Shawangunks.

Access

Take the New York State Thruway to Exit 16 (Harriman). Take NY Route 17 (the Quickway) west 29 miles to Exit 114, Highview. Turn left at the end of the exit ramp onto Old Route 17 (Sullivan County Route 171) and go down the hill 0.7 miles. As the road makes a hairpin turn to the left, there is a turn right on a gravel road to the old Wurtsboro High Line O&W Rail Station (now a VFW post) where there is parking, and where a white trail leads in about 0.1 miles to the Long Path.

Parking

0.00 Old Wurtsboro High Line O&W Rail Station. (18T 544459E 4602949N)
4.05 Ferguson Road (still called Roosa Gap Summitville Road on most maps, 0.7 miles west of the ridgetop (Shawanga Lodge Road). (18T 547142E 4606751N)

Camping

Camping on DEC land.

Trail Description

0.00 The Shawangunk Ridge Trail turns left off Old Route 17 just east of a gravel road that leads to the old Wurtsboro High Line O&W Rail Station. This section of trail is on the New York State DEC Wurtsboro Ridge Parcels and is thus marked with blue DEC discs. The trail turns onto a piece of the abandoned New York, Ontario & Western Railroad and then immediately turns right into the woods. Across Old Route 17 from this turn is an abandoned bridge abutment. Following the rail bed in the opposite direction leads to the abandoned Highview Tunnel in about half a mile. This was the main line of the New York, Ontario & Western Railroad, which was the major travel route to the Catskills in the heyday of the Sullivan County resorts. One of the first railroads to fall upon hard times, it was abandoned in the 1950s. The trail goes north in the woods, paralleling the rail bed as it gradually climbs up toward the ridgetop.

0.10 A white-blazed side trail leads to the VFW post.

0.20 Past a stream crossing, the trail switches right and then left to gain the top of the ridge. As the trail approaches the ridgetop, the trail steepens and the forest cover begins to thin. At the higher elevations the forest is predominantly scrub oak and blueberry. As the trail reaches this dwarf forest, views begin to open up.

1.00 The trail reaches the top of the ridge, turns north and comes to a section of rock slab where there are spectacular views up and down the ridge. This is the junction with the Long Path. To the south you can see the Basha Kill Wildlife Management Area. This is an excellent area to watch migratory birds. To the west you can see the Village of Wurtsboro below, with NY Route 17 in the distance crossing the mountains to the west. Just to the north you can see Wurtsboro Airport, where it is common to see airplanes towing gliders aloft to float above the updrafts created by the ridge. To the far north the Catskill Mountains can be seen. Beyond this vantage point, the trail follows the western slopes of the ridge. Unlike the northern Shawangunks, where the most interesting topography is in the east, the southern Shawangunks are much more interesting on the western side. Development reaches high up on the ridge on the east side, as witnessed by the gravel road that is just east of our vantage point. This gravel road is part of a failed subdivision that would have resulted in houses being built on the mountaintop; before that could happen, however, the owner went bankrupt and the state purchased the land. Going north follow the directions in Section 11 along the Shawangunk Ridge, which brings you in 3.05 miles to Ferguson Road. To continue southeast into Orange County, turn right on the Long Path, and you will reach Shawanga Lodge Road after 0.5 miles following the description in Section 10.

Backpacking the Long Path

By Ed Walsh

Afoot and light-hearted I take to the open road,
Healthy, free, the world before me,
The long brown path before me leading wherever I choose.

—Walt Whitman

This guide is written to assist hikers who wish to hike the Long Path from end to end in a single trip. It may also be useful to anyone planning a shorter backpack on the Long Path.

Until recently it was almost impossible to hike the Long Path in a single trip, although a few intrepid backpackers have done it. The stretches of private property crossed by the trail and the long road walks necessitated by the closing of sections of the trail, made a continuous trip a major undertaking. However, the opening of the Shawangunk Ridge Trail (SRT) and the co-alignment of the Long Path with the Appalachian Trail to reach the SRT have made such a trip feasible.

It is now possible to backpack the entire length of the trail, but it still requires quite a bit of planning. It is not possible to camp out along the trail for its entire length. Some nights it will be necessary to hike to a motel or a nearby campground.

This section will tell you which sections of the trail are open for camping and will list facilities nearby where overnight camping or other accommodations are available for those sections where camping is not allowed. Just because a motel or campground is listed in this booklet does not guarantee its quality. The accommodations were chosen based solely on their distance from the trail. It is hoped that hikers will send reports on the facilities listed and these will be included in future editions of this guide. No reference is made to suggested tent sites where overnight camping is allowed. It is up to the hiker to find these on their own. Clearly a backpacker on the Long Path should have experience in map reading and a good "woods sense".

This booklet does not give instructions on how to backpack. It is presumed that a hiker attempting to thru hike this trail in a single trip has some backpacking experience. However, due to its proximity to major population centers, the southern section is a good place to hone your backpacking skills.

Camping

Lean-tos or shelters located on the Long Path are three sided, open front structures with wood floors. They are usually buggy and almost all have resident mouse populations. In the Catskills, porcupines are a serious nuisance. They love anything salty, so hang your boots as well as your food. The Catskills and New Jersey are also home to black bears. Although bears are usually not a problem, you should know how to protect your food supply. The shelters are all first come, first served up to capacity, usually 6 to 8 people. Groups of three or more should not use the shelters unless there is remaining room left in the late afternoon. They should be ready to make room for through hikers arriving late. Except for the Appalachian Trail section and the Catskills, shelters or lean-tos are rare. A tent is a necessity for backpacking this trail.

Although the Long Path passes through many State parks in its southern section, overnight camping is restricted to Harriman State Park and there only within 100 yards of a lean-to.

Camping is allowed on State land in the Catskill Forest Preserve and in State Reforestation Areas as long as your campsite is 150 feet from any trail, road or water and below 3500 feet in elevation. Camping for more than three days in the same place requires a permit, as does camping with a group of ten or more. Permits can be obtained from the DEC. Only dead and down wood may be used for a campfire. A backpacking stove is highly recommended.

Overnight camping is not allowed on private property traversed by the Long Path. Permission to hike on these parcels was granted only after negotiations with the landowner. Please remember that you are a guest there. Do not do anything that might jeopardize these agreements. Campfires, horses, mountain bikes and motor vehicles are not allowed on private property crossed by the Long Path. Most of the private property is closed during big game hunting season. Some of this land is open for hunting, which usually extends from the Monday before Thanksgiving until the second week in December. For specific dates, write to the New York State Department of Environmental Conservation, Division of Fish and Game, State Campus, Albany, New York, 12226. The Trail Conference also maintains its own list of hunting seasons for areas under it's purvey. See http://www.nynjtc.org/trails/hunting for more information. For your own safety do not hike on these sections during the hunting season.

Post Offices

The Long Path passes by or near 21 Post Offices. A list appears in the back of this chapter. Many long distance backpackers arrange a series of mail drops along the way by mailing food or supplies to themselves. This helps to lighten their load and allows the hiker to purchase his food in bulk and save money. The package should be addressed to the hiker c/o General Delivery with the words, "Hold for Hiker Arriving on or about..." on the package. Post Offices are not obligated to hold these packages for more than 30 days, so if you are planning a long trip it will be useful to prepare these food drops ahead of time and have a friend or family member mail them to you as you hike. It's a good idea not to seal these packages until they are ready to mail. Hikers usually find that they have packed too much food (or not enough) or have forgotten to include some useful piece of equipment. The Post Offices are usually open Monday through Friday from 8:00 AM to 5:00 PM and on Saturdays from 8:00 AM to noon.

How to Use This Guide

The sections listed here correspond to the sections in the Long Path Guide. The distances given are south to north. If camping is not allowed on a section that cannot be reasonably hiked in a day, directions are given to the nearest public accommodation (campground or motel).

Section 1

George Washington Bridge to US Route 9W at Lamont-Doherty

Lean-tos	None
Camping	None
Lodging	There are many hotels in Fort Lee; the closest to the Long Path is the Tollgate Motel (201-944-5332) located directly across the street from the beginning of the trail. Of course, New York City is just across the bridge.
Food	There are many restaurants and stores located in Fort Lee. The gas station at mile 1.15 offers Dunkin Donuts, vending machines, telephones, water and restrooms.
Post Office	None

Section 2

US Route 9W at Lamont-Doherty to Nyack (Mountainview Avenue)

Lean-tos	None
Camping	None
Lodging	Both of these motels are expensive >$95 per night Super 8 Motel 845-353-3880. located right on the trail before it crosses NY Route 59 Best Western Motel 845-358-8100. 0.50 miles east on Route 59
Food	The village of Piermont has restaurants and delis. At the intersection of Route 59 is a convenience store, a McDonald's and a Kentucky Fried Chicken Restaurant. 0.75 miles east on Route 59 is the village of Nyack with many restaurants and food shops. 0.30 miles west on Route 59 is a pizza shop and laundromat 0.80 miles west on Route 59 is a Grand Union supermarket, pharmacy, and restaurant.

Post Office Palisades 10964 - mile 0.90 continue straight on Washington Spring Road across 9W for 0.10 miles. Piermont 10968 - mile 3.15 after crossing the Sparkill Creek, turn west onto Piermont Avenue for 20 yards.

Section 3

Nyack (Mountainview Avenue) to Long Clove (US Route 9W)

Lean-tos   None

Camping   None. Although the Long Path traverses much State land in this section, camping is not allowed. Ed & Eudora Walsh (845-429-8550) will allow through hikers to camp in their backyard if prior arrangements are made. Bus service to and from the trail is available for most of this section.

Lodging   Raintree Motel 845-268-5600. At mile 5.50, Landing Hill Road, turn left for 0.20 miles past the firehouse, then right for 1.00 miles to US Route 9W. The motel is across the street on the left. Holiday Court Motel 845-268-3300. At mile 5.50, Landing Hill Road, turn left for 0.20 miles past the firehouse, then right for 1.00 miles to Route 9W. The motel is 0.20 miles north (right) on 9W. Green Inn Motel on the Lake 845-268-6836. At mile 5.50, Landing Hill Road, turn left for 0.20 miles past the firehouse, then right for 1.00 miles to Route 9W. The motel is 0.10 mile farther north on Route 9W.

Food   There are restaurants both north and south on US Route 9W from the intersection with the park road at Rockland Lake. From the northern end of this section there is a restaurant, bakery and laundromat 1 mile south on NY Route 303.

Post Office None

Section 4

Long Clove to Mount Ivy

Lean-tos   None

Camping   None. Although the Long Path traverses much State land in this section, camping is not allowed. Ed & Eudora Walsh (845-429-8550) will allow through hikers to camp in their backyard if prior arrangements are made. Bus service to and from the trail is available for most of this section.

Lodging   Rockland Motel 845-354-1373. 1.30 miles south on US Route 202 (mile 6.80) in Mount Ivy.

Food   From the southern end of this section there is a restaurant, bakery and laundromat 1 mile south on Route 303. South Mountain Road, mile 1.00, turn left west, 0.25 miles is a deli.

US Route 202, mile 6.80, right (north) onto Route 202 is a deli, restaurant, pizzeria, bank and laundromat. 0.50 miles left on 202 is a large shopping plaza with a supermarket, pharmacy, bank, laundromat and restaurants.

Post Office Mile 6.80 turn left (south) onto US Route 202 for 0.90 miles.

Section 5

Mount Ivy to Lake Skannatati

Lean-tos   Big Hill Shelter mile 5.60 Water is available at stream crossing 1.10 miles south on LP or follow LP to AT&T right of way, turn left and follow for 1 mile to Breakneck Pond.

Camping   In Harriman State Park camping is only allowed within 100 yards of a shelter.

Lodging   Rockland Motel 845-354-1373. 1.30 miles south on US Route 202 (mile 0.00) in Mount Ivy

Food   Route 202, mile 0.00, right (north) onto US Route 202 is a deli, restaurant, pizzeria, bank and laundromat. 0.50 miles left on 202 is a large shopping plaza with a supermarket, pharmacy, bank, laundromat and restaurants.

Post Office Pomona 10970 mile 0.20 continue on US Route 202 for 0.90 miles

Section 6

Lake Skannatati to intersection with the Appalachian Trail

Lean-tos   Cohasset Shelter mile 4.45. 0.85 miles past the intersection with the Appalachian Trail, north on the original Long Path. Shelter is made of corrugated metal, no water. Note that this shelter is primarily for the use of a girl's camp. Be prepared to vacate if they request to use it. (To continue on the suggested route the hiker must backtrack to the intersection of the AT). Distance from Big Hill Shelter – 8.15 miles. Fingerboard Shelter mile 1.50 north on the Appalachian Trail (please note that the LP follows the Appalachian Trail south here. To continue on the suggested route the hiker must backtrack 1.50 miles). Water 0.50 miles on blue blazed side trail at Lake Tiorati. Distance from Big Hill Shelter—8.80 miles.

Camping   In Harriman State Park camping is allowed only within 100 yards of a shelter.

Lodging   None

Food   None

Post Office None

LP/AT Section

Harriman Park to High Point State Park

Lean-tos   Wildcat Shelter. Water from a hand pump Distance from Cohasset Shelter–13.65 miles. Wawayanda Shelter mile 27.90. 0.10 miles from the AT on blue-blazed side trail. Water available at park headquarters, 0.40 miles from the shelter on another blue blazed trail. Distance from Wildcat Shelter–12.10 miles. Pochuck Mountain Shelter mile 44.80. 0.10 miles from the AT on a blue blazed side trail. Water may be available from a stream south of Route 565. Distance from Wawayanda Shelter–13.10 miles. High Point Shelter mile 52.20. 0.10 miles from the AT on a blue blazed side trail. Water available from streams near the shelter. Distance from Pochuck Mountain Shelter–12.60 miles.

Camping   Mile 14.90. Three tent sites, fire ring and hand pump (during summer only). Distance from Fingerboard Shelter–14.90 miles.

Lodging   Tuxedo Motel 845-351-4747. 2.10 miles east on Route 17. Breezy Point 2.00 miles east on Route 17A. Willowbrook Inn Bed and Breakfast 0.80 miles west on Warwick Turnpike. Appalachian Motel. 1.80 miles east on NJ Route 94 in Vernon, NJ. Hostel. St. Thomas Episcopal Church in Vernon NJ. Apple Valley Inn 973-764-3735. 1.10 miles west on Sussex County 517 in Glenwood, NJ Reservations requested at least one day in advance. Backtrack Inn. 0.40 miles west on Lott Road in Unionville, NJ. Hostel with bunk space for 4 people. High Point Country Inn 973-702-1860. 1.40 miles east on NJ Route 23.

Food   Red Apple Rest, 2.10 miles south on Route 17. West Mombasha Road, 0.60 miles west is a deli. NY 17A, west 1.60 miles is a deli. East 2.00 miles to Greenwood Lake with a supermarket, deli, restaurants and pizza. Long House Road, 0.70 miles west is a small market and pizzeria. Warwick Turnpike, 0.20 miles east is a farm market. 1.50 miles east is a restaurant. Barrett Road, 1.80 miles west is a deli. NJ Route 94, 0.10 miles west is a farm stand. 2.40 miles east is Vernon, NJ with supermarkets, restaurants, delis, and a laundromat. County Route 517, 1.10 miles west in Glenwood is a farm market and deli. NJ Route 284, west 0.40 miles is a small grocery store. Lott Road, 0.40 miles west in Unionville is a grocery store, restaurant and pizza. High Point State Park, 0.60 miles from the park office is a swimming area and snack bar

Post Office   Arden, NY 10910 - 0.70 miles west on Route 17 Southfields, NY 10975 - 2.10 miles east on Route 17 Bellvale, NY 10912 - 1.60 miles west on Route 17A, inside general store Greenwood

Lake, NY 10925 - 2.00 miles east on Route 17A New Milford, NY 10959- 1.80 miles west inside store Vernon, NJ 07462 - 2.40 miles east on Route 94 Glenwood, NJ 07418 - 1.10 miles west on Route 517 Unionville, NY 10988 - 0.40 miles west on Lott Road

Shawangunk Ridge Trail

The Shawangunk Ridge Trail, which is part of the Long Path, begins at the High Point Monument. 0.50 miles from the High Point Shelter turn right, north on a blue-blazed side trail which leads to the monument. Cross the parking lot and follow the Cedar Swamp Trail north. 1.50 miles from the Appalachian Trail, the Long Path leaves the Cedar Swamp Trail and turns left paralleling the eastern edge of Cedar Swamp on a woods road. The Aqua blazes of the Long Path begin here.

Section G1

High Point State Park to US Route 6 and Hathorn Boulevard

Lean-tos	None
Camping	No overnight camping is allowed in this section
Lodging	High Point Motor Lodge 201-702-1860. 1.40 miles east on NJ Route 23
Food	None
Post Office	None

Section G2

Route 6 and Hathorn Boulevard to Route 211 and Otisville Road

Lean-tos	None
Camping	American Family Campground, Guymard Turnpike, Godeffroy, NY. 845-754-8388. Hot showers, pool, cabins, laundry. April 15 to October 15. At mile 4.90 turn left on Guymard Turnpike and cross the bridge. 1.80 miles west on the Guymard Turn pike, on the left. Caters mainly to RV's. Distance from High Point Shelter–16.70 miles. Otisville Campground, 1 Grange Rd., Otisville, NY 10963 845-386-5104 hot showers, laundry. Turn right onto Route 211 for 1 mile to Highland Ave. (County Route11) Follow Route 11 1.4 miles to Grange Rd. Turn left. Owner will shuttle hikers to and from the trail. Distance from American Family Campground–7.10 miles.
Lodging	None
Food	Otisville 1 mile right on Route 211. General store, pizza.
Post Office	Otisville 10963 - 1 mile right, on Route 211

Section G3

Route 211 and Otisville Rd. to Old Route 17 and O&W right of way

Lean-tos   None

Camping   Otisville Campground, Grange Rd., Otisville, NY. 2.50 miles
               from the trail on Grange Road, off Mt. Hope Road (County
               Route 11) southeast of Otisville. Distance from American
               Family Campground – 7.10 miles

Lodging   Valley Brook Motor Inn, 201 Kingston Ave (US Route 209),
               Wurtsboro, NY 12790, 845-888-0330

Food   Otisville 1 mile right on Route 211. General store, pizza.
               Wurtsboro, mile 9.00, supermarket, restaurants, deli.

Post Office   Otisville 10963 - 1 mile right, on Route 211. Wurtsboro 12790
               - mile 9.30, on the trail

The town of Wurtsboro is a good place for a layover day. A motel, restaurants, supermarkets, and pharmacy are all within walking distance. You can
also rent a glider at the nearby airport. If you have run short of equipment
or more specialized supplies, you can restock at the Catskill Hiking Shack,
259 Sullivan St in Wurtsboro.

Section G4

Old Route 17 and O&W right of way to Long Path

Lean-tos   None

Camping   Berentsen's Campground, RR 2 Box 63C, Bloomingburg, NY
               845-733-4984. May 1 to October 15.Hot showers, cabins,
               toilets. $10 per night. Mile 1.00, turn right for 0.50 miles to
               Shawanga Lodge Rd. Turn left for 0.65 miles to Crane Road.
               Turn right for 0.70 miles to Roosa Gap Rd. Turn right for 1
               mile.

Lodging   None

Food   None

Post Office   None

Section 11

Shawangunk Ridge Trail to Sam's Point Preserve

Lean-tos   None

Camping   Berentsen's Campground, RR 2 Box 63C, Bloomingburg, NY
               845-733-4984. May 1 to October 15. Hot showers, cabins,
               toilets. $10 per night. Mile 1.00, turn right for 0.50 miles to
               Shawanga Lodge Rd. Turn left for 0.65 miles to Crane Road.
               Turn right for 0.70 miles to Roosa Gap Rd. Turn right for 1

mile. Mile 5.60, the trail enters the DEC Roosa Gap parcel of the Forest Preserve. Camping is allowed 150 feet away from water or trails. No water.

Lodging   None
Food   None
Post Office Cragsmoor

Section 12

Sam's Point Preserve to Jenny Lane

Lean-tos   None
Camping   None
Lodging   None
Food   None
Post Office Cragsmoor

Section 13

Jenny Lane to Riggsville

Lean-tos   None
Camping   Camping is permitted on State land at the end of this section.
Lodging   Chelsea Motel 845-626-3551 or 5152. At mile 3.40 continue on US Route 44/55 for 0.40 miles. Motel is on the left. Distance from Roosa Gap –23.95 miles. Continental Motel 845-626-4000. At mile 3.40 continue on Route 44/55 for 0.50 miles. Motel is on the right.
Food   JJ's Place, My Little Ranch, F&J Mountain View Diner at the intersection of US Route 209, also a pharmacy and laundromat
Post Office Kerhonkson 12446–mile 3.90, on the right just before the steel bridge.

Section 14

Riggsville to Bull Run

Lean-tos   None
Camping   Camping is permitted on State land at elevations below 3500 feet and at least 150 feet from water or trails. Water is available at Vernooy Falls, mile 1.70, intermittently along the trail and at Sundown. Distance from Kerhonkson motels to State land – 9.80 miles. Sundown primitive campsite is at the junction of Peekamoose Road at mile 9.65. No facilities. Water available from Rondout Creek.

Lodging	None
Food	None
Post Office	None

Section 15

Bull Run to Denning Road

Lean-tos	Bouton Memorial lean-to - mile 5.20, 0.20 miles on a side trail. Water from a spring on the LP. Distance from Sundown – 5.20 miles
Camping	Camping is permitted on State land at elevations below 3500 feet and at least 150 feet from water or trails.
Lodging	None
Food	None
Post Office	None

Section 16

Denning Road to Woodland Valley

Lean-tos	Terrace Mountain lean-to - mile 8.60, 0.90 miles on a side trail. Water available. Distance from Bouton lean-to – 11 miles
Camping	Woodland Valley State Campground 845-688-7647. Mile 11.20, May 15 - October 12, showers, flush toilets, $9.00. Distance from Terrace Mountain – 2.60 miles. Camping is permitted on State land at elevations below 3500 feet and at least 150 feet from water or trails. There are designated campsites between Slide and Cornell Mountains.
Lodging	None
Food	None
Post Office	None

Section 17

Woodland Valley to Phoenicia

Lean-tos	None
Camping	Woodland Valley State Campground. Mile 0.00, $9.00. Distance from Terrace Mountain – 2.60 miles. Camping is permitted on State land at elevations below 3500 feet and at least 150 feet from water or trails.
Lodging	Phoenicia Inn 845-688-7500. Mile 5.75, turn left on Main Street in Phoenicia. The Inn is about 75 yards on the right. Cobblestone Motel 845-688-7871. Turn left onto Main Street

in Phoenicia. In 0.10 miles turn right on Route 214. The motel is 0.20 miles on the right.

Food	There is a grocery store, restaurants and pharmacy in Phoenicia. Brio's Restaurant is highly recommended.
Post Office	Phoenicia 12464 – At the intersection with Main Street, continue straight ahead for about 75 yards. The Post Office is on the right.

Phoenicia is a good town for a layover day. Besides resupply, you can spend the day fishing or tubing on the Esopus.

Section 18

Phoenicia to Silver Hollow Notch

Lean-tos	Baldwin Memorial lean-to - Mile 3.20. Pipe spring, 50' to left of trail. Distance from Woodland Valley – 8.95 miles. Tremper Mountain lean-to. No water. Mile 4.00 Distance from Baldwin lean-to - 0.80 miles.
Camping	Camping is permitted on State land at elevations below 3500 feet and at least 150 feet from water or trails.
Lodging	Phoenicia Inn 845-688-7500. Turn left on Main Street in Phoenicia. The Inn is about 75 yards on the right. Cobblestone Motel 845-688-7871. Turn left onto Main Street in Phoenicia. In 0.10 miles turn right on Route 214. The motel is 0.20 miles on the right.
Food	There is a grocery store, restaurants, and pharmacy in Phoenicia.
Post Office	Phoenicia 12464 - At the intersection with Main Street continue straight ahead for about 75 yards. The Post Office is on the right.

Section 19

Silver Hollow Notch to Platte Clove Road

Lean-tos	Mink Hollow lean-to - Mile 4.40. Distance from Tremper lean-to - 11.20 miles
Camping	Camping is permitted on State land at elevations below 3500 feet and at least 150 feet from water or trails.
Lodging	None
Food	None
Post Office	None

Section 20

Platte Clove Road to Palenville

Lean-tos   None

Camping   Camping is permitted on State land at elevations below 3500 feet and at least 150 feet from water or trails.

Lodging   Arlington House Bed and Breakfast. Mile 10.00, continue on Route 23A for 0.30 miles. Palenville House Bed and Breakfast 518-678-5649. Mile 10.00 continue on NY Route 23A for 0.40 miles, $60. Waterfall Motel 518-678-9306. Mile 10.00 continue on Route 23A for 0.40 miles, then turn right on NY Route 32A for 0.5 miles. Catskill Mountain Lodge 518-678-3101. Mile 10.00 continue on Route 23A for 0.40 miles, then turn right on Route 32A for 1 mile. Motel and restaurant

Food   Mile 10.00 - continue 0.20 miles to Palenville, which has a deli, and a general store with Coleman fuel available.

Post Office Palenville 12463 - Mile 10.00 continue on Route 23A for 0.30 miles.

Section 21

Palenville to North Lake

Lean-tos   None

Camping   North Lake State Campground 518-589-5058. Mile 4.80. 219 sites, showers, swimming $16 reservations recommended. Distance from Mink Hollow – 24.90 miles. Camping is permitted on State land at elevations below 3500 feet and at least 150 feet from water or trails.

Lodging   Arlington House Bed and Breakfast. Mile 0.0, continue on Route 23A for 0.30 miles. Palenville House Bed and Breakfast 518-678-5649. Mile 0.00. Continue on Route 23A for 0.40 miles, $60. Waterfall Motel 518-678-9306. Mile 0.00 continue on Route 23A for 0.40 miles, then turn right on Route 32A for 0.5 miles. Catskill Mountain Lodge 518-678-3101. Mile 0.00 continue on Route 23A for 0.40 miles, then turn right on Route 32A for 1 mile. Motel and restaurant

Food   Mile 0.00. Continue 0.20 miles to Palenville, which has a deli, and a general store with Coleman fuel available.

Post Office Palenville 12463

Section 22

North Lake to Batavia Kill

Lean-tos	Batavia Kill lean-to. Mile 9.80, 0.25 miles on a side trail. Water available from stream. Distance from North Lake – 10.05 miles
Camping	North Lake State Campground. Mile 0.00. 219 sites, showers, swimming $16 reservations recommended. Camping is permitted on State land at elevations below 3500 feet and at least 150 feet from water or trails.
Lodging	None
Food	None
Post Office	None

Section 23

Batavia Kill to Route 23

Lean-tos	Batavia Kill lean-to. Mile 0.00, 0.25 miles on a side trail. Water available from stream. Elm Ridge lean-to. Mile 7.40, water from a pipe spring 0.1 miles south. Distance from Batavia Kill – 7.40 miles
Camping	Camping is permitted on State land at elevations below 3500 feet and at least 150 feet from water or trails.
Lodging	Kopper Kettle Inn and Restaurant 518-734-3575. 2.50 miles west on NY Route 23. Hamilton Motel 518-734-3190. 2.80 miles west on Route 23.
Food	Kopper Kettle. 2.50 miles west on NY Route 23. Village of Windham, 3.60 miles west on Route 23 has restaurants, delis and a small grocery.
Post Office	Windham 12496 – 3.90 miles west on NY Route 23

CAUTION: Water is scarce throughout the next 3 sections especially during the summer months.

Section 24

Route 23 to Greene County Route 10

Lean-tos	None
Camping	Camping is permitted on State land at elevations below 3500 feet and at least 150 feet from water or trails. Only the first 0.75 miles of the LP in this section is on State land. The rest of the trail is on private property and camping is not permitted.
Lodging	Kopper Kettle Inn and Restaurant 518-734-3575. 2.50 miles west on Route 23. Hamilton Motel 518-734-3190. 2.80 miles west on Route 23
Food	Kopper Kettle. 2.50 miles west on Route 23. Village of

Windham, 3.60 miles west on Route 23 has restaurants, delis and a small grocery.

Post Office Windham 12496 – 3.90 miles west on Route 23

Section 25

Greene County Route 10 to Greene County Route 32C

Lean-tos   None

Camping   The first 0.55 mile are on private land, camping is not allowed. The remainder of this section is in a State Reforestation Area. Camping is permitted on State land at elevations below 3500 feet and at least 150 feet from water or trails. Distance between State lands – 10.10 miles

Lodging   None

Food   None

Post Office None

Section 26

Greene County Route 32C to West Conesville

Lean-tos   Huntersfield lean-to. Mile 4.40, south on a spur trail. No water at lean-to. Distance from Elm Ridge lean-to – 16.90 miles

Camping   Camping is permitted only on State lands in this section. Watch for signs indicating private property.

Lodging   None

Food   Waterfall House Restaurant. Mile 12.60 at the intersection of Prattsville Road and NY Route 990V.

Post Office None

Section 27

West Conesville to Doney Hollow

Lean-tos   None

Camping   Nickerson Park Campground 607-588-7327. Mile 3.30, hot showers (coin operated), pool, laundry & store. $15. Distance from Huntersfield lean-to – 11.50 miles. Max V. Shaul State Campground 518-827-4711. Mile 8.75, 6.70 miles north on NY Route 30 from the intersection with West Kill Road. 32 sites, hot showers, flush toilets. Open mid-May through mid-October. $13

Lodging   None

Food   Waterfall House Restaurant. Mile 0.00 at the intersection of

Prattsville Road and NY Route 990V. The Blenheim House Restaurant. Mile 8.40 on left side of NY Route 30 after bridge over the West Kill.

Post Office Gilboa 12076 - Mile 1.50 on the trail. North Blenheim 12131 - Mile 8.40, on the trail opposite West Kill Road.

Section 28

Doney Hollow to West Fulton

Lean-tos Rossman Hill. Mile 5.85, water 100 yards in front of the lean-to from a well, may be dry in summer, fill up at streams before lean-to. Distance from Nickerson's – 13.25 miles

Camping Camping is allowed throughout the Eminence State Forest. Watch for private property signs toward the end of this section near West Fulton. Distance to State land from Nickerson's – 7.10 miles. Max V. Shaul State Campground 518-827-4711. Mile 8.40, 4.00 miles to the right on West Fulton Road and another 0.20 miles north on NY Route 30. Water is readily available throughout this section. The streams at mile 4.10 and 4.55 and the well at mile 5.80 may be dry in summer.

Lodging None

Food None

Post Office West Fulton 12194 - Mile 8.70, turn right onto West Fulton Road for 0.20 miles.

Section 29

West Fulton to Middleburgh

Lean-tos None

Camping Camping is allowed in the State Reforestation Areas, 150 feet from trails or water. There is private property at the beginning and the end of this section. Max V. Shaul State Campground 518-827-4711. Mile 0.00, 4.00 miles to the right on West Fulton Road and another 0.20 miles north on NY Route 30. It can also be reached by heading south on NY Route 30 for 3.00 miles from the intersection with Hardscrabble Road, mile 7.65. 32 sites, hot showers, flush toilets. Open mid-May through mid-October. $13

Lodging On Hardscrabble Rd, cabin for rent by backpackers—stove, refrigerator, shower, hot water, and sleeps 5. Contact Ken & Jan Parkes 518-872-4532.

Food Mile 8.70, 0.10 miles south on NY Route 30 is a farm stand. Mile 11.75, 1 mile north on Route 30 is a Grand Union supermarket. On Main Street in Middleburgh – Mrs. K's Restaurant, Stewart's & Red Barrel (not recommended, may not be friendly to hikers) on left, Hubie's Pizzeria & Restaurant on right.

Post Office West Fulton 12194 - Mile 0.00, turn right onto West Fulton Road for 0.20 miles. Middleburgh 12122 - Mile 11.75, follow the LP for an extra 0.15 miles.

Section 30

Middleburgh to Albany County Line

Lean-tos Cotton Hill - Mile 6.75, no water at lean-to. Get water at mile 6.15 at small stream just before crossing Treadlemire Rd. or at a pump (not reliable) on Treadlemire Road opposite a green barn (the pump may need to be primed). Distance from Rossman Hill lean-to – 21.40 miles

Camping Camping is allowed in the State Reforestation Areas, 150 feet from trails or water. At mile 9.45, the trail enters private land. Distance between Patria and Cotton Hill State Forests – 9.75 miles

Lodging None

Food Mile 0.00 Middleburgh has delis, restaurants and grocery stores and a bank.

Post Office Middleburgh 12122 - Mile 0.15 on the trail

Section 31

Albany County Line to Switz Kill

Lean-tos None

Camping Camping is only allowed on the State Reforestation Areas in this section, not in the Wildlife Management Area. State Forest is reached at 3.60 miles and continues until the Long Path reaches Beaver Road at mile 5.05. Distance from Cotton Hill State Forest – 5.95 miles

Lodging None

Food None

Post Office None

Section 32

Switz Kill to East Berne

Lean-tos None

Camping	Cole Hill State Forest. Miles 2.75 through 4.75. Distance from Partridge Run Wildlife Management Area–11.45 miles
Lodging	None
Food	None
Post Office	None

Section 33

East Berne to John Boyd Thacher State Park

Lean-tos	There is a lean-to in John Boyd Thacher Park but it is not available for overnight use.
Camping	The beginning of this section is entirely on private property and the end is in John Boyd Thacher State Park. Neither allows overnight camping. Camping is available at Thompson's Lake State Campground, 4 miles from Thacher Park on NY Route 157. 518-872-1674. 140 sites, hot showers, flush toilets, swimming. $15. Distance from Cole Hill State Forest – 11.45 miles
Lodging	None
Food	None
Post Office	None

Section 34

John Boyd Thacher State Park to Route 146

Lean-tos	None
Camping	Thompson's Lake State Campground 518-872-1674mile 3.55, turn left and follow paved Stage Road to its intersection with Route 157. The campground is approximately 1 mile to the left. Open May 1 through Columbus Day. 140 sites, beach, hot showers, flush toilets. $15
Lodging	Appel Inn 518-861-6557. 590 NY Route 146 in Altamont. Bed and Breakfast, 4 rooms, $60-$80 per night
Food	None
Post Office	None

Distances Between Accommodations

	Miles	
Fort Lee to Nyack	22.65	Motel
Nyack to Rockland Lake	5.50	Motel
Rockland Lake to Mount Ivy	10.20	Motel
Mount Ivy to Big Hill Shelter	7.10	
Big Hill to Cohasset lean-to	8.15	
Cohasset to Wildcat shelter on the AT	13.65	
Wildcat to Wawayanda shelter	12.00	
Wawayanda to Pochuck Mountain shelter	13.10	
Pochuck to High Point shelter	12.40	
High Point to American Family Campground	16.70	Fee
American Campground to Otisville Campground	7.10	Fee
Otisville to Roosa Gap	19.05	
Roosa Gap to Kerhonkson	23.85	Motel
Kerhonkson to Riggsville (1)	9.80	
Riggsville to Sundown	10.10	
Sundown to Bouton lean-to	5.20	
Bouton to Terrace Mountain lean-to	11.00	
Terrace Mntn. to Woodland Valley Campground	2.60	Fee
Woodland Valley to Baldwin lean-to	8.95	
Baldwin to Tremper Mountain lean-to	0.80	
Tremper to Mink Hollow lean-to (2)	9.80	
Mink Hollow to North Lake Campground	24.90	Fee
North Lake to Batavia Kill lean-to	10.05	
Batavia Kill to Elm Ridge lean-to	7.40	
Elm Ridge to Huntersfield lean-to (3)	16.90	
Huntersfield lean-to to Nickerson Park Campground	11.50	Fee
Nickerson Park Campground to Rossman Hill lean-to (4)	13.25	
Rossman Hill to Cotton Hill lean-to (5)	21.40	
Cotton Hill to Partridge Run Reforestation Area	8.75	
Partridge Run to Cole Hill State Forest	9.55	
Cole Hill to Thompson's Lake Campground	11.45	Fee

(1) Between Riggsville and Woodland Valley the trail is in the Catskill Forest Preserve for 28.85 miles. Camping is allowed anywhere as long as you are 150 feet from trails, roads or water.

(2) Between Mink Hollow and NY Route 23 in East Windham the Long Path is in the Catskill Forest Preserve for 45.6 miles. Camping is allowed anywhere provided you are at least 150 feet from trails, roads or water.

(3) The trail is mostly in Reforestation Areas for 10 miles. Camping is allowed with the same restrictions as above. Watch for private property boundaries.

(4) The LP enters the Eminence State Forest 7.10 miles from Nickerson Park Campground.

(5) Camping is allowed in the State Forests in this area.

Post Offices

Palisades, NY 10964*
Piermont, NY 10968*
Pomona, NY 10970*
Arden, NY 10910*
Southfields, NY 10975
Bellvale, NY 10912
Greenwood Lake, NY 10925
New Milford, NY 10959
Vernon, NJ 07462
Glenwood, NJ 07418
Unionville, NY 10988*
Otisville, NY 10963*
Wurtsboro, NY 12790**
Kerhonkson, NY 12446**
Phoenicia, NY 12464*
Palenville, NY 12463*
Windham, NY 12496
Gilboa, NY 12076**
North Blenheim, NY 12131**
West Fulton, NY 12194*
Middleburgh, NY 12122**

* Located within 1 mile of the trail
** Located on the trail

Transportation

Red and Tan Lines 845-356-0877 from	Bus service along US Route 9W Fort Lee to Haverstraw
International Bus Service 201-714-9400	New York City to Mount Ivy
Transport of Rockland 845-634-1100	Bus Service in Rockland County
Short Line Buses 201-529-3666	New York City to Mountainview
Adirondack Trailways Buses 800-858-8555	New York City to New Paltz and the Catskills

Addresses and Phone Numbers

New York-New Jersey Trail Conference
156 Ramapo Valley Road
Mahwah, NJ 07430-1199
201-512-9348

Palisades Interstate Park Police
845-786-2781

New York State Department of Environmental Conservation
Region 3 Office - Ulster and Sullivan Counties
21 South Putt Corners Road
New Paltz, NY 12561
845-255-5453

New York State Department of Environmental Conservation
Region 4 Office - Greene, Schoharie and Delaware Counties
1150 North Westcott Road
Schenectady, New York 12306
518-357-2234

New York State Campground Reservations
1-800-456-CAMP, or www.park-net.com

Useful Publications

Fleming, June. *The Well Fed Backpacker*. Vantage Books, Random House, New York, NY, 1985

Fletcher, Colin. *The Complete Walker III*. Alfred A. Knopf, Inc., New York, NY, 1984

Hampton, Bruce and David Cole. *Soft Paths: How to Enjoy the Wilderness Without Harming It*. Stackpole Books, Harrisburg, PA, 1988

Jardine, Ray. *Beyond Backpacking, Ray Jardine's Guide to Lightweight Hiking*. AdventureLore Press, LaPine OR 97739, 2000

Manning, Harvey. *Backpacking One Step at a Time*. Vintage Books, Random House, New York, NY

Meyer, Kathleen. *How to Shit in the Woods*. Ten Speed Press, Berkeley, CA, 1989

Meyers, William J. *Harriman Trails. A Guide and History*. New York-New Jersey Trail Conference. New York, NY 1992

New York-New Jersey Trail Conference. *New York Walk Book*. New York, NY 2001

————— *Hudson Palisades Trails*. map set

————— *Harriman Bear Mountain Trails*. map set

————— *West Hudson Trails*. map set

————— *South Kittatiny Trails*. map set

————— *North Jersey Trails*. map set

————— *North Kittatiny Trails*. map set

————— *Catskills Trails*. map set

————— *Appalachian Trail in New York and New Jersey*. map set

Schaefer, Vincent J. *Vroman's Nose: Sky Island of the Schoharie County*. Purple Mountain Press, Ltd. Fleishmanns, NY 1992.

Waterman, Laura and Guy. *Wilderness Ethics: Preserving the Spirit of Wilderness*. The Countryman Press, Inc. Woodstock, VT, 1993

————— *Backwoods Ethics: Environmental Issues for Hikers and Campers*. The Countryman Press, Inc. Woodstock, VT 1993.

Long Path End-to-Enders

1. Albert (Cap) Field, Astoria NY   ?/?/?
2. Edward J. Walsh, W Haverstraw NY   7/4/91
3. Stella Green, Woodcliff Lake NJ   9/2/91
4. Edward L. Walsh, W Haverstraw NY   9/8/91
5. Lanny Wexler, Syosset NY   9/15/91
6. George Form, Hempstead NY   9/15/91
7. Susan Gerhardt, Suffern NY   9/21/91
8. Peter Heckler, Oradell NJ   9/21/91
9. James A. Ross, New Milford NJ   10/6/91
10. Roy Messaros, Franklin Lakes NJ   10/9/91
11. John Golenski, Pearl River NY   11/17/91
12. Arthur Schneier, Hyde Park NY   5/14/92
13. Mary R. Sive, Ardsley on Hudson NY   6/11/92
14. Arnold Projansky, New Paltz NY   9/5/92
15. Albert A. Mullen, Highland NY   5/14/92
16. Alan Gross, E. Swanzey NH   8/16/92
17. Alexander G. Gonzales, Dryden NY   6/23/94
18. Jack Hennessey, Naponoch NY   7/13/94
19. Joan D. James, Salisbury Mills NY   7/13/94
20. Herb Young Jr., Greenwich CT   8/1/94
21. Ray Cimera, Wayne NJ   10/1/94
22. Dick Hearn, Kinnelon NJ   10/1/94
23. Ferdinand Caiocca, New York NY   9/26/94
24. Dick Redfield, Riverdale NY   7/23/95
25. Eileen West, Pleasantville NY   7/23/95
26. Barry Gold, Woodbridge CT   5/27/95
27. Bill Pruehsner, Meriden CT   5/27/95
28. Marsha Gold, Woodbridge CT   5/27/95
29. May Ann Pruehsner, Meriden CT   5/27/95
30. Maureen McCahery, New City NY   4/19/96
31. Abe T. Allen, Plymouth CT   1996
32. Dean Guiliano, Olivebridge NY   6/8/97
33. Ernest C. Laug, Stamford, CT   7/8/97
34. Kathie F. Laug, Stamford CT   7/12/97
35. Margaret Freifeld, Mt. Kisco NY   8/3/97
36. Jane Smalley, Briarcliff Manor NY   7/12/97
37. Carolyn Harting, Bedford NY   9/7/97
38. Roeli Johansson, Bedford Hills NY   9/29/97
39. Mirjana V. Djordjevic, White Plains NY   8/16/97
40. Fran Levy, Hartsdale NY   8/22/97
41. Carole Ehleben, Bedford NY   9/6/97
42. June Fait, Long Beach NY   7/29/97
43. Virginia McMath, White Plains NY   9/15/97
44. Jack Barnes, Mohegan Lake NY   9/15/97

45. Barbro Thelemarck, North Salem NY   9/6/97
46. Julie Hobart, Bedminster NJ   8/8/97
47. Joan McNulty, Croton-on-Hudson NY   9/6/97
48. Carol Mantel, Amityville NY   8/8/97
49. Jean M. Dolen, North White Plains NY   8/17/97
50. Kathy Mario, Yaphank NY   9/27/97
51. Herbert J. Coles, Long Beach NY   7/12/97
52. Diane Bamford, Bedford NY   9/6/97
53. Carl D. Daiker, Middletown NY   9/11/97
54. David Zansalari, Bellefonte PA   9/11/97
55. James Shearwood, Long Island City NY   10/12/97
56. Marry Ann Nissley, Chalfont PA   5/31/98
57. Raymond S. Wilkin, Greenville SC   5/16/99
58. Donna L. Pasternak, Huntington WV 25701   9/22/96
59. Richard Rapold, Maplecrest NY 12454   9/19/99
60. Robert W. Novick, New Milford, NJ   9/29/00
61. Peter C. McGinnis, Poughkeepsie, NY   9/30/00
62. Henry C. Jenkins, Highland, NY   9/30/00
63. Rick Taylor, Hopewell Junction, NY   9/30/00
64. Alan Householder, Asheville, NC   5/14/01
65. Joe Fennelly, Chesire, CT   5/14/01
66. Richard K. Greve, Mt Holly, NJ   6/24/01
67. Michael Hume, Peekskill, NY   9/16/01
68. Violet Davis, Unadilla, NY   10/19/01
69. Kay Cynamon, New York, NY   10/21/01

Feedback Needed!

Please help to keep this guide up to date by sending your comments, observations and suggestions to Ed Walsh, 11 Kwiecinski Street, West Haverstraw, NY 10993-1410 or by e-mail to walshej@aol.com. Thanks and enjoy your hike.

Index of Place Names

JOIN US

NEW YORK-NEW JERSEY TRAIL CONFERENCE 1920

If you enjoy this book, we invite you to join the organization of hikers and environmentalists that published it—the *New York-New Jersey Trail Conference*. Since our founding in 1920, Trail Conference volunteers have built and presently maintain 1,500 miles of publicly accessible hiking trails in New York and New Jersey, from the Delaware Water Gap to the Catskills and the Taconics.

As a Trail Conference member, you will receive the *Trail Walker*, a bi-monthly source of news, information, and events concerning trails and hiking. The *Trail Walker* lists hikes throughout the NY-NJ region by many of our 75 member hiking clubs.

Members are entitled to purchase our authoritative maps and guides at significant discounts *(see reverse)*. Our highly accurate trail maps printed on durable Tyvek® enable you to hike with assurance in northern New Jersey, the Catskills, Harriman State Park, the Shawangunks, the Kittatinnies, Sterling Forest, and the East and West Hudson Highlands.

Trail Conference members are also entitled to discounts of 10% (and sometimes more!) at most outdoor stores and many mountain inns and lodges.

Your membership helps to give us the clout to protect and maintain more trails. If you want to experience pristine nature in the broader metropolitan New York area, you will most likely use a Trail Conference trail. As a member of the New York-New Jersey Trail Conference, you will be ensuring that public access to nature will continue to expand. So please join by contacting us now.

For rates and contact information, see reverse.

MEMBERSHIP CATEGORIES

	Individual	*Joint*
Regular	☐ $25	☐ $31
Sponsor	☐ $50	☐ $60
Benefactor	☐ $100	☐ $120
Student/Senior	☐ $18	☐ $24
Life	☐ $500	☐ $750*

* two adults at same address

Check out these other publications available from the New York-New Jersey Trail Conference:

	Retail	Members
MAPS		
Sterling Forest Trails	$7.95	$5.95
Harriman-Bear Mountain Trails	$8.95	$6.75
East Hudson Trails	$8.95	$6.75
West Hudson Trails	$7.95	$5.95
Catskill Trails	$13.95	$10.45
Kittatinny Trails	$12.95	$9.75
Shawangunk Trails	$9.95	$7.75
South Taconic Trails	$4.95	$3.75
North Jersey Trails	$7.95	$5.95
Hudson Palisades	$5.95	$4.75
BOOKS		
Hiking Long Island	$19.95	$15.95
Day Walker	$19.95	$15.55
Circuit Hikes in Northern New Jersey	$14.95	$11.95
Scenes & Walks in the No. Shawangunks	$10.95	$8.75
New York Walk Book	$19.95	$15.95
Iron Mine Trails: NY-NJ Highlands	$8.95	$7.15
Harriman Trails: A Guide and History	$16.95	$13.55
Long Path Guide	$16.95	$13.95
A.T. Guide for NY & NJ w/ 6 maps	$19.95	$15.95

NEW YORK-NEW JERSEY TRAIL CONFERENCE
156 Ramapo Valley Road • Mahwah, NJ 07430 • (201) 512-9348
www.nynjtc.org